A Fallen Angel

A Fallen Angel

The Status Insularity
of the Female Alcoholic

Florence V. Ridlon

Lewisburg
Bucknell University Press
London and Toronto: Associated University Presses

Associated University Presses
440 Forsgate Drive
Cranbury, NJ 08512

Associated University Presses
25 Sicilian Avenue
London WC1A 2QH, England

Associated University Presses
P.O. Box 488, Port Credit
Mississauga, Ontario
Canada L5G 4M2

The paper used in this publication meets the requirements
of the American National Standard for Permanence of Paper
for Printed Library Materials Z39.48-1984.

Library of Congress Cataloging-in-Publication Data

Ridlon, Florence, 1946–
    A fallen angel.

    Bibliography: p.
    Includes index.
    1. Women—Alcohol use. 2. Alcoholism—Psychological
aspects. 3. Deviant behavior—Labeling theory.
I. Title.
HV5137.R54   1988   362.2'92'088042   86-47992
ISBN 0-8387-5115-6 (alk. paper)

PRINTED IN THE UNITED STATES OF AMERICA

**To J. Peter McCormick
In Loving Memory**

Contents

Acknowledgments

When I first began examining the literature on alcoholism in 1970, I was struck by the paucity of studies on female alcoholics. Since then, work in that area has increased dramatically but still lags far behind that on male alcoholics. My initial goal was to contribute to this underdeveloped area of research which would have remained my focus were it not for the insistence of my friend and mentor, Ephraim H. Mizruchi, that this was not enough. He suggested I discuss what I had observed in theoretical terms. The concept of status insularity developed from the need to explain what I saw taking place among female alcoholics. I am grateful to him for encouraging the theoretical orientation of this work.

The National Institute of Mental Health (Grant no. MH11840-02) provided the funds necessary to support the initial inquiry. The research reported in the Appendix would have been impossible, however, without the assistance of a group of dedicated professionals who answered queries, allowed me access to their clinics and halfway houses, and in some cases administered questionnaires. I am particularly indebted to Reen Bacon of Spencer Halfway House, Newark, Ohio; Kitty Riddle Culkin of Talbot Hall, St. Anthony's Hospital, Columbus, Ohio (currently in private practice in Boca Raton, Florida); Charles Hoyt and Carolyn Close of Riverside Methodist Hospital, Columbus, Ohio; Gerry Gilbert, executive director, and Phil Gerhardt of Brick House, Syracuse, New York; Tom Goulet and Jenny Perleoni of the Onondaga Council on Alcoholism, Syracuse, New York; Judy Grossman and Kim Pagel of Regional Alcoholism Clinic and Rescue Mission, Inc., Syracuse, New York; Mike Jackson of Serenity House, Zanesville, Ohio; M.A.R.C., Cambridge State Hospital, Cambridge, Ohio; Jayne Mazzarella of Merrick Hall, Women's General Hospital, Cleveland, Ohio; Katie Mitchell of Clifton Springs Hospital and Clinic, Clifton Springs, New York (currently coordinator of Family Services, Pathways Treatment Center, Lynchburg, Virginia); and Larry Smith of Molly Stark Hospital, Lewisville, Ohio.

The Library of Congress staff and facilities were graciously made available to me while I was researching this book. Dave Kelly deserves special recognition for offering his vast expertise on numerous occasions and doing it with a wholeheartedness that is unique to him.

Bloomfield College's president, Merle Allshouse, and the dean, Gary

9

Confessore provided office space and an academic atmosphere without which it would have been impossible to write.

Other friends and colleagues played very special roles in guiding my work, offering suggestions, and providing much needed moral support. Their deeds are too many to list but not their names: Mary Anderson, Marian and Jerry Batson, Dawn Bouw, Florence and Thomas Conway, Doris Corbett, Dave Hanson, Bill Johnson, Meg Ksander, Edward C. Mazique, Marilyn Nouri, Thomas Pastorello, William Pooler, Jim Ridlon, Mae and Frank Ridlon, Manfred Stanley, Howard Taylor, Dorothy Wheeler, and George Zito.

A special debt of gratitude is owed to Susan Granai who cheerfully read every draft of every chapter. Her suggestions were inevitably correct and her sociological expertise faultless. The finished product is much the better for her efforts. She provided a friendship and a collegial relationship that made working on this book a memorable experience.

Matt Silberman, my editor at Bucknell, made the task of altering the manuscript not only worthwhile but pleasant. He reviewed the manuscript for its potential and helped me to make the most of what was there. The book is much improved thanks to his tireless work and intelligent critiques.

On a personal level two people made this book possible. My husband, Robert W. Wheeler, and my friend, J. Peter McCormick, provided the support and encouragement that only these two very special people could give.

A Fallen Angel

1

The Insulated Status of the Female Alcoholic

Female alcoholism is no longer a matter of slight concern. Recent estimates of the number of women who have problems with alcohol addiction in the United States have risen to as high as five million. [1] Yet much less attention (both academic and popular) has been directed to the female alcoholic. The main explanation for this can be found in what we expect of women in our society.

Those opposed to the women's liberation movement argue that women like being on a pedestal, but they do not discuss what happens when a human (both male and female) disease such as alcoholism knocks a woman off her lofty perch.

When I began to study the female alcoholic in the early 1970s, two unexplained and interesting findings emerged from the literature. One was the lack of research focusing on female alcoholics. The other was that women were less likely than men to be labeled alcoholic, frequently remaining undiagnosed through many years of excessive drinking. Both facts, I came to believe, could not be explained without a better understanding of the impact of the status of female in our society on drinking values, norms, and behavior.

Why do we not discuss female alcoholism more openly and honestly? Why is more research money directed toward studies of male alcoholics? Why do hospitals and halfway houses not have adequate space for female alcoholics? Why are people more critical of female alcoholics? Why do women become full-fledged alcoholics more rapidly than men do once they start drinking heavily?

Answers to these questions are not found in genetics nor psychology, although both certainly play some part in alcoholism, but in the status of women in our society. The social position accorded to a woman as a result of her sex has a great effect not only on how she behaves but also on how others behave toward her. For this reason, it is important to look at alcoholism from a sociological perspective.

History of the Research on Female Alcoholics

Until the late 1960s, very little research was done on female alcoholics. A literature review in 1972 reports only twenty-eight articles published in

English,[2] although many thousands of articles had been written about male alcoholics.[3] This is a clear indication of how little interest and research money had been spent on female alcoholics. Given the voluminous work done on male alcoholics, it is not an exaggeration to say that, until recently, female alcoholics were largely ignored.

Since the early 1970s, information about female alcoholics has flourished. Many excellent literature reviews exist[4] covering over one hundred sources. Several annotated bibliographies have appeared detailing from 159[5] to 488[6] studies. Popular books about what it is like to be an alcoholic female and how to be successfully rehabilitated[7] have also started appearing. The National Council on Alcoholism in 1976 finally established the first national office to deal specifically with the problems of women. And even an organization similar to, but separate from, Alcoholics Anonymous, Women for Sobriety, has been formed to deal with the special problems that alcoholic women face.[8]

Although in the past few years, more time and energy have been devoted to understanding female alcoholics, it is important to note that despite the impressive increase in research, it remains a very small portion of the overall work on alcoholism. Even granting that there are a larger percentage of male alcoholics, research on women has still failed to keep pace with the proportion they form of the overall alcoholic population. Until recently, it was argued in most standard sources on alcoholism that the ratio of men to women was about 5 to 1 or 6 to 1.[9] Estimates of the current ratio vary, depending on the setting in which the statistics are gathered: from 11 to 1 in prisons,[10] to 3 to 1 in inpatient clinics,[11] to 1 to 1 in private physicians' offices.[12] In testimony and material submitted to the Senate Subcommittee on Alcoholism and Narcotics in 1976, the estimated ratios ranged from 3 to 1[13] to 1 to 1.[14] It appears safe to say that at most there are three alcoholic men for every alcoholic woman. A look at recent abstracts in the *Journal of Studies on Alcohol*[15] finds that out of 273 abstracted works, only 12 relate to females. Of these, one is an animal study, and one deals with the popular topic of fetal alcohol syndrome.

Women are also shortchanged on services. Dr. Jean Kirkpatrick in a Women for Sobriety publication notes that "the federal government financed 574 programs for men and only 14 for women."[16] She also asserts there are 600 halfway houses for men and only 30 for women.[17] Although these numbers are increasing, whatever ratio we accept and however great the recent advancements, the amount of research being done on female alcoholics and the availability of treatment for their illness does not approach the amount we would expect given their prevalence in U.S. society. No matter what the exact number of female alcoholics, the problem is serious and deserves more extensive attention.

Many authors have argued that the recent intensified interest in women who drink has followed an increase in their numbers.[18] Others claim it is not only that the number of women who drink has increased but there has also been a drastic rise in the number of female alcoholics.[19] It is certainly true that most statistics do show a large growth in the number of female alcoholics. Whether this is due to an actual expansion in the numbers or a greater willingness of people to deal with the problem of female alcoholics is questionable.[20] Whatever the cause for the apparent increase in numbers, it is difficult to believe that so few female alcoholics existed prior to 1970 that they were not worthy of study. The reports of higher numbers of female alcoholics have clearly been an incentive for the increase in research and facilities, but it cannot be a complete explanation.

One obvious answer to why so few studies had been done on female alcoholics is that most researchers until recently were men. With the increase in female researchers has come a greater consciousness of issues of importance to women. The *Statistical Abstract for the United States* shows a startling change in the ratio of men to women who received their doctoral degrees in 1970 compared to 1980. In 1970, 23,091 degrees were conferred.[21] Of these, 2,906 were women.[22] The ratio of men to women had dropped slowly from 1950 (9.14 to 1)[23] to 1960 (8.28 to 1)[24] to 1970 (6.95 to 1).[25] However, in 1980, the ratio changed dramatically to 3.37 to 1, with 9,672 of the 32,615 graduated being women.[26] In the social sciences, which one would expect to be a particularly relevant group of fields, the ratio of men to women for 1970 was 7.20 to 1,[27] and in 1980, it dropped to 1.37 to 1.[28] It is not surprising that research in all areas of women's studies increased during this time. However, even this large jump in female Ph.D.s has not come close to equalizing the amount of research or the treatment facilities available to female alcoholics.

Women had drinking problems long before research specialists took a major interest in them. As early as the 1930s and 1940s,[29] serious scholars were doing research and writing about alcoholic women. For that matter, from the writings of ancient Greece and Rome, we learn that even then excessive drinking among women was considered a problem.[30] Why then did most researchers, writers, and health specialists choose to ignore the problem of alcoholism in women until recently? And why does it still not receive the recognition one would expect, given the magnitude of the problem?

The Labeling Perspective

The lack of research was not the only curious finding. Available data on female alcoholics indicated that in one way there was less societal reaction to their deviance. Although there might be more "moral indignation" expressed at seeing a woman drinking heavily, there appears to be actually less inclination toward "action directed to its control."[31]

One of the most persuasive perspectives for understanding deviance is labeling "theory." However, the protection female alcoholics receive from the labeling process does not fit with one of the major assumptions of the labeling perspective, which indicates that those in power are the most likely to be protected and the underdogs[32] labeled deviant and stigmatized.[33] The data necessitated a new look at the tenets of labeling theory in an attempt to explain why so little attention had been directed toward female alcoholics and why they were less likely to be labeled.

Within the labeling perspective, deviance does not result simply from wrongdoing,[34] but from how people and organizations treat a person's beliefs or actions. The emphasis is on process. Deviance is not seen as an either–or proposition. A person's self-concept is continually shaped and reshaped by the fluid processes of social interaction. An individual is no longer deviant or nondeviant; instead, there are shades of deviation, different degrees of commitment to the deviant role, and different ways of looking at the deviant act. Those who define an act as deviant and enforce rules about it in essence create the deviance, not the person who goes against their definition.

Once an act is labeled deviant and an individual is stigmatized,[35] the self-concept may change in response to the societal reaction to his or her deviation. The individual can no longer view the deviance as part of a proper societal role but is often pushed toward acceptance of his or her role as a deviant. Lemert has called the potential responses to these labeling and stigmatizing processes secondary deviation:

> Secondary deviation is deviant behavior, or social roles based upon it, which becomes means of defense, attack or adaptation to the overt and covert problems created by the societal reaction to primary deviation. In effect, the original "causes" of the deviation recede and give way to the central importance of the disapproving, degradational, and isolating reactions of society.[36]

Simplistically, Lemert's argument can be diagramed as follows:

Activity → Labeling → Stigmatization → Self-Concept Change → Secondary Deviation

No diagram can portray with complete accuracy the complexity of the process that labeling theorists are describing. While label and stigma are theoretically separable, the interrelationship between the two and even the order in which they occur are not clearly delineated in the literature or everyday life. Many activities that some consider deviant are never labeled as such, and secondary deviation can, and according to theory, is expected to, have an effect on the initial deviant activity. Secondary deviation is not an easily identifiable entity, but an ongoing process that, as Lemert defines it (and as I use it), involves "societal insults to identity."[37] Therefore the arrows are one directional in only a very simplified diagram of a process that should be considered interactional.

By focusing on aspects of the social structure that affect the likelihood of someone being labeled deviant, we can (1) explain what we see happening to female alcoholics, (2) make an important contribution to the basic theoretical model, and (3) partially correct for the critique of labeling theory that suggests it ignores the influence of the social structure on the deviance process.[38]

Status Insularity

Certain statuses offer a degree of insularity to those who occupy such places in the social order. I use the term status insularity to refer to the property of a social position that decreases the likelihood that an occupant of that status will be labeled deviant. For example, studies have shown that whites often possess insularity when compared to blacks or other minority groups; the rich when compared to the poor; and in most cases, the powerful when compared to the powerless in our society. It is also true that, with respect to certain types of deviance, women occupy a more insulated position than men.

Status insularity not only makes it less likely for the occupant of a certain position to be labeled deviant, but once labeled, the severity of the sanctions imposed may also vary. Although not part of the definition of status insularity or my initial hypothesis, the literature on female alcoholics led me to speculate about how status insularity affects the degree to which someone is stigmatized.

Generalizing from data on female alcoholics, it would seem that if a member of a relatively privileged position is labeled, he or she will be stigmatized with greater vehemence. To label the holder of an insulated status means the labeler has to confront the normative order and / or the power structure that has defined that status as privileged. There are norms, values, and forces (both legitimate and illegitimate) in our society that predispose people to assume that those in certain positions are unlikely to be deviant. If this assumption is to be contradicted, stronger forces must be mustered than against those in a status unprotected by such insularity. More severe criticism can be expected of those who have, in spite of their position, committed deviant acts of such magnitude as to justify public sanctions. For example, we can more easily understand the theft of a purse by a youth from a ghetto neighborhood who has had a bad upbringing and is poor than the same behavior by a youth from a wealthy family where there would seem to be no justification for such an action.

We would further expect that severe stigmatization of the individual (symbolic or physical) would lead to more extensive damage of his or her self-concept and a greater amount of secondary deviation.

This extension of labeling theory can be diagramed as follows:

Status Insularity
| |
Activity → Labeling → Stigmatization → Self-Concept Change →
Secondary Deviation

In this model, status insularity is a conditional variable predicting that someone who belongs to a privileged status is less likely to be labeled if he or she deviates. It is further hypothesized that there will be an increase in stigmatization if labeled, a more damaging effect of stigmatization on the individual's self-concept, and greater secondary deviation.

It is important to keep in mind that these hypotheses did not come from theorizing about how the labeling process works but are derived from what has been observed about alcoholics. Although the concept of status insularity is considered generalizable to other kinds of deviance, it is possible that the additional hypotheses about stigmatization and secondary deviation are not applicable.

An attempt was made to understand the data that existed on alcoholics. Female heavy drinkers appeared to have a certain amount of status insularity; when labeled, they tended to be more heavily criticized than men. Observations and firsthand accounts claimed that female alcoholics have lower self-esteem than male alcoholics. The women appeared to be subject to more secondary deviation than men, as evidenced by greater pathologies associated with their alcoholism and the accelerated rate at which they became full-fledged alcoholics (telescoped development). The hypothesized relationship can be diagramed as follows:

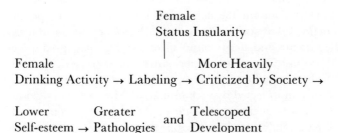

Female
Status Insularity
| |
Female   More Heavily
Drinking Activity → Labeling → Criticized by Society →

Lower   Greater   and Telescoped
Self-esteem → Pathologies   Development

Secondary deviation and low self-esteem are not being equated in this formulation. Although it is basic to the labeling perspective and to much of sociological thinking that other people's perceptions of us influence how we view ourselves (see chapter 6), a change in self-concept is not part of the secondary deviation process that has been of particular interest to social theorists. It is the behavioral manifestations that have intrigued sociologists:

the increase in deviant conduct, the adjustments in life style made to accommodate the new definition of self, or other modifications of behavior in response to labeling and stigmatization.

Lemert has argued that a change in self-concept is an integral part of the secondary deviation process: "Devaluation of the self on society's terms ordinarily has a sequel of internal or psychic struggle, greatest where the sense of continuity of the self is massively threatened."[39]

However, the exact role played by the change in self-concept has not been specified. In fact, some recent quantitative research has shown that the relationship between self-concept and secondary deviation is anything but a clear one.[40] The self-esteem variable in the present text is used to describe part of the secondary deviation process that has been observed by researchers to affect alcoholics.

Low self-esteem is not always the outcome of labeling and stigmatization. Deviance theorists have enumerated various effective ways in which individuals and groups protect their self-concept from the assaults leveled by a moralistic society.[41] There are some forms of deviance in which researchers have argued fairly persuasively that being labeled deviant actually increases the individual's self-esteem. For example, much of the literature on delinquent subcultures argues that the delinquent achieves status he or she could not achieve in society in general by identifying with a delinquent subculture in which nonconformity to middle-class values is lauded.[42] The delinquent subculture can serve to increase a youth's self-esteem, since his or her status is increased in the eyes of the peers.[43] Similar results have been shown for homosexuals where being committed to the deviant identity seems to accord the homosexual better psychological adjustment than only partial commitment.[44]

Some labels may be positive, and even negative labeling may have some positive effects, such as making treatment available to alcoholics. Deviance theories, however, generally deal with negative labeling and its detrimental effects on individuals. This study assumes that the label of alcoholic is negative and does lead to stigmatization. The alcoholics in my research and in most other studies are found in rehabilitative settings, indicating they have accepted the alcoholic label and the desirability of recovering. Therefore, this negative aspect of labeling is of particular interest.

Labeling theory predicts that those in positions of power are less likely to be labeled. Since women are generally in less powerful positions than men in our society, the question of why female alcoholics are less likely to be labeled was unanswered and unanswerable by the labeling perspective.

The Status of Women in American Society

In modern American society, ascriptive statuses are not so important as they were in the past. As Coser and Rosenberg have noted, "The growth of modern industrial society produces tremendous differentiation of functions. Although age and sex continue to be relevant factors in status ascription, the occupational determination of status and the occupational definition of role assumed unprecedented importance."[45] Thus what were at one time consistent social positions (characterized as applying for the person across what Merton[46] has called status-sets), may now be applicable for a given status only under certain circumstances. Consequently, a woman's status may cause a different reaction when combined with other statuses.

The rapidly changing roles associated with womanhood may also be a factor in lessening the impact of status insularity. A woman's status in American society carries with it numerous and diverse role expectations. Coser and Rosenberg state that "in general, status is problematic when roles are vaguely or ambiguously defined. Thus, women, mothers-in-law, adolescents, and the aged are suspended in a painful and doubtful position across the American social scene."[47]

Status insularity appears to be applicable to women under only certain circumstances. For example, we expect status insularity will accrue to a woman's position for such forms of deviance as alcoholism and homosexuality. Yet we do not expect this insularity to apply to the female status if the occupant is promiscuous or mentally ill. Gender, then, may be a weaker predictor of insularity in different types of deviation than a relatively more consistent position, such as socioeconomic status. The status of gender may protect women under certain circumstances, while gender may be a status that insulates men under other circumstances.

Although gender may not be the best predictor of insularity, it is an interesting example within the alcohol literature of how the likelihood of being labeled is related to the degree of stigmatization. It is hoped that, as has been the case with other work in this field, "research in the sphere of alcohol and society can make simultaneous contributions to the solution of immediate social problems and to the development of general theories of social processes."[48]

Sources of Insularity

At least two sources other than power appear to be important in determining status insularity; they are: (1) social evaluations based on cultural definitions, which refer to entrenched norms and values that are part of our society and do not always coincide with the power structure; and (2) structural features of social organization, such as physical and social distance patterns that differentially affect variables like segregation and visibility. How these two sources protect female alcoholics from labeling will be discussed at length in a critical examination of the available material on female alcoholics (chapter 2).

Hypotheses

Three separate hypotheses are suggested based on how status insularity seems to function for female alcoholics; (1) first, women are less likely than men to be labeled alcoholic. (2) Secondly, if women are labeled alcoholic, they will be more heavily stigmatized. (3) Finally, if female alcoholics are more heavily stigmatized, then women are more likely than men to have lower self-esteem and suffer various forms of secondary deviation.

Research and firsthand accounts and observations of female alcoholics are reinterpreted and analyzed from the perspective of status insularity and these three hypotheses. There is ample evidence to support the first hypothesis that women are less likely to be labeled alcoholic (see chapter 2), although the degree of their insularity appears to be declining in recent years (see chapter 3).

A discussion of labeling theory and stigmatization is included to place the stigmatization process of female alcoholics in a larger perspective (see chapter 4). Analysis of existing studies support the second hypothesis: Women are generally more heavily stigmatized than men (see chapter 5).

The literature also supports the contention that female alcoholics are subject to more secondary deviation, which shows up in their greater pathology and telescoped development, as it is called by professionals working with alcoholics (see chapter 6). If women do suffer from telescoped development and greater pathology which did not exist prior to their alcoholism, then it is reasonable to assume that their self-concept has been damaged by the stigmatization process.

As an indication of damage to self-concept, hypothesis 3 also argues that women's self-esteem will be lower than men's due to the greater stigmatization. The literature was least persuasive on this aspect of the theoretical model due to a paucity of comparative research on the self-esteem of male and female alcoholics. What is available is presented in the discussion of the secondary deviation process in chapter 6. In order to supplement published material on the self-esteem of male and female alcoholics, a sample (see Fig. A.1 on p. 118) of male and female heavy drinkers who have not been labeled alcoholic and males and females who were in rehabilitative settings and therefore affectively labeled alcoholics were compared on the Self-Regard score of the Personal Orientation Inventory (POI) to determine if female alcoholics actually do have lower self-esteem. Other status insular positions were also compared to noninsular positions on Self-Regard to demonstrate the potential usefulness of the concept in explaining other forms of deviant labeling. A very brief summary of these findings are presented in chapter 6. Details of this exploratory research and findings from the POI and other questionnaires are reported in more detail in the appendix.

The implications of these findings are reserved for chapter 7, which examines how status insularity should be conceptualized and whether further research is warranted by the findings from analysis and research. If a convincing case can be made from the existing research that women are less likely to be labeled, more severely stigmatized, and subject to lower self-esteem and more secondary deviation, then the supposition that status insularity functions as hypothesized is plausible. Showing that female alcoholics have a greater amount of secondary deviation and proportionately lower self-esteem than male alcoholics and that alcoholics in other status insular positions have lower self-esteem would support the view that status insularity plays an important role in the labeling process.

Alcohol and the Traditional Roles of Women in Society

Women have not shown up in clinics nor jails nor been reprimanded publicly for their alcoholism because they have been protected in our society. Their social position makes it less likely that people will call them deviants of one sort or another. As mentioned in chapter 1, certain social positions or statuses (in this case, gender) offer those who occupy them insulation from being identified as a deviant. In sociology, this identification process is called labeling and will be discussed at length in chapter 4.

Coining a new term, such as status insularity, is of little use unless it explains something we did not previously understand. What is it about a woman's social position that protects her from being labeled alcoholic even if she has serious problems associated with her drinking? And how does this differ from a man's social position?

As noted previously, there are two sources of status insularity that pertain to the woman who drinks excessively: social evaluations based on cultural definitions and structural features of social organization. Power, which is the more commonly discussed source of protection from labeling is not applicable to the status of female, although it may be applicable to a particular woman through one of her other status positions.

Social Evaluations Based on Cultural Definitions

Judgments of others are partially based on values shared with other members of the culture. This value system assists us in making decisions about the appropriateness or inappropriateness of behavior for ourselves and others. Based on these cultural definitions, decisions are made about the way men and women should act or the roles they should play: What is acceptable or unacceptable behavior. To a large degree, how others believe a person should behave depends on the individual's sex.[1] There are some situations in which gender is irrelevant, but generally others expect certain behavior from us based on our sex, and if our actions do not match these expectations, we may be judged harshly.

An interesting study by Inge K. Broverman et al. illustrates that sex-role stereotypes not only differ for men and women but also that male qualities tend to be more valued.[2] A group of seventy-nine clinically trained psychologists, psychiatrists, and social workers (both men and women) were divided into three groups. One group was asked to choose the mature, healthy, and socially competent adult male traits from a list of 122 items. The second group was asked to describe the mature, healthy, and socially competent adult female, using the same list. A third group was asked to describe the mature, healthy, and socially competent adult person. The researchers found that these experts, whose jobs required dealing with people on a regular basis, had very different concepts of the healthy man and the healthy woman. Their ideals were very much like the stereotypes that many of us share about men and women. They suggested that "healthy women differ from healthy men by being more submissive, less independent, less adventurous, more easily influenced, less aggressive, less competitive, more excitable in minor crises, having their feelings more easily hurt, being emotional, more conceited about their appearance, less objective and disliking math and science."[3]

As the researchers concluded, this seems like a very strange way to describe an adult! And when the ideals of the two groups were compared with those of the third group, which described the healthy adult person, it was found that the ideal healthy adult person was much like the healthy adult male but very different from the female.

The authors concluded that this double standard for health occurs because clinicians feel that to be healthy, people should adjust to restrictions placed on them by society, even if they keep an individual from achieving his or her full potential. This does not mean clinicians dislike women but that they reflect the same stereotypes shared by most people in society. The study clearly demonstrates that standards and expectations are different for men and women and even "experts" on human relations expect people to abide by them in order to be healthy and well-adjusted. These roles are restricting in some ways and have a considerable effect on the way people relate to one another in society.

This is not the only research to support the contention that the qualities males and females possess are not only different but also are valued differently and that health professionals are no less judgmental than the rest of society.[4] Men and women both rate the characteristics they associate with the ideal male higher than those they associate with the ideal female and in other ways indicate they devalue the work and the success of women.[5]

Although this research is very convincing, it does not mean that everything in our lives is determined by gender; other factors also come into play. A person's socioeconomic status, personality, physical appearance, skills, and so forth, all play a part in how people respond to us. We generally take more than one attribute into consideration when making decisions about other people.[6]

This research indicates the accuracy of Friedland et al.'s conclusion that "so called stereotypes—whether based on race, sex, occupation or some other external attribute of the person—are used as tentative cues to the probable attitudes and personality characteristics of others, rather than as invariant indicators of such underlying qualities."[7] Thus someone's gender gives us certain cues or tells us what to expect from that person and also how we are expected to respond to the person. We also receive other cues from an individual, and these, too, play a part in our behavior. All of these cues combined give us certain boundaries within which we expect someone's behavior to fall if it is to be acceptable. But each individual interaction varies and is never fully determined by the stereotypes we hold.

Traditional Roles

Traditionally, women have been viewed as the preservers of morality, charged to uphold the moral and spiritual values of our society.[8] Whatever the traditional value—chastity, loyalty, honesty, cleanliness, charity, or sobriety—women were expected to adhere to it more closely than did men. Women have been placed on a pedestal and accordingly expected to behave as the embodiment of all the values we as a society hold dear.

To some degree, women have been worthy upholders of morality, since, in our society, they are more traditional or conventional than men. Women are more likely than men to accept official standards of morality and propriety, and this is evidenced in their drinking attitudes and behavior.[9] As a California survey showed, women are less likely to drink in bars, enjoy getting drunk, or to be heavy drinkers.[10] Although women are more likely to drink now than in the 1960s when this research was conducted, more recent surveys still show that women are less likely to be heavy drinkers.[11] In a survey in the San Francisco area, Genevieve Knupfer found that on every question (frequency of drinking, amount of drinking, and disapproval of drunkenness), women were more likely than men to support strict social standards.[12] It was also "typical of both sexes to think it worse for a woman to drink too much."[13] Similar results were found in a sample from the state of Washington. "Both sexes at all status levels reported more intolerance toward drunkenness in women than in men."[14] Dissimilar beliefs about drunkenness for men and women also appear to exist when individuals from different races are interviewed. A study of primarily black residents in a low-income housing development in the midwest revealed that half of the men and three-quarters of the women thought it was acceptable for a man to get drunk. Only a quarter of both sexes expressed the opinion that it was alright for women.[15] Apparently, the double standard for drinking has gone unchallenged by individuals despite their gender, social status, or race.

Given the progress made in the 1970s toward equality of the sexes, people might no longer be willing to admit on a questionnaire how they feel about

female alcoholics. Therefore, in my research, I asked not only how they felt
about women being alcoholics but also what they believed others thought of
women drinking heavily. [16] This gave respondents the opportunity to appear
unprejudiced themselves while putting the blame for discrimination against
female alcoholics on others. As predicted, an overwhelming majority of the
sample (72 percent), both alcoholic and nonalcoholic, female and male, felt
that *others* criticize women more for drinking heavily (see table A.1), and
female alcoholics believed this most strongly (81 percent). However, only a
small percentage (26 percent) of the sample said *they* felt it was worse for a
woman to be an alcoholic (see table A.2).

Despite some people apparently not wanting to admit to prejudice against
female alcoholics, many still bluntly speak their mind. Alluding to the alleged
superior morality of women, a male alcoholic, unmarried, 32-year-old clerk
said, "Women should be the fairer sex, more gentle, and so forth. Therefore
getting drunk is an about face for a woman. Men just show their ass when
drunk."

This view of woman's better character was held despite the fact that this
young man's mother had a drinking problem. A married 52-year-old who is
labeled alcoholic and self-employed said, "My wife should be stronger than
her desire." According to this man, alcohol allowed him to "escape all my
responsibilities"—apparently something he thought his wife should be able to
do without. A 55-year-old millwright, who is separated from his wife, stated
he thought it was worse for a female because "I was taught to respect
women."

Although women have been expected to behave better than men, they have
not been granted political or economic power that would allow them to enforce their supposed superior morality. Instead, women were expected to
devote full time and effort to the domestic realm. A man can contribute to
family life by being a provider and yet still be drunk every evening. [17]
If alcohol does not undercut a man's ability to support his family, then his
main role is undamaged by excessive drinking. Men, single or married, who
claim it is worse for a man to be an alcoholic say it is because the man is the
breadwinner.

The roles of wife and mother, however, require constant attention. And in
the past, a woman's success and prestige in the world depended on how well
she married and how well she managed a household. If a woman drinks excessively, it is bound to affect the family, and as Hirsh notes, "It is bound to
disintegrate the very bedrock upon which her status and prestige rest." [18]
Men and women agree that the woman's demanding role in the family makes
it worse for her to be an alcoholic. An alcoholic, 48-year-old mother of three
notes that "A woman is the foundation of home life. When this foundation
falls apart everything falls apart." According to a young (19-year-old), single,
alcoholic woman, "Society places a woman into a role of mother, wife, and

so forth. When she starts to drink she tends to neglect her family and then is put down because she doesn't fit in her role that was set down."

Jan Clayton, a recovered alcoholic and actress testifying before a Senate Subcommittee Hearing on women alcoholics stated:

> Society told us we were particularly rotten when and if we drank because we rocked the cradle and were consigned to that damned pedestal for soothing, for being wise, understanding, tolerant, loving, cooking, serving, and if necessary, adding to the family coffers. It was bad enough to fail, but failure because of booze was far beyond the well-known pale. It was disgusting. [19]

There is clearly a different standard of morality for drinking and drunkenness for men and women. Both male and female respondents were aware of the double standard, and most appeared to accept it. The majority of the explanations in my research referred to this double standard. Respondents gave similar reasons why it was worse for a woman to be an alcoholic—"It's more socially accepted for men than women;" "because of our society and its social standards;" and "double standard in society, double guilt complex for women." One well-to-do, 42-year-old housewife agrees with the social standards and puts her opinion succinctly, "A drunken woman is disgusting."

This attitude is not unique to American culture. In ancient Rome, wine drinking by women was punishable by death. Accounts exist of Roman men executing their wives not only for drinking but also for the intent to drink (stealing the keys to the wine cellar). There have been times in more recent Western history when it was common to see a woman drinking. However, it is interesting to note that no matter how acceptable it was for a woman to drink, at no time was it considered proper for a lady to be drunk. [20] Our history has taught us that the two words lady and drunk are indeed contradictory and mutually exclusive terms.

Sexual Promiscuity: The Drunken Slut

The roles of wife and mother and the vast responsibilities they entail would be enough to ensure a woman's condemnation for excessive drinking. However, another cultural value plays a part in how female alcoholics are treated: the double standard of sexual morality. Despite the equalizing efforts of the women's liberation movement, chastity and sexual restraint are still prized for females in this country. Men, historically and in the present, have had fewer moral restrictions placed on their sexual behavior.

From the beginning of civilization, there has been a connection made between drinking and involvement with sex. Wine drinking by women was punishable by death in early Rome because it was believed to be linked

directly with adultery.[21] It was feared that if a woman opened herself to one
male vice, drinking alcohol, she might open herself to another, sexual promiscuity. Researchers have found that "the danger that the release of
inhibitions caused by alcohol might lead women to violate approved standards of sexual restraints is very prominent in people's minds."[22] In fact, some
people think excessive drinking and promiscuity are directly linked. A
husband's angry comment to his wife about her alcoholism sums up this connection: "You're nothing but a drunken slut."[23] By her own account, she
was indeed drunk, but there was nothing in her actions to indicate lewd
behavior. However, in anger the two words were automatically joined in her
husband's mind; and they are automatically joined in the minds of many
people.

As Dr. Susan B. Anthony, a recovered alcoholic, told the Senate Committee during their 1976 hearing on alcohol abuse among women:

> We are suspect of being either prostitutes or not quite nice women, a
> problem men do not have. Therefore we are looked down upon far more
> than the man alcoholic at any level, no matter whether we are upper class,
> lower class, bottom; because there is the added sexual note with the woman
> alcoholic. She is not considered in the same sort of light that the male
> alcoholic is because of the stigma that the woman may be sexually loose in
> morals.[24]

Even a recovering female alcoholic is still suspect of sexual laxity. "When a
man recovers he is a hero... when a woman recovers she is an ex-prostitute."[25]
A recent conference of the Association of Halfway House Alcoholism Programs of North America reported an exchange that reflected this well:

> I represent the non-alcoholic wife who has sat now in A.A. meetings for
> fifteen years and watched the alcoholic woman "wiggle" into meetings,
> and they just have a "different look about them" than we do. I don't know
> how they do it, but they cause a sparkle in the eyes of men (and they can't
> help themselves).[26]

The inference is clearly that since these women are recovering alcoholics,
they have had vast sexual experience. If this nonalcoholic woman's description is accurate, even the men in Alcoholics Anonymous believe this, since
their eyes sparkle when they see these women.

Early research on the female alcoholic tended to perpetuate the stereotype
of her as promiscuous.[27] Case studies highlighted the sexual behavior of the
women they interviewed.[28] Most of the cases reported involved what have
been called the sociopathic female alcoholic[29]—the one who has expressed
"severe pervasive antisocial behavior" usually prior to a drinking problem.
Only a small minority of female alcoholics are sociopathic,[30] yet researchers

have presented these women as if they were representative of the overall female alcoholic population.

Recent research has provided findings that contradict commonly held beliefs regarding the sexual laxity of female alcoholics. The majority of the work has indicated that instead of becoming promiscuous, excessive drinking by females diminished sex drives and decreased sexual activity.[31] Generally, female alcoholics tend to find sexual relationships very unsatisfying and even painful.[32] "The popular image of the scarlet woman is a fiction—promiscuity is appropriate to only 5 percent of all women drinkers. Most of the other 95 percent complain of diminished interest in sex."[33]

This small percentage of promiscuous female alcoholics is frequently brought to the public's attention and serves to strengthen the stereotype of the drunken slut.

Female alcoholics seldom are bawdy and promiscuous, seeking all the sex they can find. Despite scientific findings, however, the stereotype is hard to eradicate.

Traditional roles in our society, therefore, have two distinct effects, one is to keep a woman from becoming an alcoholic, the other is to condemn her if she does. These roles have in essence afforded women what Knupfer has called "cultural protection" against alcoholism.[34] They are protected in that the standards discourage women from drinking and especially from drinking heavily. The double standard for morality and especially sexual morality in our culture has meant that, in the past, women were not likely to go against such strong taboos. The threat of imminent moral condemnation and disgrace if they did become alcoholics was an incentive that kept them from turning to alcohol to solve their problems.

Men are at times encouraged to drink to prove their masculinity, women, on the other hand, are discouraged from drinking. There are no prescriptive norms telling women how to drink; only proscriptive norms preventing them from drinking, from drinking in public, from being in a bar, and the like.[35] Once women start drinking, as Straus and Bacon have pointed out in their analysis of Mormon drinking behavior, "extremes are likely since the behavior itself represents rejection of social rules."[36] Although alcoholism is certainly not encouraged in men, there are some positive role models of heavy-drinking and even alcoholic males. Ernest Hemingway, Dylan Thomas, and Babe Ruth were all admired despite their problems with alcohol, no such image exists for women. There is nothing romantic about the life of the alcoholic woman, while the hard-drinking, hard-living male has at times been glorified.

Leniency of Labeling Agents

The stricter standards of morality for women not only protect them from becoming alcoholics, but also insulate them so that people are not likely to label them alcoholics even if they have problems. Although a family normally acts to insulate its members, the need for loved ones to shield male drinkers from the public's awareness is often outweighed by the desire to help them. A woman is so heavily criticized for alcoholism, however, that her family and friends are more likely to overlook her drinking than to encourage her to seek assistance.[37]

Some theorists argue that this family protectiveness may stem less from love for the woman than from a desire to preserve the family's self-image.[38] A husband's attempt to shield his wife may be due to fear that exposure would reflect on his ability to manage his household or even on his masculinity.[39] One husband on learning of his wife's drinking problem reacted in a manner that emphasizes this common response to an alcoholic wife: "I was righteously indignant. She was making me look bad! If my superiors and associates learned that I couldn't handle my own wife, they might logically assume that I couldn't handle my business responsibilities."[40]

A research report indicates that some physicians attempt "to protect their injured male pride by treating their alcoholic wives with little else than drug combinations which can also lead to cross-addictions."[41]

Whatever the actual reason for protection that a woman receives from her family, to save the alcoholic or the family from embarrassment and / or moral condemnation, it helps her remain hidden from the public. She therefore does not show up in clinics, halfway houses, and at Alcoholics Anonymous (A.A.) meetings. It can be argued that because her alcoholism is hidden and her family and friends help to hide it even more than they would for a man, alcoholism in women becomes a more serious problem.[42]

Not only are family and friends less likely to label a woman an alcoholic, physicians hesitate even to ask questions about drinking let alone to tell a woman that her problem is alcohol. In some research done on A.A. members in 1975, Jane James found that one half of the ninety women interviewed had tried to discuss their drinking problem with other people and had been told they were not alcoholics.[43] The majority of the people they tried to speak to were physicians (five of them were psychiatrists). This means that one-fourth of the forty-five women tried to get help for their drinking problem from a medical doctor and failed. Forty-five of the women interviewed by Marian Sandmaier in 1980 saw physicians when they were drinking alcoholically, and only seven of these doctors confronted them with their drinking problem.[44] These are discouraging statistics!

Physicians and many alcohol professionals share stereotypes about alcoholics, both male and female, with the rest of the community. As the Broverman study indicated, those who deal with alcoholics are subject to the same stereotypic beliefs as the rest of us. Responses by professionals who work with alcoholics to questionnaires measuring attitudes and beliefs about alcohol and alcoholism showed that "the professionals tend to reflect the opinions and biases of the community within which they work."[45] Others found that there was a "significant core of negative sentiment toward the alcoholic on the part of community hospital and agency personnel."[46] Personnel who thought of the alcoholic as a troublemaker were less likely to accept him or her as a patient for treatment. These negative attitudes are reflected in other studies of health professionals.[47] Interviews with 161 physicians, showed that many had especially negative feelings about female alcoholics. The physicians believed that these women had more personality disorder, less insight, and were less likable than their male counterparts.[48]

If physicians have negative attitudes toward alcoholics in general and especially female alcoholics, little knowledge of the disease, and like the rest of the community are unwilling to face the problem, then female alcoholics can expect little assistance from physicians in their recovery from alcoholism.

Frequently, doctors are just too busy to see through the obvious symptoms a patient is suffering to the disease of alcoholism. In a 1972 survey of physicians in private practice, researchers learned that doctors with larger practices diagnosed the same number of patients as alcoholic as those who treated many fewer patients.[49] Physicians who see a large number of patients, therefore diagnose a smaller proportion of them as problem drinkers or alcohlics. As the deputy director of a mental health clinic told the Senate in 1976, "The busy practitioner is often more apt to pick up the anxiety, miss the depression, and thus prescribe a tranquilizer such as Valium or Librium."[50] The deputy director also noted that overlooking the alcohol problem is even more likely to happen if the patient is a woman. In a 1972 survey, only about one-half of the fifteen thousand physicians in private practice who were surveyed believed that a patient can ever recover from alcoholism.[51] It is no wonder physicians do not make time for the alcoholic!

It was only in 1956 that the American Medical Association acknowledged that "alcoholism must be regarded as within the purview of medical science." Many doctors, therefore are severely lacking in training about alcoholism. A magazine article gives the example of a physician who could not recognize the symptoms in his wife, although she had been drinking heavily for eleven years. During this time, she had sought treatment from five consulting physicians and eight psychiatrists before her disease was finally diagnosed. The doctor brings together the reasons for not labeling his wife an alcoholic in his very candid explanation of what happened. "Denial, pride, nearness to the problem, plus absolutely no education about the disease all prevented me from grasping the real problem. Neither the first eight psychiatrists nor the five consultants nor I could make the diagnosis for eleven years."[52] What women frequently do receive from physicians are prescription drugs, which end up leading to a cross-addiction.

Mental illness is a disease more likely to be associated with women than alcoholism, and over the years, mental illness has become a more respectable disease—a position that alcoholism has yet to fully achieve. "At the clinical level... alcoholism continues to be viewed with the ambivalence, often expressed in feelings of derision, disgust and anger such as were accorded other mental illnesses a generation ago."[53] Some theorists have argued that since it is more acceptable for a woman to be mentally ill than alcoholic, physicians are more likely to label them in the least injurious way.[54] Nervousness and hysteria are uncensurable female ailments that do not have a link to sexual promiscuity.

A divorced woman describes how her husband failed to mention her alcoholism when they went through divorce proceedings even though he left out nothing else: "All the most secret areas of my life beginning with my sexual abuse in childhood, to my brother's death, my therapy, and my hospitalizations, were made public by my husband. He never mentioned my alcoholism—that would have injured his image more seriously than an emotionally dysfunctional wife."[55]

Mental illness does not cast aspersions on either the spouse, parents, children, or friends, who tend to feel guilt by association with a female alcoholic. They believe it is partially their fault, and given that many people (physicians included) see alcoholism as secondary and caused by some underlying problem, it is not an unreasonable assumption.

Some of the women who campaigned for prohibition were coming home and using the patent medicines of their day, which contained up to 50 percent opiates or alcohol.[56] Pills and prescribed medicines are very acceptable for women, and some doctors seem ready to oblige the woman who complains of nervousness, jitteryness or depression. The statistics on prescribed drug use are clear. Women use prescription drugs to a much larger extent than do men. A 1971 survey in New York state found that the largest percentage of those who frequently used antidepressants were unemployed housewives (45.9 percent of the users).[57] Almost twice as many women as men in a California survey regularly used sedatives, stimulants, and tranquilizers.[58] A national survey published in 1973 showed that greater prescription drug usage among women was a national phenomenon. Women (29 percent) were more than twice as likely as men (13 percent) to use psychotherapeutic drugs (especially tranquilizers and sedatives) on a regular basis.[59]

Physicians are willing to prescribe these drugs for women and women are likely to go to "Dr. Fixit," as one recovering alcoholic called physicians, for remedies to overcome the effects of alcohol.[60] As testimony before the Senate Subcommittee on Alcohol Abuse in Women noted, "What is also known, and of greater concern, is that sedatives and tranquilizers when used in combination with alcohol, a distressingly more frequent occurrence, are additive (synergistic) and compound the toxic and lethal effects of the two substances."[61] Physicians are more likely to prescribe drugs for women with alcohol problems and therefore they are likely to end up with an even worse problem than the male alcoholic due to the devastating effect of this cross-addiction. This is true no matter to which socioeconomic group a woman belongs. In a 1974 sample, 42 percent of the alcoholic women used tranquilizers and 24 percent used sedatives while drinking. This relationship held whether the woman was poor or wealthy, and most of the drugs were prescribed.[62] A 1977 survey of A.A. members showed that 29 percent of the women were addicted to drugs other than alcohol as compared to only 15 percent of the men.[63] Instead of improving, this situation seems to be worsening: Among those A.A. members thirty years old or younger, statistics were even more shocking—55 percent of the women and 36 percent of the men were addicted to other drugs.[64]

The firsthand accounts of alcoholics and their spouses back up these statistics with startling clarity. One woman went to a psychiatrist and then a general practitioner. The psychiatrist suggested that she cut down on her drinking so that he could get a better understanding of her id or superego. Any time he directed the conversation toward her drinking, she cried and thus avoided a discussion. After months of unsuccessful treatment during which her problem with alcohol was never broached, she went to a general practitioner. She told him directly, "I drink a lot, and I think I'm an alcoholic." His response was to suggest she'd "better cut down on the drinking." He then prescribed tranquilizers, which she promptly took along with the alcohol.[65] This situation is not unique; there are similar accounts from many female alcoholics who have tried to seek assistance from the medical profession.

Another woman, for example, continually mixed scotch and valium and found that even after three suicide attempts no one ever mentioned that she might have a problem with alcohol. "Even my family doctor could not believe that a 'nice lady' like myself could be alcoholic."[66]

Family, friends, and physicians are not the only people who do not like to deal with the female alcoholic, our law enforcers also protect women from being labeled alcoholic. "There is a reluctance to impose the stigmatization of arrest, conviction and incarceration on women."[67] In California in 1957, Johnson found that "the ratio of boys to girls declined as the severity of the offenses involved lessened."[68] If females are convicted, the Uniform Crime Reports show that they are likely to receive shorter sentences. This trend continues into adulthood, and women who do show up in felony statistics tend to commit more serious offenses than do men. "This suggests that women offenders are treated with greater leniency than males and that they are brought into court only when their behavior is considered serious."[69]

This special treatment of females by the law enforcement system carries over into treatment of their alcohol-related problems.[70] Inebriated women often receive special consideration from male officers. A researcher for

Canada's Addiction Research Foundation reports that officers either appear shaken by seeing a woman in such condition or are charitable toward her. Frequently, she is sent home instead of being booked.[71] Thus, fewer female alcoholics are ever arrested.[72] This may be partially due to their tendency to cause less trouble, but it also appears to be a reflection of the inability of the legal system to come to terms with alcoholism in women.

Public drunkenness statistics from the Toronto courts support the claim that women who drink receive special police and court protection. There are more men convicted than one would expect from the percentage they form of the alcoholic population and fewer women convicted.[73] A crown attorney in Toronto's women's court discussing the disposition of female drunks said, "We're generally very lenient with women. They just plead guilty and walk out.... Usually it's enough punishment that she's spent a night in jail drying out."[74]

A 1974 survey by the U.S. National Highway Traffic Safety Administration documented that police officers who stop women for driving while intoxicated (DWI) are less likely to arrest them than men.[75] Women comprise a very small proportion (4 percent) of those who have been arrested and required to enter a drunken driver program.[76] The percentage of women arrested in Boston for DWI several years ago was even less (2 percent).[77] When the researchers investigated the records of seventy-three women who were arrested, they found that "in the case of the woman DWI offender, certain conditions, events or behaviors, must accompany the act of driving while intoxicated in order to cause the police officer to complete the arrest procedure."[78] Three-quarters of the women arrested had been guilty of some traffic violation, in an accident, or verbally or physically abusive to the arresting officer. Clearly, it takes more for the officer to decide to arrest a female than a male for DWI. Although this seems to give unequal but favorable treatment to the woman who is drinking and driving, it also protects her from getting much needed medical attention.

What the woman alcoholic faces is a combination of traditional roles and / or expectations associated with her status as a female. These roles leave no room for the image of her as an alcoholic. She is supposed to be a preserver of morality and mainly concerned with serving her husband and family. To become an alcoholic, a woman has to violate stronger cultural standards than a man who acts in a similar manner. A woman is thought to be unnatural if instead of upholding all the female virtues and performing the accepted female tasks, she has sunk to the level of the male vices of alcoholism and promiscuity. This attitude is a function of social definition. It is primarily due to the role that society expects a woman to play that her alcoholism is considered so degrading. She is not more morally reprehensible than a male alcoholic; but as a society, we have determined how she should act, and she has gone against society's dictates in the most flagrant manner.

It is no wonder then that friends, family physicians, and legal representatives are hesitant to label a woman an alcoholic. It is a severe action to take, for once labeled, she is beyond redemption in the minds of many. She is automatically a bad mother, a miserable wife, and a slut. People will ignore or deny her problem until there is no option left but to "tell it like it is."

Structural Features of Social Organization

It is not only these cultural definitions and traditional values that offer a woman status insularity and keep her from being labeled an alcoholic. Those features that affect variables, such as visibility or segregation, are called structural features of social organization. They also make it less likely that a woman will be labeled alcoholic.

Physical Location of the Housewife

Since, traditionally, the main role we expect a woman to fulfill in our society is that of a housewife, we have provided her with an ideal location in which to conceal her drinking. An American housewife is often alone for a major part of the day, affording her a great deal of privacy.

Numerous studies have shown that women are more likely to drink alone and at home.[79] As Fraser states,

> Housewives swell the ranks of female alcoholism and indeed constitute the greater proportion of heavy drinkers. They have more of an opportunity to drink than any other women, and in the case of the affluent social classes, they have more money to buy more and better booze, time and recuperative aids.[80]

A prominent psychiatrist has argued that the female's ability to manipulate environments keeps her from showing up in the official statistics as alcoholic.[81] However, women do not have an innate or learned capacity to manage their surroundings; instead, their status not only prescribes how they are expected to behave but also the location of their activities. In many traditional societies with a large extended family, although the woman was a housewife, she was unlikely ever to have much time alone. In our society, however, a household usually consists of the immediate family, with the husband at work and the children, as soon as they are five or six, in school. Thus our social structure has provided the perfect opportunity for women to be undisturbed while they drink.

Taboos against Bar Drinking

Women also drink at home because the bar has not traditionally been considered a proper place for them.[82] A 41-year-old alcoholic male in my sample made it clear that he did not think that this had changed: "I think it is OK for a man to drink at a bar—a woman looks for sex in a bar." Other male alcoholics said, "Females belong at home" and "A lady should not be out drinking." They seemed to be as concerned about the setting as the amount of drinking that was taking place. Some recent interviews conducted in the Boston area reconfirmed this view. A 62-year-old bartender in a Boston hotel was quoted as saying, "When you see a woman sitting at a bar you think she's loose. It's natural that you should think that."[83] This response is appropriate in the sense that it is "natural" in this country at this time to think of a woman who breaks conventions and is alone at a bar as loose. Clearly, this has not always or even usually been true. Rather, this is what many of us have been taught to believe about a woman who drinks a lot, especially if she is doing it alone and publicly.

Even women who work in bars are suspect. In another interesting interview from the same research, a 22-year-old female bartender in an inn north of Boston explains how critical her family and friends are of her job. Her father has two main objections, "You don't meet the right kind of people in bars," and "bargirls are bargirls and people think they're loose and easy."[84] Just being associated with the bar, which traditionally has been considered male territory, is enough to call a woman's morals into question. These attitudes toward a woman drinking in bars prevent the female alcoholic from showing up as frequently as men in public settings.[85]

Solitary drinking is considered an indicator of alcoholism among male or female drinkers. In my research, I found that those labeled alcoholic were much more likely than heavy drinkers to drink alone (see table A.3). Only 4 percent of the heavy drinkers said they usually drank alone, while 56 percent of the alcoholics usually drank alone. Moreover, female alcoholics were even more likely (by 10 percent) to be solitary drinkers than male alcoholics (see table A.4).

This pattern of drinking limits the visibility of the drinking woman and makes it less likely that people will realize she has a drinking problem and label her, further adding to her status insularity.

Settings in Which Women Seek Help

One additional factor that makes it less likely for women to be labeled alcoholic and come to the public's attention is the fact that they tend to seek help in the most private of settings. This is the one feature that is as much dependent on the manipulation of women as it is the way in which the social organization is structured. They are not as likely as men to go to rehabilitation facilities or clinics, instead, they visit general practitioners.[86]

The statistics on the ratio of male to female alcoholics who are treated in various settings supports this contention.[87] As noted earlier, the ratio of males to females varies from 11 to 1 in prison,[88] to 5 to 1 in public hospitals,[89] to 3 to 2 in private hospitals,[90] to as low as 1 to 1 in private physicians' offices.[91] Women who seek help therefore tend to do so in places that limit the number of people who will know about their problem.

Conclusion

The way female alcoholics have been treated makes little sense without understanding the status of females in our society. Traditionally, women were expected to behave in accord with their exalted position as preservers of morality. Their prestige depended largely on their roles as wives and / or mothers and their family's welfare was to take precedence over their own.

The image of a woman as an alcoholic threatens the traditional values that have defined the roles of women. If we accept that a woman can be both a lady and an alcoholic, we must change our traditional views of women. The traditional values have worked together with the physical locations in which we are likely to find women in our society to protect a woman from becoming an alcoholic (cultural protection and proscriptive drinking norms) and even more importantly, to protect her from being labeled an alcoholic even if she has a severe drinking problem (status insularity).

The idealistic way in which we have regarded women has kept us from dealing with their drinking problems. Female alcoholics have been less likely to show up in statistics, giving professionals and organizations a rationale for spending little on research and often not providing facilities for their treatment. As a society, we have been guilty of ignoring the problem of alcoholism in women with the misguided logic that since there are so few female alcoholics, it is not worth studying them separately. The belief was, and often remains, if we ignore the problem of alcoholism in women, it will somehow go away.

This has led to a catch-22 situation for the female alcoholic in our society. Knowing that she will be considered "the lowest of the low," as one alcoholic woman put it, she is unlikely to seek assistance for her problem. The moral condemnation that has prevented many women from ever turning to drink keeps them from ever recovering once they develop a drinking problem. The woman is stuck with her drinking problem or condemned as a tramp, unfit mother, or worse if she does seek help. Alcoholic women, and frequently the people with whom they come in contact, end up doing all they can to keep from identifying the problem.[92]

The unrealistic roles we proffer for women have prevented us from dealing honestly with the increasing number of female alcoholics. The more alcoholic women hide because they fear censure, the more severe their disease becomes.

3

Declining Insularity

In the first chapter, roles, stereotypes, and values were treated as static in order to present a clear picture. In the real world, however, things never remain exactly the same, society is always in flux, although at times more so than at others.

Chapter 3 focuses on roles as socially defined and therefore changeable from society to society and within a particular society at different times. I discuss the impact of changing roles on the drinking habits of women and the greater willingness of people to deal with the problems related to female alcoholism. Recent changes in roles are shown to lead to expectations for behavior that are at times contradictory for women. The possible importance of sex role confusion for explaining the increase in female alcoholism is considered. The impact of changing roles on the drinking habits of women and the greater willingness to deal with the problem of female alcoholism are also investigated. An increasing realization that the female alcoholic is not unnatural or morally reprehensible and the more public nature of her life have led to a decrease in the aspects of her status that once insulated her from being labeled. Ramifications of this decline in status insularity for female alcoholics is discussed.

Sex Roles and Their Social Definition

The past fifty years have evidenced a dramatic change in women's roles. Women's liberation, the need for the wife to help support the family, the increasing divorce rate, the growth of a modern industrial society where much of the labor is not dependent on physical strength, and the more extensive use of birth control devices have all played a part. As Riley and Marden have claimed, there appears to be a "general trend in our society toward less and less differentiation in the social behavior of men and women."[1] This means that the status of male or female is not as good a predictor as in the past of how a person will behave.

Until recently, in Western society, many of an individual's actions in certain situations could be predicted if we knew their gender. We could clearly specify which actions or attitudes were masculine and which were feminine. Only recently has "a woman's place is in the home" been replaced by "a woman's place is in the House and in the Senate too!"

Even though there have been distinctly different roles for men and women in American society (and in most societies, for that matter), this is not the only way that society can be organized. Roles are socially defined. They do not spring simply from biological differences between men and women. The same attitudes and actions may be masculine in one society and feminine in another, or as Margaret Mead showed in *Sex and Temperament*, [2] men and women may be expected to act in a similar manner. Mead studied three "primitive" societies in New Guinea and found interesting differences among them in terms of what they considered masculine or feminine characteristics. Among the Arapesh, one of the societies Mead described, both men and women were maternal, passive, and mild.

> Those who find the whole social scheme the least congenial and intelligible, are the violent aggressive men and women. This will at once be seen to contrast with our own society, in which it is the mild, unaggressive man who goes to the wall, and the aggressive violent woman who is looked upon with disapproval and opprobrium, while among the Arapesh, with their lack of distinction between the male and female temperament, the same temperament suffers in each sex. [3]

Ideal Mundugumor men and women are the opposite extreme of the Arapesh. Members of both sexes are expected to be "violent, competitive, aggressively sexed, jealous and ready to see and avenge insult." [4] Traditionally, in our society, these have been prized masculine behavior patterns. In both these societies, the ideal temperaments were similar for both sexes, although the preferred temperaments were opposite.

Unlike the two preceding societies, the Tchambuli have very diverse ideals for men and women. The women hold the real positions of power. Fishing, which is the main source of food, is a business controlled entirely by women. Whereas women are dominant, men are perceived as less responsible and more dependent. "The woman's attitude toward the men is one of kindly tolerance and appreciation." [5] The Tchambuli evidence male and female ideals almost exactly opposite to those of traditional American culture.

More current research has also shown that men and women have similar roles and share in decision-making processes especially in hunting and gathering societies. [6] Mead's work is viewed as a "bridge between the past of myths and misunderstandings, and newly emerging knowledge that better informs our thinking about ourselves." [7] Social scientists do not discount Mead's conclusions; instead, they claim she did not go far enough in showing how little the roles assigned to men and women are determined by biological differences. [8]

The research of Mead and more current anthropologists tells us two things. First, male and female roles that we tend to consider part of nature are instead socially defined. It is not unnatural for a man to be maternal, passive, or dependent, it is also not unnatural for a woman to be aggressive, dominant, or responsible. And extrapolating to our current research, it is no more unnatural for a woman to be an alcoholic than a man, although it may be defined that way in our particular society. Mead's studies showed above all else the great flexibility of human nature and the diverse ways in which men and women can be expected to behave in different cultures.

Secondly, it is not necessarily undesirable that men's and women's roles are defined in a similar manner. Mead and others show that societies manage well without such strict distinctions. Similarly defined roles may lead to less complexity and variety in the culture, but they also allow for greater individual freedom to achieve the full potential of one's natural temperament. The fact that men's and women's roles are becoming more alike or androgynous does not necessarily lead to such social problems as increased rates of alcoholism, even though alcoholism among women is often cited as the price women have to pay for emancipation and tackling career goals—one of the unwanted fruits of the women's liberation movement. [9]

Sex Role Confusion: Internal

Alcohol specialists for the past forty-five years have been saying that alcoholic women suffer from some kind of "sex role confusion." [10] Exactly what they mean by this is not always clear, but they generally believe that female alcoholics do not accept their proper role as women in our society. Female alcoholics are seen as possessing and / or valuing masculine traits. Whether this sex role confusion leads to alcoholism or is a result of alcoholism has never been convincingly demonstrated. However, it is a fairly common assumption that failure to accept traditional roles causes psychological stress that may lead to alcoholism in women.

Sharon Wilsnak made an attempt to test clinical observations of sex role confusion that had been reported in other research. The conclusion she reached was that female alcoholics identify consciously with the female role but unconsciously with styles that have traditionally been masculine. [11] This is viewed as a conflict internal to the individual, despite the author's admission that what is masculine or feminine is socially defined.

Although this research was conducted by a female, it and most of the work done on sex role confusion seem to be heavily laden with prejudicial assumptions. The measures of what it means to be masculine are so intertwined with the traditional roles of men and women and an attempt to keep women in their place that it is hard to question such research without questioning all the values of our society. A response on one of the series of tests used by Wilsnak was considered masculine if the individual answered false to the following question: "I like to accept the leadership of someone else in deciding what the group is going to do." A true response on the following item would reflect masculinity: "It is very important to do your best in all situations." The reverse responses (true and false, respectively) are counted as feminine.

It is unlikely that a successful career woman would ever be considered feminine by such psychological testing. Recent research on career women has indeed found that successful women have masculine interests and characteristics.[12] These studies do not discount the ability of such tests as those used by Wilsnak to measure certain traits. Instead, they call into question whether masculine and feminine properly describe the traits they measure. Those who interpret standard tests often confuse femininity with docility and the inability to take a leadership role.

Earlier research in the 1950s and 1960s tended to show that working women were well-adjusted only if their priorities were such that their families came first. Women who placed emphasis on careers had poor self-concepts and were seen as maladjusted.[13] Whether this maladjustment existed because of cultural roadblocks to success they faced or whether they were maladjusted and that is why they chose such a path is a question that was investigated but never answered.[14] A well-thought-out review of this research concluded that "the design, visibility, and interpretation of research relevant to social issues depends very much on the current purposes of the social organism and entrenched opinions and values."[15] People believed it was wrong for a woman to work instead of having a family, and research reflected this bias. Currently, "investigators are portraying career women in sufficient detail and perspective so that simplistic evaluation of them as good or bad, well-adjusted or neurotic, feminine or not should become obsolete."[16] This sophistication has not reached alcohol research, however, and much of that work is still based on outdated distinctions of masculine and feminine behavior.

The arguments of sex role confusion generally take women's roles as unvarying. These arguments make no room for the fact that society is always in flux and women's roles are changing rapidly. They assume it is bad or at least harmful if a woman does not choose traditional female styles as determined by standard psychological tests designed twenty years or more ago. As research discussed in chapter 1 indicated, to be a healthy woman is not to be fully an adult.

Some theorists have made the step from looking at women's drinking problems from this perspective to arguing that women should not have equality, given all the awful problems, such as alcoholism, that go with it. If we look at society in such a fixed way , it is not surprising that any change is viewed as negative.

Sex Role Confusion: Societal

A more convincing argument can be made if conflict is seen as occurring

sampled about their attitude toward their patients to see if they were as negative as past studies have shown (chapter 2). A majority of those responding
claimed that women were no more difficult to treat than men (see the
appendix). Even those who claimed that women were harder to treat indicated this was because they are looked down on by society or tend to be
further along in their alcoholism by the time they seek treatment. Not a single
response indicated the prejudicial views commonly expressed in the past that
women were more difficult to work with or had more psychological problems
than men. One respondent stated, "They quite often need continuing support," and another said, "They are more protected from consequences of
their drinking in many cases." These are the only two comments that came
close to insinuating that women are really more difficult to handle than men
in rehabilitative settings. This was a far cry from Johnson's research, which
showed physicians believe that female alcoholics have more personality disorders, less insight, and are less likable. [36] Although the small number of the
sample makes any generalizations impossible, it does show that those who
worked with alcoholics in the rehabilitative settings I sampled did not have
the stereotypical prejudice against female alcoholics that had been found in
earlier studies.

A poorer prognosis for successful rehabilitation was also used as an excuse
for not admitting female alcoholics to treatment facilities. Despite findings in
previous research, [37] the majority of the professionals who worked with the
alcoholics in my own research said there is no difference in the success rate of
male and female alcoholics (see the appendix). Of those who claimed there
was a difference, most indicated that women are more likely to be successful.
The myth of the maladjusted female alcoholic who has little chance of recovering seems to be unsubstantiated in the rehabilitative settings studied.

The increasing openness with which alcoholism in general and female
alcoholism in particular is discussed cannot help but encourage women and
their families and friends to seek assistance. Today, Elizabeth Taylor does
television interviews and discusses her addiction to alcohol. Senators wives
are willing to speak openly about their alcoholism. Even one of the most respected women in our country, Betty Ford, wife of Former President Gerald
R. Ford, has had the courage to write [38] and speak about her cross-addiction
to drugs and alcohol. Although some people would prefer that she remain
silent about her illness, most people admire Mrs. Ford for her honesty and
openness. Female alcoholics now have prominent role models for their recovery process.

Conclusion

The sources of status insularity for the female alcoholic have been somewhat undercut. Traditional cultural definitions that for so long supported
women's roles have begun to change; double standards for drinking and

sexual behavior have been questioned. The less condemnation a woman is likely to receive for admitting to her disease, the more likely she will seek help and therefore be labeled an alcoholic. These changes in attitude have also made it more likely that those in a position to label women alcoholics will not be as hesitant to do so. Increased public knowledge about alcoholism and more training for doctors have hastened these changes.

The structural features of social organization that once protected women from being labeled alcoholic have also been altered. More women than ever are working today. In 1940, 48.1 percent of the single women and only 14.7 percent of the married women living with their husbands were working. These percentages have risen steadily over the past forty years until in 1981, 62.3 percent of the single women and 51 percent of the married women living with their husbands work.[39] Being away from home during working hours eliminates the private setting that enabled female alcoholics to hide their drinking from others. This change in occupational status means that a woman's behavior is much more likely than it was forty years ago to be open to public scrutiny.

The bar, as strictly male territory, is also on the decline. One of the more dubious accomplishments of the women's liberation movement was to take legal action to integrate bars. Women are more likely today to drink in public places, and therefore public intoxication of females has also become more likely. Although this behavior has become more common for women and they cannot legally be denied access to most places, the comment by the bartender in the preceding chapter makes it clear that women who go to bars unaccompanied are still not regarded as pinnacles of virtues.

The change in women's roles, especially occupational ones, the advances of the women's liberation movement toward equality of the sexes which has led to diminishing the moral condemnation of female alcoholics, the greater willingness for alcohol facilities to treat women, and the greater publicness of women's lives have all lead to a decline in the status insularity that once protected women from being labeled alcoholics. Today, they are more likely to be labeled but also more likely to be treated for their illness. Protection from labeling may have been viewed as gallant but it also kept many women from receiving the help necessary to recover. The price of emancipation may well be more alcoholic problems for women; however, it is also means that those who do have a problem are now more likely to receive the treatment they so desperately need.

All status insularity for female alcoholics has not disappeared. They are still more likely to remain hidden from public view and less likely to receive treatment or by other means be labeled an alcoholic. When we look at what we know about alcoholics, their drinking patterns, their problems, and their needs for a successful recovery, it is clear that gender is still an important variable in explaining the differences we find among alcoholics and will remain so for years to come.

4

Labeling Theory and Stigmatization

A person commits an act (drinking too much, robbing a bank, embezzling from a corporation, and so forth) and in doing so breaks the written or un-written rules by which we live. If discovered, that person may be called a deviant. When we speak of the deviant, in everyday conversation, we tend to focus on his or her personal attributes or environment. Thus when discussing Jane who is an alcoholic, we are likely to note that she is depressed, imma-ture, has inadequately adopted the feminine role, or other such individual characteristics. On the other hand, we may be concerned that she has an unhappy marriage, a job that puts her under too much pressure, comes from a broken home, or is affected by other environmental factors. This is not only how most of us look at the deviant, but also how sociology has traditionally viewed the deviant. The concern has generally been to explain why any particular individual or group goes against and / or disrupts the orderly way in which our society is organized.

Deviance from the Labeling Perspective

Since the 1960s, labeling theory has become popular in sociology. This theory or perspective attempted to change how we view deviation. Instead of concentrating on the deviant individual, labeling theorists are interested in the way other people react to deviation and those who deviate. For example, the question was no longer, What is it about a person or a person's environ-ment that makes him or her smoke marihuana? Instead, the interest shifted to how people would go about labeling the marihuana smoker deviant. What process does the smoker go through to become a regular user? How is a person emancipated from the controls of society that keep most of us from ever becoming regular users (for example, limiting supplies by legal means, the need to keep one's smoking from others who would not approve, and the belief that it is immoral)?[1] From this perspective, it is not the deviant act that matters but how others perceive and react to the person's behavior.

Social groups create deviance by making the rules whose infraction constitutes deviance, and by applying these rules to particular people and labeling them as outsiders. From this point of view, deviance is *not* a quality of the act the person commits, but rather a consequence of the application by others of rules and sanctions to an "offender." [2]

In an excellent and comprehensive review, Edwin Schur argues that one of the main points of labeling theory is: "Deviant individuals and situations involving deviant behavior result not simply from discrete acts of wrongdoing or departure from norms; they also reflect patterns and processes of social definition." [3] An act or a series of acts may vary from the acceptable social norms, but these individual acts do not define deviance. Those who create and enforce the rules have it within their purview to decide what will and will not be treated as deviant behavior.

Although popularized in modern sociology by labeling theorists, these ideas are not new. In 1877, when speaking of prostitution, the social historian William Lecky noted that the extreme censure that women confronted meant that once guilty of one indiscretion, they were cast in the role of prostitutes for life.

> Acts which naturally neither imply nor produce a total subversion of the moral feelings, and which, in other countries, are often followed by happy, virtuous, and affectionate lives, in England almost invariably lead to absolute ruin. Infanticide is greatly multiplied and a vast proportion of those whose reputations and lives have been blasted by one momentary sin, are hurled into the abyss of habitual prostitution—a condition which, owing to the sentence of public opinion and the neglect of legislators, is in no other European country so hopelessly vicious or so irrevocable. [4]

It is easier to understand this perspective by citing another example. If a man is walking down the street and speaking loudly, apparently to himself, some people are likely to think and say that he is crazy. If he frightens some people and they complain to the police, he may be put in a mental hospital for examination. If those who examine him believe that he is potentially dangerous to himself or others he may be locked up in an institution for the remainder of his life. Now suppose we have a little more information about the man. We learn that he is from a country where it is believed that a man can speak directly with his God and that this conversation should take place in a loud voice whenever one needs assistance. When he was walking down the street, the man in question was seeking guidance on how to solve one of his problems. Clearly, he would not be considered insane in his own culture, where everyone behaved in a similar manner. However, in ours he may be labeled a deviant, lose all his privileges, and be institutionalized until he stops his crazy behavior.

This example may seem far fetched. Nothing like this could really happen, since if this man were picked up and taken to a hospital, psychiatrists would immediately recognize that he was sane. A study by D. L. Rosenhan makes this supposition questionable.[5] Eight people volunteered to gain admission to twelve different hospitals by claiming that they heard voices. They were admitted to eleven of the hospitals with a diagnosis of schizophrenia and to the twelfth as having manic-depressive psychosis. Once admitted, they reverted to their usual personalities and with the exception of their name and occupation told the truth about themselves and their histories. Despite their normal behavior, the length of time that they were kept in the hospital ranged from seven to fifty-two days, with an average of nineteen days. None of the staff (from attendants, to nurses, to psychiatrists) in any of the twelve cases ever suspected they were sane, although the patients became suspicious of them and questioned their presence in the hospital. Hospital reports written about these pseudopatients altered the events of their lives and their attitudes to fit the original diagnosis. When these patients were eventually released, the diagnoses were not changed, and eleven of their records showed schizophrenia in remission.

In our typical way of looking at deviance, we would not question those who label the deviant. Instead, we would ask what it is about the individual or the individual's environment that makes him or her crazy? Labeling theory focuses our inquiry instead on the problem of being labeled deviant and draws our attention to those who actually do the labeling. By doing this it has shown that in most instances deviance is not just a case of either you are or you are not. Rosenhan's study indicates the sane are not sane all the time (we all do things that are considered irrational or illogical) and the insane are not always insane (remember, it was the patients who realized the pseudopatients were faking).

In the Rosenhan study, once the patient was labeled schizophrenic all of his or her other actions were interpreted in terms of this illness. Very rational behaviors, such as taking notes, were described as an aspect of their pathological behavior. This label often does not disappear once the patient leaves the hospital. Since the attitudes of the public toward the mentally ill are often suspicion, fear, and hostility,[6] "the label sticks, a mark of inadequacy forever."[7]

The Impact of Stigmatization

Other theorists have also shown us that labeling is not just a matter of semantics. Name calling can be a powerful means of keeping other people from violating society's accepted norms and if they do, of punishment. Stigmatization or the "process of attaching visible signs of moral inferiority to persons, such as invidious labels, marks, brands, or publicly disseminated information"[8] can have a detrimental effect on the rule-breaker. These stigmas frequently[9] serve to impede the process of reforming the individual and instead push him or her further into the deviant role.

The implications of this theoretical orientation for methodology have been to move away from the statistical correlations and predictions of earlier deviance research. Most research conducted by labeling theorists uses participant observation or ethnography in an attempt to present reality from the viewpoint of those involved.[10] Thus, the main works associated with the labeling perspective have been descriptive and do not lend themselves to the standard empirical testing that some sociologists would like.[11] However, the more broad-minded labeling theorists admit that traditional research using comparisons of individual characteristics and official statistics can at least play a complimentary role in labeling analysis.[12]

Some quantitative research presents "tests" of labeling theory. An entire book by Walter Gove examines studies that claim to determine the veracity of what he defines as labeling theory's basic tenets. Although I believe his attempt is admirable, I must agree with Schur and John I. Kitsuse[13] that some of Gove's propositions are misguided and oversimplified. Despite Gove's contention that there is little support for the main propositions of labeling theory, a great deal of empirical research shows, to the contrary, that a description of deviance is not complete without insights from the labeling perspective. Instead, it is difficult not to conclude with Schur that "the central idea of the societal reaction perspective is incontrovertible, in the sense of being so well-established and so central to the sociological enterprise as to be (insofar as we can ever say it) undeniable, that is, true."[14]

There are several areas of deviance where persuasive studies using statistics demonstrate the importance of the stigmatization process.[15] This research frequently shows the powerful negative influence of the stigmatization process on the individual. A study by Schwartz and Skolnick tests the indirect consequences of legal sanctions for two different occupational positions.[16] Four different folders were prepared for use in job applications for unskilled laborers. The folders differed only in the individual's involvement with the legal system. One folder indicated the person had been arrested and convicted of assault; the second that he had been tried for assault but acquitted. The third person's record also indicated he had been tried and acquitted, but in addition, his folder included a letter from the judge attesting to the not guilty verdict and reiterating that innocence must be presumed. The fourth folder did not mention any criminal record. Four groups of twenty-five employers were asked to hire a person from one folder. Nine expressed an interest in the person who had no record, six in the person who was acquitted and had a letter from the judge, three in the person who was acquitted but did not have an accompanyng letter, and only one in the person who was found guilty. The researchers drew two conclusions from this. First, that even after a person has paid his or her debt to society, there are informal negative sanctions that affect the person's life. Secondly, even those whom we presume innocent are affected by negative sanctions simply because they were charged with a crime. Schwartz and Skolnick also studied the effect of malpractice suits on doctors to see if the effects of labeling were similar. Fifty-eight physicians who had been sued for malpractice were interviewed. The researchers found that very little occupational harm came to physicians who had been sued. Fifty-two reported no negative effects from the suit on their practice; five of the six others reported their practice improved and only one that the practice had declined. This research showed not only the impact of legal stigma on individuals, but also demonstrated that those with low occupational status are the most likely to suffer detrimental effects from this stigmatization process.

Similar research was carried out more recently in the Netherlands in an attempt to see if the stigma of a criminal record impeded youths from securing a job.[17] Researchers found that 52 percent of those with no criminal record received a positive response to their application, 32 percent of those convicted once for theft, and only 26 percent of those who had lost their license once for drunken driving. The authors concluded that the "experiment shows conclusively that ex-delinquents are stigmatised when they apply for employment."[18]

Alcoholism does not lend itself as easily to discussion from the labeling perspective as some other forms of deviation, especially since the physiological aspects of the disease distinguishes it from many other kinds of deviation. However, the limitations of Gove's propositions are obvious from this analysis. Somehow the facts that the most common labeler of an alcoholic is a member of his or her own family and that official agencies are not eager to label alcoholics are seen as contradicting the tenets of labeling theory. With the exception of rather superficial categories, such as whether the label accounts for maintaining deviant behavior, the effects of being labeled an alcoholic is never considered. Instead, Gove reduces secondary deviation to the much more simplified notion of a self-fulfilling prophecy. Kitsuse correctly points out the inaccuracy of using this concept to describe Lemert's more sophisticated work.[19] One section of Gove's book concludes from an analysis of the available research that "the process of labeling in alcoholism is rather different from that imagined by the labeling hypothesis."[20] To the contrary, the only way to describe a portion of what can be observed in the life course of the alcoholic is by using the labeling perspective. Although it does not account for all that is taking place and some aspects of alcoholism are not taken into consideration, this does not discount the usefulness of labeling theory or its analysis of stigmatization. The basis for the present research is to modify the labeling perspective to allow it to explain more of the factors we see in alcoholism and deviance.

Critiques of Labeling Theory

Some critiques of labeling theory are justified by the foci of the research that have come out of this perspective. It is not my purpose to review all of them. However, several of the more serious criticisms will be mentioned briefly to give insight into the concept of status insularity.

THE ORIGINS OF DEVIANCE

Labeling theory does not explain some of the most pressing questions people want answered about deviance. For example, it tells us nothing about the origins of deviance. "What causes crime?" "What accounts for increases or decreases in crime rates?" "How can crime be reduced?"[21] Initial rule breaking is of minimal importance to the labeling theorist, and therefore he or she ignores the social contingencies that may lead to deviation.

"There is a premise in the writing of the labeling theorist that whatever the causes of initial rule-breaking, they assume minimal importance or entirely cease operation after initial rule-breaking...."[22] There is no reason to believe that a person's commitment to deviancy totally changes once he or she is labeled. To the contrary, it would make more sense to view the initial commission of a deviant act and the continued commission of deviant acts as part of some overall totality. Labeling theory ignores the social contingencies that lead to deviance, which results in a denial that the individual may have some reason for breaking the rules. As Nettler suggests, this tends to obscure our understanding of deviance "by shifting the locus of causes from actors to their judges."[23] The unwillingness of the labeling approach to investigate the origins of deviance comes from its narrow focus on the social-psychological aspects of deviance and its lack of concern, and therefore knowledge, of the structural.

DETERMINISTIC APPROACH TO THE INDIVIDUAL

Despite their deep concern for the underdog, labeling theorists have also been criticized for a deterministic approach to the individual. Deviance and deviant careers are not chosen by the individual, but forced on him or her by a reacting society. "Typifying deviants as passive receptors in an all-powerful social mechanism, labeling theory views actors as more acted upon than acting."[24]

According to labeling theorists, the causes of adult behavior lie in the people who respond to that behavior. In essence, others are responsible for a person's actions. As Gouldner says,

If this is a liberal conception of deviance that wins sympathy and tolerance for the deviant, it has the paradoxical consequence of inviting us to
view the deviant as a passive nonentity who is reponsible neither for his
suffering nor its alleviation—who is more "sinned against than sinning."[25]

Labeling theory overlooks the possibility of diversified constructions of
reality. Choices are available only within the confines of the official definitions.

Lemert, despite his key role in shaping labeling theory, admits to this
particular weakness in his later work. He expresses it so well that he is worth
quoting at length:

> Labeling unfortunately conveys an impression of interaction that is both
> sociologistic and unilateral: in the process deviants who are "successfully
> labeled" lose their individuality; they appear as Bordua (1967) says, like
> "empty organisms" or as Gouldner (1968) puts it, "like men on their
> backs" (Walton 1973). The extreme subjectivism made explicit by the
> underdog perspective, reflecting sympathy for the victim and antipathy
> towards the establishment, also distorts by magnifying the exploitive and
> arbitrary features of the societal reaction. But more important, it leaves
> little or no place for human choice at either level of interaction.[26]

Human choice exists for the deviant as well as the official labeling agent
before, during, and after deviation. Deviants choose from many possible
courses of action, and officials choose from a multitude of rules when deciding
whether or not to impose a label as well as which rule should actually be
applied. Lemert argues that there is "little... in labeling theory which deals
with this kind of conflict and choice making in the context of pluralism of
groups so conspicuous in modern society."[27]

THE PERMANENCE OF A LABEL

Since labeling theorists do not treat the deviant as a person who acts but as
one who is acted upon, they have presented deviant careers as inevitable and
ignored the possibility that people may be "delabeled" or "relabeled." These
processes have received little attention in the labeling literature because of
the assumption of the permanence of deviant careers. Trice and Roman[28]
show through the use of A.A. that delabeling and relabeling do occur. In the
case of alcoholics, assigning deviant labels actually helps change deviant
careers. Blacks, who are less likely to be labeled as alcoholics, have less chance
of extricating themselves from deviant careers.[29] Research indicates two
findings that run counter to the assumptions or at least contrary to the focus
of most labeling analyses: (1) Labeling is not always permanent, and (2)
labels can be helpful in assisting people to escape deviant careers.

STRUCTURAL ASPECTS OF DEVIANCE

The lack of concern with structural aspects of deviance is perhaps the weightiest charge leveled against labeling theory. "It is not that structural analysis... is precluded in the social reaction perspective, but rather that it remains consistently under-applied."[30] Theorists have chosen to focus on the individual deviant and to ignore the structural and historical aspects of his or her deviation. This has led to a "decontextualized"[31] deviant; one without a history or a place in the social structure.

Labeling theorists focused on an important aspect of deviance that had been largely ignored: the effects of social control on the deviance process. Other aspects of deviance, however, were overlooked in their effort to explain the workings of this one process. As Davis notes,

> An exclusive focus on confrontations between the labeling group and the persons it seeks to label overlooks such complex structural features of organizational life as status hierarchies, unofficial norms among labelers, conflicting ideologies of different agencies and informal power structures that operate to undermine or alter agency goals.[32]

Both labeling theorists and some of its critics tend to overlook the societal norms and values that play such a large part in determining people's response to deviation. The severity with which people view breaking a particular rule, beliefs about how rule-breakers should be punished, and even the prestige of the labeling agencies all play a part in the effect of the labeling process on the deviant. Different social conditions lead to different types and rates of deviation, which cannot be fully explained by focusing only on people's response to rule breaking.

As some commentators have argued, the narrow focus of the labeling theorists have led to a critique of the middle-range establishment. Even though they are the immediate enforcers of the norms and laws, they are certainly not the only force in society that sustains the social order. By focusing on the micro-setting, labeling theory never offers a critique of the overall system and therefore leaves the original power structure unchallenged.

In his comments on Becker's work, Gouldner probably summarizes best this criticism of labeling theory: "With all its humanistic merits, [they fail] to see that men—superiors as well as subordinates—may be powerfully constrained by institutions, by history, and indeed by biology."[33]

NOT A THEORY OF DEVIANCE

The criticisms discussed lead to a general question of whether labeling theory is actually a theory. Many labeling theorists do not, in fact, claim that it is a formal theory with related and testable propositions. Kitsuse[34] accepts Gibb's[35] terminology of a " new conception of deviance" or "perspective," and Schur sees societal reaction as "a central orienting concept"[36] or an "approach,"[37] Glassner suggests "labeling studies,"[38] and Scheff refers to it as a "sensitizing theory."[39]

As many critics have noted, there are numerous aspects of deviance that labeling theory does not illuminate.[40] Schur admits in his review of the field that some acts are more adequately explained by the labeling perspective than others: "Borderline forms of deviance seem to be especially good candidates for labeling analysis and those deviations on which widespread consensus exists (homicide, incest, and so on) less promising candidates."[41]

There is little doubt that labeling, as far as it has developed, gives only a partial explanation and a partial view of the complex aspects of deviance. Until it broadens its focus to include the structural features of deviance and seeks to answer many of the important questions posed by various theorists,[42] the labeling perspective cannot be treated as a formal theory.

The Labeling Perspective and a Focus on Insularity

If the labeling perspective were as broadly conceived as some labeling theorists claim it should be,[43] then most critiques of it, with the exception that it is not a formal theory, would be invalid. However, the evaluation of labeling theory cannot be formulated on possible achievements within this perspective; it must be based on actual work done within the field.

The issue is whether it makes sense to expand labeling theory in certain directions. The concept of status insularity was created by looking at what labeling theory cannot explain in the area of alcoholism. Systematization, expansion to include research on the structural and historical facets of deviance and a clarification of what aspects of deviance it does and does not explain, are necessary ventures if labeling theory is to give us a more complete picture of deviance.

Using Schur's conception of what should be accomplished by labeling theory, it is possible to show how status insularity can increase knowledge in areas that have been left relatively untouched by labeling theorists. Schur claims that three levels of analysis come into play or three "audiences": (1) the society-at-large—groups responsible for general reactions to behavior; (2) individuals (including significant others) with whom the individual interacts; and (3) the official and organizational agents of control.[44] "It is on this third audience that the labeling approach has especially focused until now, but... this audience is only one of several important research targets suggested by the labeling orientation."[45] As noted, most labeling analysis has focused on middle-level officials and the impact of their labeling on the deviant. Status insularity offers a way of including the other two audiences, especially the society at large, by looking at what makes it more or less likely that a person will be labeled. Three variable features of this societal audience are:

1. The *social evaluations based on cultural definitions* which help to guide our behavior, tell us what it is about a certain status that makes members more or less likely to be labeled for a certain type of deviance. As noted earlier (see chapter 1), the fact that resistance to labeling does not always coincide with power differentials is important. To understand the labeling process, it must be put in the cultural context of the society at large. The degree of insularity and whether it is declining or increasing, as discussed in the previous chapter, forces us to consider the place of norms and values in some historical context. By examining the status of the person being labeled, we provide the social and historical context that has been missing from most labeling analysis. What these assumptions mean for how labels are applied by significant others and officials (see chapter 2) ties the society at large together with the other two audiences. Social evaluations based on cultural definitions dictate to some degree how family and friends and officials, such as physicians and police, will respond to the female alcoholic.

2. *Structural features of social organization* also deal with the overall arrangement of society and help explain why a deviant in a particular status is labeled. It is clearly not just the individual nor the officials who determine the structures that enhance the possibility of a deviant being found and labeled or hidden and unlabeled.

3. *Power*, the third variable mentioned as a source of status insularity, also deals with the society at large. Although not applicable to female alcoholics, for most status insular positions power would be the primary variable. It is also one of the aspects, as previously discussed, that labeling theorists have been criticized for omitting from their analysis.

Status insularity then, is a tool to allow us to look at some of the key components that have been missing from labeling analysis: power differentials, structural features of society, and normative and historical contexts. At the same time, it manages to tie the three audiences together in a coherent analysis. Clearly, status insularity does not allow us to look at these aspects in all the ways that effect the deviance process, but for the labeling aspect at least, these variables are analyzed.

Status insularity also bridges another gap that labeling analysis has thus far left unfilled: "The specification of labeling processes can also provide a picture of the intervening social mechanism through which the effects of structural, situational, and social-psychological variables that have been the main concern of traditional deviance analysis are mediated."[46] This is exactly what status insularity seeks to describe: One of the intervening social mechanisms by means of which cultural, structural, and power aspects of society can be better understood. By focusing on status insularity, the effect that these three variables have on applying deviant labels is investigated.

Schur concedes that power and conflict are important aspects of deviance that have been neglected by labeling theory. "For our purposes, however, it may be more useful to consider power differentials as significant determinants of susceptibility and resistance to labeling processes than to build such differentials into a definition of deviance."[47] This is what the status insularity hypotheses have attempted to accomplish. In this formulation, power is one variable that does determine "susceptibility and resistance to labeling." Schur emphasized that the likelihood of individuals becoming involved in the labeling process varies,[48] and yet he has not dealt with the specifics of how and why certain people become involved. Labeling theory asks three questions: "By what processes does the individual come to feel and act like a deviant?" "How is the rule against behavior X applied?" "Why is behavior X a 'crime'?"[49] Consistent with the labeling perspective and yet unasked by most theorists is "Why is the rule against X applied to person A and not person B?" This is the status insularity question, and it provides a way of studying power and yet not oversimplifying and claiming that power is the only variable involved.

Conclusion

The refocusing argued for by the use of status insularity is not an attempt to change the basic orientation of labeling theory. Instead, it is a way of trying to expand the work done within this perspective to include areas that should be of concern to labeling theorists but as yet have not been given the proper attention. It is certainly one way of combatting some of the major criticisms of labeling theory. Lemert, in discussing labeling theory's break with earlier work on deviance, focuses on the crux of the issue: Labeling theory has encountered the "perennial problem of sociological theory, namely how to establish a connection between symbolic systems, social systems, and physical systems without denying the obvious fact that human beings make choices that affect as well as are affected by the system."[50] Functionalists were, in the extreme, guilty of reifying the system. Labeling theorists, in their attempt to correct this error, are, in the extreme, guilty of ignoring the system. Status insularity is a way of focusing on the structural aspects related to labeling in an attempt to approximate more closely the actual balance between the individual and the social system. Clearly, one concept cannot correct all the problems within labeling theory. However, status insularity is an attempt to push for more in-depth study in areas that labeling theorists have largely ignored.

The Societal Reaction to Female Alcoholics

The prediction of greater stigmatization and greater secondary deviation of the individual in an insulated status is not part of the basic definition of status insularity, but an extension of the concept based on available data on female alcoholics. The research indicates that females are less likely to be labeled alcoholic, more heavily stigmatized, and therefore subject to a greater degree of secondary deviation. Evidence has been offered for the first of these hypotheses in chapter 2; chapter 5 explores existing evidence in support of the latter two insularity hypotheses.

Stigmatization of Female Alcoholics

A good deal of material was presented in chapter 2 to substantiate the proposition that there is a greater stigmatization of female alcoholics. However, it is worth looking at the data in a more systematic manner to gain a better understanding of the amount of support there is for this hypothesis. Evidence is available from four different types of sources to corroborate that female alcoholics are more heavily stigmatized than male alcoholics: journalistic and expert opinions, firsthand accounts, quantitative studies, and the inaccessibility of treatment facilities for female alcoholics.

Journalistic and Expert Opinions

Studies have shown convincingly that the woman who drinks is more heavily criticized than any drinking man. Her assault on the bottle represents the breaking of a more rigid taboo, the shattering of a deeply divined image of femininity. Regardless of her social or economic status, the woman alcoholic faces greater castigation and rejection from a less tolerant society. [1]

Articles and books written by experts on alcoholism seem unanimous in agreeing that the female alcoholic is subject to a greater amount of censure than is the male alcoholic. [2] The experts' opinions are also reflected in more journalistic style articles that rely on experts for their information. [3]

Professionals who work in rehabilitative settings confirm this viewpoint. In my study of specialists in the field of alcohol abuse, I found that they felt females were subject to greater criticism by other patients than were males (see the appendix). Their reasons for this view were diverse. One indicated it was female behavior patterns, such as dependency that infuriated men. Most argued, however, that it was caused by a double standard for men and women. Such a belief was stated strongly by the director of a women's program: "In my past clinical experience, males stated there was nothing worse or more disgusting than a woman alcoholic." As the director of a halfway house put it, "Females accept the fact of alcoholism among males. Males always appear shocked when a female walks in." A nurse who supervised another clinic said, Men "tend to place them [women] in one category (the drunk hustler who neglected her children)." In this short phrase, much of the reason for criticism of female alcoholics is summarized: the double standard in regard to sex and the role of a woman as a mother in our society. Several practitioners noted that women were "much more accepting than males" who were alcoholic. Others added that it was not only that men were less accepting of female alcoholics, but so were other women.

It should be reiterated that the sample was much too small to enable me to make generalizations. However, the opinions of these professionals are of particular interest, since they ran the clinics and halfway houses from which the alcoholic sample was drawn. If these professional observed greater censure of women, it is likely this affected some of those women who answered the questionnaires.

At best, experts would be accurately describing how others react to female alcoholics. Conceding that the experts may not be unbiased themselves, as the Broverman study (chapter 2) and other research suggest (see the discussion in chapter 2), at worst they would be giving their own prejudicial opinions, which are to some degree a reflection of views held by the public. [4] Either way, their opinion gives us a general understanding of the public consensus on female alcoholics. [5]

Firsthand Accounts

Literature written by female alcoholics or in which alcoholic women are interviewed also supports the contention that they are more heavily stigmatized. [6] All accounts by female alcoholics mention how critical others are of their drinking problem. This material is presented in detail in chapter 2.

Quantitative Studies

There are a few quantitative studies that lend credence to the premise that female alcoholics are more severely stigmatized. Most of these, however, do not actually show that women are more severely stigmatized but that people believe it is worse for a woman to drink excessively or to be an alcoholic. A study conducted on a sample of A.A. women found they said that it was

worse for a woman to drink excessively than a man.[7] As noted earlier, a
California survey showed that members of both sexes believed it was worse
for a woman to drink too much. These studies do not actually show that
female alcoholics are more heavily stigmatized, but that would be a logical
extension of the findings; that is, if people consider it worse for a woman to
drink heavily or to be an alcoholic, it would seem to follow that they would
be censorious of her.

There is an interesting section on perceived social rejection in a recent
book by Eileen Corrigan on women receiving treatment for alcoholism.[8] Of
the female alcoholics who were questioned about whether they felt rejected in
some way, 47 percent said they experienced no rejection. Corrigan tended to
discount the percentages by indicating that it was an area in which women
found it difficult to respond honestly.[9] Another of Corrigan's findings supports this interpretation: Even though alcoholic wives said they were not
rejected, fifteen of the twenty husbands interviewed said they disapproved
and were openly critical of their wives.

In my research, I found that when directly asked if others including spouse
(see table A.5), relatives (see table A.6), and friends (see table A.7) were
critical of their drinking problem, female alcoholics were no more likely to
say yes than were male alcoholics. I did not have corresponding data from
spouses, relatives and friends of the alcoholics against which to check the
accuracy of these responses. However, other findings from my research that
supported the greater criticism of women did seem to contradict these data:
Female alcoholics were the subgroup most likely (81 percent) to express the
opinion that others were more critical of female heavy drinkers (see table
A.1), and the majority of the alcohol practitioners agreed that other patients
were more critical of female alcoholics (see the appendix).

The literature on sex differences indicates several possible reasons why
women are not as likely as men to say others are critical of them. First of all,
there is a vast amount of research that indicates that males are more aggressive than females.[10] Females are also less likely to perceive aggression than
males. One researcher found that even when people were given incentives to
recall aggression, fewer girls remembered aggression than did boys.[11] Other
researchers studing recall of aggression from films that were viewed found
girls recalled less aggressive content than did boys.[12] A group of 8–16-year-
olds were shown one violent and one nonviolent picture in a stereoscope; boys
reported seeing the violent scenes more often than the girls.[13] In a tachis-
tosopic presentation of aggressive scenes, a longer exposure time was needed
for girls to recognize the picture.[14] This answer does not seem completely
satisfactory, however, since female alcoholics' response to how critical others
were of them (chapter 2) evidenced that they were apparently able to perceive the hostility of others toward female alcoholics.

Another, and perhaps more satisfactory explanation, stems from evidence that women choose answers to personality questionnaires more on the basis of social desirability than do men.[15] It is possible that female alcoholics did not think it was acceptable to indicate that people in their lives were not helpful; such a response could be interpreted as blaming one's drinking problem on others.

Perhaps the most convincing explanation can be found in the literature on dissonance. "Dissonance is a feeling of personal unworthiness (a type of anxiety) traceable to rejection of oneself by other people either in the present or in the past."[16] There are a number of ways to escape dissonant situations in order to achieve "cognitive consistency," including accepting another's definition of self or misinterpreting how others feel so you do not perceive they are rejecting you. This seems like a plausible psychological explanation, which has a sociological counterpart in balance theory.

> Despite certain differences, the central hypothesis common to all varieties of the theory is that given initial unbalance or inconsistency, the focal person will undergo high tension (discomfort, pressure, drive, etc.), which in turn will cause him to change one or more orientations (relations) in the direction of balance or consistency.[17]

Alcoholics were raised with much the same value system and cultural definitions as their spouses, relatives, and friends. They are as likely as their labelers to believe that alcoholism is wrong. If we accept another's criticism of ourself, it lowers our sense of self-worth and brings the situation back into balance. If this were true, we would expect alcoholics, both male and female, to have lower self-esteem than the heavy drinkers in our sample. The results supporting this proposition are presented in the next chapter.

For female alcoholics, the word guilt may be especially appropriate. Guilt, according to English and English, is the "realization that one has violated ethical or moral or religious principles, together with a regretful feeling of lessened personal worth on that account."[18] Jean Kirkpatrick, the founder of Women for Sobriety, claims that

> All women in our culture feel a modicum of guilt for not being "perfect," for not fitting the unrealistic mold that American society has cast for them. For alcoholic women, this guilt is unbearable at times.... Women alcoholics have this strong feeling of having failed as a wife, as a mother, as a sister or daughter, as a woman.... On the other hand, the male alcoholic feels much remorse for having hurt his family... his wife and his children. He rarely feels guilt, and he never feels the same as women do.[19]

A study of clusterings of commonly reported alcoholism symptoms found that male and female alcoholics were surprisingly similar:[20] Eight basic dimensions were found in both groups. However, one factor found among women had no counterpart among men—the cluster characterized by anxiety, shame, and guilt.

Women have violated more rules than men; therefore, it is likely female alcoholics will agree with others' criticism of them and not be critical of others' behavior toward them. As noted in chapter 2, female alcoholics are aware of the criticism of others, but they apparently accept this censure.

These explanations of why women, when asked about other's reactions to them did not report that they were more critical than did men are plausible. It is also possible, however, that these women were not criticized more by their significant others. Questions about the criticism of others should be asked again in future research in various ways to try and understand exactly what is taking place.

Other quantitative material indicates that females are more heavily stigmatized. As noted earlier in chapter 2, many studies have shown that females are more likely to drink alone. These findings have been interpreted as an indication that women drink alone because they are more severely criticized for heavy drinking. My research on alcoholic women indicates that women who are heavy drinkers and those who are labeled alcoholics are both more likely to be solitary drinkers than their male counterparts (see tables A.3 and A.4). It would seem that even before a woman is labeled an alcoholic, she feels pressure to curtail her drinking in public.

Findings on divorce rates are hard to place in our simplified diagram of labeling. In most research, a higher rate for female alcoholics is considered evidence that women are "sicker" or subject to greater psychopathological problems than male alcoholics.[21] Divorce can alternatively be seen as a female alcoholic's response to the censure of others or secondary deviation. Since I do not interpret the husband's being less likely to "stand by" the alcoholic wife as simply a result of her greater pathology, the data will be presented in this section on stigmatization. However, this example makes it clear that the dynamic labeling process cannot be fully explained by static categories.

Both male and female alcoholics show a higher number of broken marriages than the general population.[22] Only 4.8 percent of the males and 6.6 percent of the females in the United States were divorced in 1979.[23] In my study of alcoholic women, among heavy drinkers, only 5 percent were separated or divorced; the labeled alcoholics, however, showed a divorce or separation rate of 36 percent (see table A.8).

Researchers have tended to argue that there is greater marital instability among female alcoholics,[24] sometimes reaching a break-up rate as high as 90 percent.[25] Findings that men are less receptive to participating in treatment with their wives lends some credence to the argument that men are less likely to be supportive and remain with alcoholic wives. In a two-year follow-up of 251 patients, one of the main observations was that husbands of alcoholic wives were very difficult to involve in the program. The men did not "come in, call or otherwise complain as did their female counterparts attached to the male patients."[26] When the husbands were contacted, almost every one of them responded defensively; common opening statements were "I didn't cause it" or "It's not my fault."[27]

Popular literature and newspapers have repeated these contentions about the high break-up rate in the marriages of female alcoholics.[28] Everyday observations also seem to support these findings. After attending Al-Anon meetings, the husband of a female alcoholic observed: "I found that the 'weaker sex' often prove themselves stronger than many men in the face of living with a practicing alcoholic. They don't seem to cut and run so often."[29] One of the female alcoholics in my sample said, "Most men look down on women alcoholics. But most women will put up with men alcoholics longer."

Although the evidence strongly supports a high divorce rate for alcoholic women, some samples show marital disruption as equally distributed between both sexes.[30] In my study, only a small difference existed in the separated or divorced rate for male and female alcoholics (see Table A.9). Schuckit and Morrisey have suggested that "for men, marital stability varies directly with occupational status, while the relationship between occupational status and marital stability is not so straightforward in the case of women."[31] Other variables therefore, especially socioeconomic ones, should be considered when comparing the divorce rate for male and female alcoholics.

Even if female alcoholics do have a higher rate of marital instability, the reason why is far from clear. Frequently, their marital problems are attributed to what is believed to be a larger amount of pathology in general among female alcoholics.[32] This general pathology is discussed in detail later in this chapter. If marital instability is viewed as an integral part of the stigmatization process, however, it changes how we view the high divorce rate among female alcoholics.

The stereotype of the spouse of the male alcoholic versus the spouse of the female alcoholic gives us some insight into beliefs about how men and women are expected to behave toward an alcoholic spouse.

> A recent article in the London *Times* points this out in reporting the results of a random sampling of people's reactions to alcoholics. The most common view of the male alcoholic was, "The poor soul ! His wife drove him to it!" and of the female alcoholic, "The poor husband. He deserved better than that!"[33]

These opinions from a random sample do not vary greatly from the portrait presented by clinical reports. Clinical descriptions of wives of alcoholics from 1937 to 1959 pictured them as "aggressive, domineering women who married to mother or control a man."[34] This view holds that the wife married a man who was or would be an alcoholic because of her own neurotic needs. Therefore, she has a stake in preventing her husband from discontinuing his drinking.[35]

More current and systematic research has shown that wives of alcoholics are actually "normal personalities" of varying types.[36] Their marriage to an alcoholic places them in a stressful situation, and they show some personality dysfunction as a result of the problems they confront. Less dysfunction seems to be evidenced the longer the husband is abstinent.[37] As Gomberg aptly notes, "That it should have taken three decades to arrive at this view makes one wonder."[38]

It especially makes one wonder since there is no such negative view of the husbands of alcoholic wives; as a matter of fact there is almost no view of the husband of an alcoholic wife. In reviews of research on the female alcoholic,[39] authors include sections on women who are married to alcoholic men instead of discussing the spouse of the alcoholic woman. This does not seem unusual once it is realized that there is almost no research on the spouse of the alcoholic female. An extensive annotated bibliography[40] on female alcoholism lists thirty-two sources in a section on the alcoholic's spouse; of these, only one includes husbands of alcoholic wives. The remainder refer only to women who are married to alcoholic men.

This negative image of the spouse of the male alcoholic provides him with excuses for his alcoholism. If he becomes an alcoholic, it would appear that people frequently believe it is his wife who drove him to it. Whereas the nonexistent image of the spouse of the female alcoholic is a reflection of the attitude that women should not be alcoholics and if they are, it is no one's fault but their own. Clearly, a double standard exists that maintains it is more acceptable for a man to be an alcoholic. Therefore, different attitudes and behaviors are acceptable for the spouses of male and female alcoholics. Women are expected to stand by their alcoholic husbands more than men are expected to stand by their alcoholic wives. As Ruth Maxwell contends,

> Society's attitude toward the female alcoholic is a significant factor in preventing her husband from being both more responsible and more effective. Society offers no excuses for her alcoholism. She has not been forced into it by all the extenuating circumstances which society uses as contributing factors for the male alcoholic.... Society if it doesn't actually support the husband in his desertion of his alcoholic wife, does little in the way of helping him to do anything else.[41]

Higher divorce and separation rates for women alcoholics in this view are seen as arising from the societal pressures a man must face if his wife is an alcoholic. It is not considered part of his proper role to stand by his wife once she is labeled an alcoholic. However, "standing by" is a female virtue prized in a good wife. If she is also considered to be partially to blame for his alcoholism, as clinicians for years purported, then the least one would expect of her is to stand by her husband during the recovery process. High divorce and separation rates do not result from a woman's greater pathology, but are part of the double standard in alcoholism that pervades all aspects of the female alcoholic's dealings with people. It is part of the greater stigmatization she receives because her drinking and alcoholism are less acceptable.

Inaccessibility of Treatment Facilities

"Treatment facilities of all types and kinds lag in providing adequate treatment for women."[42] Of the estimated 251,000 people who were served by programs funded by the National Institute on Alcohol Abuse and Alcoholism in 1979, only 24 percent were women.[43] This possibly reflects the misconception that there are few female alcoholics who need help; however, this misconception may not be accidental. One researcher claims that the needs of female alcoholics are unmet due to the male bias in collecting data, which strongly underrepresents the number of women who have alcohol problems.[44] These figures in turn provide excuses for not funding more programs and opening more facilities for women.

It is also possible to view the inaccessibility of treatment facilities as an indication of the negative attitude that society holds of alcoholic women.[45] As mentioned in chapter 2, some physicians have especially negative feelings about female alcoholics.[46] Other groups dealing with the alcoholic in treatment also describe female alcoholics in an uncomplimentary way. Police rate alcoholic women as more "foolish, feminine and dangerous."[47] One study found that alcoholic women who were referred to the psychiatric emergency room of a hospital were less likely to be admitted to the alcoholism unit of the hospital (16 percent) than were men (44 percent). And this same sample of female alcoholics was more likely to be admitted to the psychiatric unit (24 percent) when compared to men (10 percent).[48] Another source cites the case of a Washington, D.C. businesswoman who was placed in a locked cell in a psychiatric ward because the hospital did not have an alcoholism program for women.[49] Whatever the actual reason for this differential treatment of male and female alcoholics, it prevents women from receiving treatment primarily for their alcoholism. As Christenson and Swanson claim, "These moralistic attitudes towards women interfere with objective research, severely hamper, and often times deny women proper medical treatment."[50]

In facilities that do admit women, most of the programs are geared to the needs of male alcoholics and ignore women's problems.[51] Research has shown that the same factors may not be important for success in treating men and women.[52] After forming an all-women therapy group, Ardelle Schultz found a larger number of women came to her center for treatment. During this time, the percentage of women who completed the treatment program rose from 35 to 59 percent; eighteen months after discontinuing the separate women's group, the number dropped back to 38 percent. [53]

Another rationale for not admitting women to treatment facilities is that they are harder to treat and less likely to be successfully rehabilitated. [54] Some research has disputed these beliefs, [55] and as expected, practitioners in my sample who worked with female alcoholics did not adhere to these stereotypes.

Secondary Deviation

In his earlier work, Lemert argues that "as long as it is satisfactorily rationalized, dissociated, or otherwise dealt with as part of a socially acceptable role, or even a sociopathic role," [56] then inebriation remains primary deviation. Secondary alcoholic deviation "refers to drinking which is motivated by the conception the drinker has of the self as that of a drunkard, a sot, an inebriate, an alcoholic or a drunken bum." [57] This change in self-conception has been brought on by some societal reaction to the person's drinking. Alcohol then becomes for the alcoholic a means of coping with criticism and resultant guilt feelings. The point at which the transformation from primary to secondary deviation occurs is difficult to pinpoint. [58]

In Lemert's model, the change in self-conception is a motivation for secondary deviation; it is an intervening variable between stigmatization and secondary deviation. From this perspective, we would expect a change in the female alcoholic's self-concept (that is, a decline in self-esteem) to lead to secondary deviation.

Due to censure, the alcoholic's self-esteem is lowered, and he or she is prone to greater deviation from the norms of acceptable drinking behavior and actions associated with drinking behavior (for example, suicide, marital disruption, affective disorders, and the like). Female alcoholics are thought to be subject to more secondary deviation of two general types than male alcoholics. The "disapproving, degradational and isolating reactions of society" [59] lead to (1) a greater pathology and (2) telescoped development in female alcoholics.

Theoretically, these three aspects (greater pathology, telescoped development, and self-esteem) are distinguishable. They have been discussed as separate issues in the literature, with self-esteem emerging only recently as a unique problem for female alcoholics. The term pathology is so general, however, that it could include both telescoped development and low self-esteem. Since they are all part of the secondary deviation process, it is perhaps not surprising that there is a conceptual relationship between the three. This overlap is evidenced in research that has focused on the female alcoholic's responses to the societal reaction to her deviation.

The low self-esteem of female alcoholics is of particular interest to me because it is the least well researched of these three aspects, yet it is frequently listed in the literature as crucial to understanding female alcoholics. Also, although self-conception is an integral part of the secondary deviation process as described by Lemert (and for that matter of any socialization or resocialization process), it has not been given a great deal of attention by sociologists, who perhaps wish to avoid its psychological overtones. The evidence and the implications of the research findings on greater pathology and telescoped development of female alcoholics are discussed in this chapter to indicate the direction research has taken with regard to the secondary deviation of female alcoholics. The importance of self-esteem in the secondary deviation process will be reserved for the next chapter.

Greater Pathology

The literature abounds with studies proving that women suffer from a greater number of pathologies than men, both psychological and physiological,[60] as well as a reasonable number showing that such is not the case.[61] Data on suicide attempts, affective disorders, and greater marital instability have all been used to argue that female alcoholics are more abnormal; other data have shown that male alcoholics have a more disturbed personality.[62]

There are three possible explanations for these discrepancies; first of all, as Lisansky has effectively argued,[63] it is conceivable that the female alcoholic is more disturbed by the time she receives assistance due to the socially disturbing consequences that she experiences because she is a woman. In this view, the female alcoholic starts out no more maladjusted than her male counterpart, but stigmatization of a woman is so much greater that it has a more damaging effect on her self-concept, and therefore she behaves in a more abnormal way (secondary deviation). This would explain why so many findings indicate that some female alcoholics have more psychopathological problems. At the same time, it would also explain why this is not true for female alcoholics who do not respond to stigmatization with secondary deviation.

Secondly, as Lisansky argues[64] when she compares women who were in the outpatient clinic with those in her state farm sample, there are striking differences between subgroups of female alcoholics. She found a greater degree of psychopathology in the outpatient sample. Her suggestion that differentiation has to be made between various groups of female alcoholics is a sensible one, but it is seldom followed. Just as there is no male alcoholic personality, a topic which has been discussed at length in the literature,[65] there is no reason to assume that alcoholism among women is uniform. Sociological and psychological studies have been lax in attempting to encompass this diversity even in research on male alcoholics. "By adhering strictly to our American ideas about 'alcoholism' and 'alcoholics' (created by Alcoholics Anonymous in their own image) and restricting the term to those ideas, we have been continuing to overlook many other problems of alcohol which need urgent attention."[66] Research on female alcoholics, which has only recently begun to expand, naturally falls behind studies on male alcoholics in its attempt to encompass this heterogeneity.

A few recent reviews have highlighted the differences among female alcoholics.[67] In interviews conducted with thirty-four female A.A. members,[68] three separate groups of female alcoholics were distinguished. A small percentage (12 percent) had no personality maladjustment and still became alcoholic. The other two larger groups either had personality maladjustment or a strong emotional crisis that preceded their alcoholism. Other work has distinguished between primary female alcoholics and those with severe affective disorders that preceded their alcoholism.[69] Demographic variables have also been shown to play a role in the form that alcoholism takes.[70] Case histories of both male and female upper-class alcoholics indicate that they drink for the same reasons as those in other socioeconomic statuses but possess a greater ability to remain hidden from labeling agents.[71]

The research conducted thus far has shown that alcoholism is not a unidimensional illness. Contradictory studies on female alcoholics may reflect researchers tapping different subgroups while failing to be cognizant of the diversity that exists among female alcoholics. As with male alcoholics, factors other than their gender status have to be taken into consideration.

Thirdly, the methods of testing may be another source of contradictory findings on the greater sickness or abnormality of female alcoholics. As discussed earlier in chapter 2, female alcoholics by their behavior vary more from society's standards than do male alcoholics. The woman who violates the strong taboos against heavy drinking is more likely to be viewed as neurotic because the standard of measurement is different for males and females.[72] The Broverman study, discussed at length in chapter 2, makes it clear that women are not diagnosed as healthy as men even if they do not drink.[73]

The weight of the evidence indicates that women do experience more problems than their male counterparts. It is likely that many of these pathologies are a response to the societal reaction to the deviation of the female alcoholic, as Lisansky suggested. All three of the reasons play some part in confusing the interpretation of the results of research that compares male and female alcoholics. However, it is undeniable that female alcoholics' greater pathology is a form of secondary deviation, not the result of a more disturbed personality.

Telescoped Development

In a 1952 report, the World Health Organization put forth the hypotheses that women begin to drink later in life than men and become alcoholic within a shorter period of time.[74] This rapid development of alcoholism among women has come to be called telescoped development and is supported by the large majority of the studies that compare male and female alcoholics.[75]

Even though there is agreement about the process occurring, there are differing opinions about why it occurs. The World Health Organization contended that telescoped development was the result of the moral condemnation, ostracism, and guilt feelings suffered by female alcoholics. In other words, the acceleration of the alcoholism process was a form of secondary deviation. Others argue it results from the greater pathology of female alcoholics and therefore alcoholism should be viewed as a reflection of some other primary disorder.

For the greater pathology or the telescoped development of women, the question of directionality cannot be answered without the unlikely event of a controlled experiment. However, there is one study that indicates that the greater problems of alcoholic females are a reaction to the greater criticism they meet. In a sample of 192 male and 77 female alcoholics in England, Glatt found that "in the majority of patients studied, asocial and antisocial behavior started only after several years of excess drinking, leading the author to speculate that these tendencies are probably the result and not the cause of excessive drinking."[76]

Although some of the evidence is contradictory, there is enough research to support the contention that at least part of the greater pathologies evidenced by female alcoholics and the rapid pace at which they become full-fledged alcoholics (telescoped development) are due to the greater amount of stigmatization they received. The next chapter turns to the role that low self-esteem plays in this secondary deviation process.

Self-Esteem and the Status Insularity of Female Alcoholics

By studying alcoholics or interviewing those who work with alcoholics, a great deal of data have been amassed to show that low self-esteem is the plight of male alcoholics.[1] As Fitts concluded in reference to male alcoholics, "The overall picture is clear. It is rare for a person with a healthy, realistic self concept to be an alcoholic, and it is rare for a true alcoholic to have a good self concept."[2]

Most researchers claim, however, that low self-esteem tends to be an even worse problem for female alcoholics.[3] Frequently, however, authors provide no corroborating data, assuming its existence can be taken for granted.[4] Recent discussions on the special difficulties of being an alcoholic female tend to focus on self-esteem as a major hurdle to be overcome if women are to recover.[5] The research supporting this contention will be discussed at length in this chapter.

Conceptualizing Self-Esteem

The main obstacle to discussing self-esteem effectively is the inexactness of the concept, which has been used differently by almost every theorist and interchangeably with a long list of other concepts, including self-respect, self-concept, self-worth, and ego-strength. An extensive analysis of the use of the concept led Wells and Marwell to conclude that "any attempt to derive a fairly rigorous definition of self-esteem (or its parallel constructs) from the literature is likely to be frustrated by the current state of vagueness and fragmentation."[6]

Formalizing the concept becomes more difficult because it is part of our everyday vocabulary. Since people believe they know what self-esteem is, they do not feel the need to define it precisely. This leads to three serious problems: First, the reliance on a common sense definition makes it appear that we are dealing with the same phenomenon despite the different intuitive definitions and different means of testing used. Clearly, this is not the case and comparing findings from different situations is often fallacious. It is possible that many of the contradictory findings could result from this lack of consistency in the definition. Secondly, treating self-esteem as if its meaning

were consistent and understood obscures the rationale behind the concept.
Self-esteem is a value-laden term with an underlying assumption of what is
normal and good. A theorist's belief about the degree of ego-strength or self-
esteem that is good for a person has an effect on how he or she defines the
concept. Thirdly, since everyone knows what self-esteem is, the concept is
introduced in many studies without being placed in a larger theoretical
framework. When it comes to conclusions, however, self-esteem has often
played a crucial role in the explanation, even though it was not initially one
of the key variables.

The Sociological Roots of Self-Esteem

The concept of self-esteem is more frequently associated with psychology
than sociology. In truth, however, self-esteem has deep and respectable roots
in the field of sociology.[7] The sociological underpinnings of the concept and
its place within acceptable sociological theory are briefly discussed in order
to make it clear that research in this area is clearly within the realm of
sociology. If the creation of the self and self-esteem were not viewed as having
a social basis, a theory such as Lemert's secondary deviation would not be
possible. Although some symbolic interactionists have objections to any sort
of standard testing, the Iowa School has developed a reputable body of research using such standardized tests as Kuhn's Twenty Statements Test.

Early sociological analysis of self was founded on the work of William
James and the pragmatists.[8] In accord with James, Charles Horton Cooley
claimed that the important aspects of society were not in the world but in our
minds: "The imaginations people have of one another are the social facts of
society."[9]

Cooley described what he called a "looking-glass self." "A self-idea of this
sort seems to have three principal elements: the imagination of our appearance to the other person, the imagination of his judgment of that appearance
and some sort of self-feeling."[10]

Sociological theorist Don Martindale alleges that Cooley's looking-glass
self is hardly more than "a neat re-statement of James''social-self'."[11] However, it can also be argued that the importance of Cooley's work lies in the
emphasis he placed on the social aspects of self. For Cooley, a concept like
self-esteem could not be precisely defined.[12] Despite this lack of conceptual
clarity, self-feeling played a crucial role in his looking-glass self, and Cooley
does suggest several ways in which pride or self-esteem can be achieved.[13]
Increased self-esteem comes mainly from seeking rewards through approved
behavior, successful comparisons with other people, and by conforming to
group standards.

George Herbert Mead agreed with Cooley and James that the explanation
of self was to be found in reflexive experiences, "but the theory that the

nature of the self is to be found in such experiences does not account for the origin of self."[14] It is an explanation of the origin of self that dominates Mead's theory.

He argued that there are two main stages in the development of self. In the first, "the individual's self is constituted simply by an organization of the particular attitudes of other individuals toward himself."[15] This can be seen in play, where a child learns to take the role of the other. The child's behavior is organized around stimuli to which he or she learns appropriate responses. The child plays at responding as both student and teacher, child and parent.

The second stage finds the self "constituted not only by an organization of these particular individual attitudes, but also by an organization of the social attitudes of the generalized other or social group as a whole to which he belongs."[16] This stage is illustrated by the game, in which the child not only takes the role of the other but must also take the role of everyone else in the game. This means that the child must understand and accept the attitude of the generalized other toward the social activity itself and act on this acceptance. Mead uses the example of a ballplayer who not only has to be able to take the role of all the other players in the game but must also understand the relationship of these roles to each other.

The medium through which the self develops in these two stages to full self-consciousness is communication. A self is possible only when a person becomes an object to him- or her-self. Role-taking is the underlying process requisite to the production of self, and essential to role-taking are gestures and significant symbols. "The essence of the self... is cognitive: it lies in the internalized conversation of gestures which constitutes thinking.... And hence the origin and foundations of self, like those of thinking, are *social*."[17]

Mead kept James's distinction between the "I" and "me" in explaining how the self is structured. "The 'I' is the response of the organism to the attitudes of other; the 'me' is the organized set of attitudes of others which one himself assumes."[18]

The realization of the self in a social situation occurs in two ways. First, as members of the community, we possess a certain amount of self-respect because we live up to what is considered right (for example, keeping our word, meeting our obligations, and so forth). Mead argues that this type of self-respect is never enough for a person. The second way in which we achieve self-realization is by comparing ourselves to other people and finding ourselves better. This instills a sense of superiority—not a self-centered, bragging superiority, but an enjoyment of one's own successes. Inferiority complexes are the opposite of these feelings of superiority; they "arise from those wants of a self which we should like to carry out but which we cannot."[19]

Mead opened up an avenue for the study of self-esteem within a social context through his discussion of self-realization. It has been argued that a major step was taken toward analyzing self-esteem when Mead described the "generalized other." [20] By means of this concept, "we can account for a more global, cross-situational sense of self rather than just an atomistic collection of situational selves, a necessary idea if we wish to refer to a person's *overall* self-esteem." [21] This is especially true for empirical research that treats the self as static during its investigation.

Any current research on the self in sociology is based on work by these theorists. Since the self is at least partially socially determined, study of the self by sociologists is meaningful. That the self in addition to being socially determined is also not a fixed entity but a process makes possible typologies of secondary deviation, such as Lemert's, that explain increased deviation as a function of a change in self-concept brought about by social condemnation. [22]

Symbolic Interactionism and Self-Esteem

"Symbolic Interactionism probably represents the theoretical setting where self-esteem is most firmly embedded in a larger conceptual structure." [23] Although self-esteem is not of primary concern to symbolic interactionists, it logically has an important place in their theories, since the process of self-conceptualization is the means by which the individual is linked to the social structure. A mind arises in the social process when the individual becomes self-conscious or aware of the self as an object.

Society is defined as human beings who are interacting; [24] thus society is an ongoing process not a fixed entity. The symbolic interactionists are "fundamentally committed to the active *creation of meaning* and thus human being(s)." [25] Society is based on the minds and selves of individual members while at the same time the creation of minds and selves is based on a social process. [26] Using self-conceptualization to explain how the individual becomes part of society and society becomes a part of the individual provides a concept of self-evaluation, such as self-esteem, with a coherent conceptual framework.

There are two major traditions within symbolic interactionism: the Chicago School and the Iowa School.

The Chicago School

The Chicago School, derived directly from Cooley and Mead, is associated with a group of sociologists from the 1930s and 1940s from the University of Chicago and current thinkers of similar persuasion. Herbert Blumer, a spokesman for the Chicago School, has given a clearly stated presentation of the basic premises of symbolic interactionism and what he sees as the methodological implications of these assertions. [27] The three main propositions derived directly from Mead are: (1) human beings act on the basis of meanings, (2) these meanings arise out of social interaction, and (3) these meanings are dealt with in an interpretive process by the person.[28] What Blumer calls the "root images" or basic beliefs of symbolic interactionism are also based on Mead but differ in emphasis from the Iowa School of symbolic interactionism. Using root images, Blumer discusses the importance of process, role-taking, the individual, self, and interaction; continually stressing the importance of the individual and downplaying the importance of society.

Blumer goes on in his essay to comment on what he considers the methodological implications of symbolic interactionism. A wide gap exists between his techniques of study and those promoted by the Iowa School. Blumer argues strenuously for an "empirical" investigation of the social world. His use of the word empirical differs greatly from what has traditionally been meant. Blumer believes that one should not start with a preconceived theory to test, with unverified concepts, or conventional or standard research procedures. Firsthand observation of the individual in social relationships is the only way to be "true" to the data. To avoid preconceived notions, theories must be constantly revised as research continues. Blumer argues that soft data are the only truly empirical data and exploration and inspection (the close analysis of data collected through exploration) are the only acceptable ways of developing sociological theories.

The Iowa School

Members of the Iowa School (Manford Kuhn and his students and associates at Iowa University) also take their lead from Cooley and Mead. However, they differ in the elements they emphasize and how they believe it is possible to operationalize the concepts. There is clearly less interest in process, which leads to the possibility of more standard empirical research. The Iowa School advocates see their task as operationalizing the basic concepts of Mead's theory and testing them empirically through the use of questionnaires. Instead of focusing on the self-in-process, members have done static tests of the consequences of Mead's hypotheses[29] or sought to document statistically the relationship between delinquency and self-concept.[30] Perhaps because of their emphasis on measuring and studying the self-concept with traditional methodologies, the Iowa tradition has produced a much more sizable literature on self-concept and self-esteem.[31]

The methodological distinction between the Iowa School and the Chicago School is based on what the two schools consider empirically valid. Blumer argues that quantitative measures are an invalid way of testing a social reality constantly in flux, while members of the Iowa School believe that in order to prove the validity of Mead's abstract theory, it has to be operationalized and quantitatively tested.

The Compromise

Clearly, all work by symbolic interactionists does not fit neatly into one of these two schools of thought. Although they seem diametrically opposed due to their testing methods, this does not mean that symbolic interaction theory cannot use work from both traditions. Several theorists have indicated how quantitative and qualitative research can be used in studies that treat people as subjects rather than objects.[32] As Glaser and Strauss state, "In many instances, both forms of data are necessary—not quantitative used to test qualitative, but both used as supplements, as mutual verification and, most important for us, as different forms of data on the same subjects, which when compared, will each generate theory."[33]

Arnold Rose attempted to summarize systematically the assumptions of symbolic interactionism and at the same time to exclude neither the participant-observation research of the Chicago School nor the quantitative research of the Iowa School.[34] Some aspects of his summary clearly disagree with Blumer's rather dogmatic interpretation. There is no question whether certain aspects exist but rather of the importance of these aspects to understanding society. No sociologist denies the existence of culture, roles, structure, and society; however, Blumer deemphasizes them in his interpretation of symbolic interactionism. For Blumer, the point is to stop focusing on these as fixed entities. Instead, they are changing, fluctuating, and recreated every time people interact. Rose treats them more as fixed entities—not totally static but certainly more stable than Blumer implies. Blumer makes an attempt to move away from the standard view of society as "an established order of living, with that order resolvable into adherence to sets of rules, norms, values, and sanctions that specify to people how they are to act in their different situations."[35] For Blumer, it is useless to study a system without studying the people. It is individuals at various places who interact, and how they interact and what they do are a function of how they interpret the situation within their own set of meanings. After his critique of viewing culture, role, structure, and society as fixed entities, Blumer makes a disclaimer: He concedes that indeed people do have historical linkage and what has taken place before is of some importance to how they will act in the present. Rose emphasizes the importance of meaning, symbolic solutions, and individual choice but contends that society "precedes the individual"[36] and places certain limits on his or her behavior. After discussing culture, role, structure, and society as having real and important influences on our behavior, Rose makes a disclaimer in the opposite direction. He must explain how if these entities have such an impact on us individuals are not totally culturally determined.

This expanded emphasis on structure allows Rose not to discount research from either school. He neither denies the importance of process nor the possibility of examining in a static way symbols that are clustered together to form roles or structures.

The differences in perspectives and empirical techniques evidenced in the choice of articles for his book on symbolic interactionism[37] indicate Rose's belief in the importance of work from both the Chicago and the Iowa schools. He insists there is a coherence to the articles he has collected for his book, and he believes this stems from the "common theoretical tradition which informs their work."[38] In an article in which he offers insights into neurosis from a symbolic interactionist perspective, Rose indicates the value of both of these types of research: "Observations of human behavior in a variety of settings have supported this conception and recently Manford Kuhn has undertaken laboratory experiments which demonstrate that one's opinion of oneself is significantly influenced by a sharp negative reaction from others concerning oneself."[39]

Both types of data are seen as indicators of the truth or falsity of Mead's theories. This interpretation of symbolic interactionism validates the investigation of self-esteem through descriptive or "exploratory"[40] research as well as quantitative research.[41]

These distinctions between schools of how important structure is and what is empirical are crucially important in guiding any research design. It is clear from the present study and previous discussions that my sympathies lie with Rose who argues that both quantitative and qualitative research can make important contributions.

Research on Self-Esteem

Self-Esteem Differences by Gender

In order to comprehend the meaning of self-esteem differences between male and female alcoholics, it is necessary to know what male and female self-esteem differences are in the general population. If the differences that are argued to exist between male and female alcoholics simply reflect differences found in the nonalcoholic population, then neither alcoholism nor the stigmatization that takes place after labeling could be said to play a part in the self-esteem disparity.

From extensive research,[42] several conclusions can be reached: (1) Society places less value on female qualities, and (2) women expect to do worse on a given task, especially if it is competitive. With the vast amount of data supporting these findings, it would be logical to expect males to have higher self-esteem. Despite these findings, no consistent sex differences are found on overall tests of self-esteem.[43] Since there appear to be no significant self-esteem differences between the sexes in the general population, if a difference is found in self-esteem between male and female alcoholics, we can hypothesize that it results from alcoholism and the stigmatization process to which male and female alcoholics are subjected.

There are a number of possible explanations why, even though they share these beliefs about their abilities, women do not have lower self-esteem. The most plausible is first of all that success for women is defined differently than it is for men; they use different scales to judge themselves and therefore do not compete against men.[44] Secondly, women are less likely than men to feel responsible for their actions[45] and therefore may not see failure as their fault.

The Before-or-After Debate

As with the greater pathology and telescoped development discussions, there is a before-or-after debate for the low self-esteem found in female alcoholics. Researchers tend to concur on the existence of low self-esteem, but there are no conclusive arguments about whether it precedes or is a consequence of alcoholism.

A strong sociological argument can be made that it is the more disturbed woman who would be likely to be drinking heavily in the first place. Jellinek hypothesizes that "In societies which have a low degree of acceptance of large daily amounts of alcohol, mainly those will be exposed to the risk of addiction who on account of high psychological vulnerability have an inducement to go against the social standards."[46]

As Knupfer notes, this could also be true of subgroups within the population of one society: "The rate of alcoholism among subgroups in the culture will vary if there is an appreciable differentiation in the drinking practices and attitudes toward alcohol for those subgroups of the culture."[47]

Following this logic, we would expect women to be less likely to drink heavily, since such behavior is less acceptable for them than for men. Only those women who have a high psychological vulnerability would go against stringent social standards: "It is very possible that in a culture which does not look favorably on women drinking excessively, women who are both deprived and maladjusted are more vulnerable to alcoholism."[48]

According to some theorists, alcoholism in women is not the primary illness; men are more apt to be primary alcoholics whose drinking has not been preceded by some affective disorder. Women alcoholics, on the other hand, are likely to have preexisting emotional disturbances.[49]

Other research indicates low self-esteem is a predisposing factor among women who will become alcoholics. In a study of sixty-nine middle-aged female alcoholics in a counseling clinic, Wood and Duffy found that a common bond between the women was their feeling of worthlessness and inadequacy, which overshadowed their superior talents and beauty.[50] The researchers concluded that the low self-esteem they saw in these women was acquired while they were growing up. In studying a sample of female alcoholics from a state hospital, Kinsey reached a similar conclusion: [51] "Inadequate or distorted self-concepts" lead a woman to alcoholism. It is hypothesized that the women did not feel sufficiently close to either parent to turn to one of them when in trouble or lonely. This inability led to the respondent's distorted self-image and feelings of inadequacy and unattractiveness. Although only 59 percent of the patients interviewed felt this way, Kinsey still considered his material to be persuasive. Both of these studies are subject to criticism based on methodological problems arising from how an individual interprets her past experiences.

By far the most convincing argument is made by those who see low self-esteem as neither exclusively a before nor after problem. Even though low self-esteem was seen as a precipitating factor among the women in the state hospital sample just discussed, Kinsey did not discount the negative effects of labeling on the female alcoholic:

> The consequences of drinking intensify the inebriate's failure to find favorable definitions from others (except inebriates) or to meet the requirements of mature adult roles. There emerges, consequently, a vicious circle in which predisposing factors lead to alcohol usage, which in turn intensifies the predisposing "traits." [52]

As noted in chapter 5, we have not isolated an alcoholic personality syndrome or certain predisposing factors that all alcoholic women possess. There does seem to be a reasonable possibility that some women who drink have a poor self-image before they start drinking heavily. Evidence is even more convincing, however, in support of the belief that women are more heavily criticized for their drinking. Since women are more heavily criticized and there is no evidence they form effective means of defense (such as subcultures and the like) against these attacks on their self-concept, a negative self-esteem resulting from being labeled alcoholic seems even more possible.

In writing about her observations of a sample of one hundred men and one hundred female alcoholics, Curlee noted that alcoholism in women tended to be more closely linked with a specific problem or situation in their lives. [53] The women were already questioning their self-worth, so that the criticism they received for heavy drinking led to a vicious circle. The sense of worthlessness and depression they experienced when they found themselves alone was compounded by the feeling that they were "weak-willed and degraded drunks." In-depth interviews with twelve female alcoholics in another study showed that they consistently had low self-esteem and alcohol "lowered this self-esteem to zero." [54] Female alcoholics in California were shown to have inadequately developed coping devices; "they were classified as vulnerable, dependent, self-defeating and distrustful." [55] Such research does not preclude the possibility that the prealcoholic woman had been unsuccessful in developing coping devices before the advent of her alcoholism.

A clear before-or-after separation in the discussion of the female alcoholic's self-esteem seems to be impossible and unnecessary. Both types of studies add to our knowledge of the female alcoholic. Even if low self-esteem is a factor in a woman becoming an alcoholic, given current attitudes toward female alcoholics, an increasing assault on her self-esteem seems to be all but inevitable.

An individual's self-concept is in a state of continual modification and alcohol addiction is unequivocally a process during which one's self-image undergoes certain changes. A theoretical model that delimits clear steps is not meant to divide our image of reality into discrete and separable parts. Instead, it attempts to clarify some points of the possible progression. Therefore, although some data exist to support the notion that females who become alcoholics may have low self-esteem before their heavy drinking, this does not negate the value of studying the effect of stigmatization on the female alcoholic's self-esteem. Research that shows changes in self-esteem during the rehabilitation process makes this clear.

Self-Esteem and the Rehabilitation Process

While techniques for assisting an alcoholic to recover may vary, there appears to be general agreement that raising the alcoholic's self-esteem is an important goal, especially among women: "The marked improvement in self-esteem of an alcoholic lady can be one of the main reasons she no longer drinks."[56]

Although one study shows no significant change in the self-esteem of participants in a three-week Alcoholic Treatment and Education program,[57] the majority of the research indicates that alcoholics' self-esteem can be significantly increased. An observer of women in Alcoholics Anonymous notes that "their self-esteem slowly begins to rise as they establish themselves in the A.A. community."[58] Different measures have been used to test those in treatment settings. The Marlowe-Crowne Social Desirability Scale,[59] the Michigan Alcoholism Screening Test,[60] and the Tennessee Self-Concept Scale[61] were all used in various studies to show the improvements that occurred over relatively short time periods (no longer than six weeks) in alcoholics' self-esteem.

However, there is some question about the long-term effect of the self-esteem changes that have been evidenced in these studies. In a study of sixteen patients in a treatment facility for female alcoholics in New Jersey, it was found that clear gains were made on self-concept measures.[62] The Total Positive, Identity, Self-Satisfaction, the Moral Ethical Self, and Behavior scales and subscales of the Tennessee Self-Concept Scale all showed marked improvement over a four-week training period. Sixteen weeks after reentering the community, the women were tested again. All of these gains were found to have been eliminated by the time of retesting. Burtle and others conclude that the results "signally demonstrate the power of society over deviant women. Highly significant gains in assertiveness and on five of the seven scales of the Tennessee Self-Concept Scale used in evaluation were eradicated or diminished after 16 weeks in the community."[63]

This result is not surprising, given my belief in the impact of the stigmatization process on the female alcoholic. It is, nevertheless, rather discouraging for the success of any particular kind of rehabilitation program. Apparently, the community's views of female alcoholics will have to be significantly altered if they are to be effectively treated.

The Self-Esteem of Female Alcoholics

There is fairly widespead consensus that alcoholics have low self-esteem. Interviews with those who work with alcoholics and studies of alcoholics show that male[64] and female alcoholics[65] have lower self-esteem than the general population.

Low self-esteem is considered an exceptionally difficult problem for female alcoholics.[66] Until recently, there were no comparative studies to support this contention other than reports by female alcoholics who wrote about their experiences.[67]

In the past twenty years as the literature on female alcoholics increased, observations of low self-esteem have repeatedly been reported by those who work with female alcoholics. It is difficult to assess the validity of much of the material because frequently it gives impressionistic accounts rather than providing the reader with information about how these observations were made. Howard T. Blane, a psychologist at Massachusetts General Hospital at the time he wrote his book, noted that women who started drinking were always "preoccupied about being inadequate and inept."[68] From in-depth interviews with alcoholic housewives, Bedell found that they accepted the view that the female alcoholic is a repulsive drunk and had an accordingly low self-concept.[69] Observations at Eagleville Hospital and Rehabilitation Center delivered in a report to the Senate Subcommittee on Alcoholism and Narcotics in 1976 concluded that "We find that alcoholic women treated at Eagleville generally identify themselves through the men they are with, have little self-esteem, and see the female experience as a negative one."[70]

Other researchers have drawn conclusions about the low self-esteem of alcoholic women, even though this was not the thrust of their research nor an area to which the data they presented were related. Frequently, the research is supported by observations, but it is not clear from the presentation just what these observations entailed. For example, some of Burtle's research did not warrant conclusions about self-esteem, yet self-esteem was introduced in a suppositional manner near the end: "It may be that the lack of self-trust, low self-esteem, and the drive to prove their womanhood may be important factors in bringing many women alcoholics into marriage, despite their lack of trust in men."[71] Although Burtle has done a great deal of research on female alcoholics, it is difficult to determine the accuracy of her statements about self-esteem from this particular article. Much of the research is inconclusive for this reason.

The technique of free drawing has been used by psychologists to measure the self-concept of alcoholics. This test combined with self-esteem questionnaires were enough to convince Langone and Langone that "the self-esteem of alcoholic women is often a good deal lower than that of male alcoholics and nonalcoholic women."[72] A study of twenty male and twenty female alcoholics in a private psychiatric hospital revealed that female alcoholics tended to characterize themselves in more deprecating terms.[73]

Two quantitative studies have specifically attempted to measure differences between male and female alcoholics by using a standardized self-esteem test. Sandra Clarke in 1974 administered the Q-sort technique to study twenty male and twenty female alcoholics.[74] She found no significant differences between the men and women in her sample. It is easy to make methodological critiques of this study from its small sample size, to the problems with the Q-sort method, to the lack of a random sample. However, perhaps the most crucial problem with interpreting the results is that the reader is not told what stage of rehabilitation the alcoholic sample has reached. Some of Clarke's sample came from an outpatient alcoholism clinic, and the rest were recruited from Alcoholics Anonymous. We would expect a person who has been in Alcoholics Anonymous for a long period of time to have achieved an increase in self-esteem. Clarke's brief report is provocative, yet it remains unconvincing as to the lack of male / female self-esteem discrepancies.

A more detailed and methodologically sounder study was conducted by Linda J. Beckman in 1978.[75] The sample consisted of 120 female alcoholics, 120 male alcoholics, 119 nonalcoholic women who were not in any treatment program, and 118 women who were not alcoholic but in treatment for psychiatric or emotional problems. Using the Rosenberg Self-Esteem Scale, it was found that female alcoholics had lower self-esteem than male alcoholics or nonalcoholic women. Beckman also found that female alcoholics did not differ significantly on self-esteem from the women who were in treatment for emotional problems. By using a follow-up questionnaire, it was discovered that after one year, the self-esteem of female alcoholics showed more improvement than that of the males. One of the possible implications of this work (although the researcher opted for bidirectional causality) is that low self-esteem may predispose a woman to either alcoholism or emotional problems. Beckman's work lends some credence to the belief that low self-esteem may be present in a woman before alcoholism.

In the research I conducted in 1978, I sampled seventy-nine females and

seventy-three males who had been labeled alcoholic and were in rehabilitative settings and sixty-two female and sixty male heavy drinkers who had not
been so labeled.[76] They were administered a fairly detailed background
questionnaire and the Personal Orientation Inventory (POI), a psychological
test that includes a measure of Self-Regard (Sr).

Several findings are particularly relevant to the discussion of self-esteem. It
was clear from this and other research conducted using the POI on alcoholic
samples,[77] that there is a major difference between alcoholics and other
populations.[78] There were major differences for both males and females on
Self-Regard and most of the other scales between those who were heavy
drinkers and those who were labeled alcoholic (see figure A.1, appendix a).
Heavy drinkers did score somewhat lower than would be expected of a
random population whose scores would likely cluster around the mean. However, the Self-Regard scores of the heavy drinkers were slightly above the
norm. Seventy-three percent of the alcoholics had a low Self-Regard score,
while only 40 percent of the heavy drinkers did (see table A.10). Alcoholics
scored lower overall on most of the scales and subscales.

Findings from this research can also be used to address the before-or-after
debate. The control sample was not a "normal adult sample"[79] as used for
comparison in other POI research, but a group who admitted to drinking
very heavily. If people with low self-esteem (especially women) are attracted
to heavy drinking, we would not expect to find the stark differences between
heavy drinkers and those labeled alcoholic that emerged from the data. Even
though this was not a longitudinal study with a sample of heavy drinkers
before and after being labeled, there is still a strong indication that those who
drink heavily are not those with very low self-esteem. Instead, these data
lend support to the contention that labeling someone alcoholic has a detrimental effect on that person's self-esteem. Once someone is in a rehabilitative
setting being treated for alcoholism, it is nearly impossible to incorporate
one's heavy drinking into part of acceptable social roles.

Findings on male and female differences on the Self-Regard scale were disappointing. Although in the predicted direction, there were very minimal
differences in Self-Regard scores between male and female alcoholics (see
tables A.12 and A.13). In an attempt to see if initial male-female differences
were blurred by attending Alcoholics Anonymous, which is generally con-
ceded to raise self-esteem,[80] the number of A.A. meetings attended was
controlled. The male-female differences increased in the predicted direction,
although the amount of the difference was still not of a particularly large
magnitude (See tables A.14 and A.15). However, there were very few people
who had not attended many A.A. meetings. To keep a reasonable sample
size, I divided the group into those who had attended eight or less meetings
and those who had attended nine or more. Future research should attempt to

locate alcoholics not currently involved in programs that attempt to raise their self-esteem and therefore perhaps more strongly influenced by the views of the larger community.

Other Effects of Status Insularity on Self-Esteem

Some research findings show that those in higher socioeconomic positions—both men[81] and women[82]—have a better prognosis for successfully combating alcoholism than do those in lower socioeconomic positions. Other research finds no relationship between socioeconomic status and prognosis for abstinence.[83] These research findings could be interpreted as negating the hypothesis that once labeled, those in more insulated positions are more heavily stigmatized. An attempt to understand contradictory findings of this sort is made in the next chapter in a discussion of power as a source of insularity.

In the meantime, however, it is important to note that research does not unanimously contradict the insularity hypotheses; in fact, several interesting findings make sense given the concept of status insularity. A study of two social classes of women was conducted on female alcoholics in the lower social stratum.[84] It was found that the higher-status women lost control over their drinking in a shorter period of time. Although not interpreted in this way, results could indicate that higher-status alcoholic women were subject to more criticism and therefore experienced a more telescoped development of their alcoholism.

In a sample of sixteen women, seven of whom were black, Burtle and others found that the ratio of successful outcomes among the black group was twice as high as among the white subsample.[85] This was true despite the lower socioeconomic status of the black subjects. As noted by the authors, this group is open to dual stigmatization, and their enhanced success rate needs some explanation.

In another study, Bateman and Peterson sent follow-up questionnaires to a large sample ($N=719$) of alcoholics who had been hospitalized in a psychiatric treatment program.[86] The questions were geared to determining which of a selected group of variables had "prognostic value for post-hospital drinking behavior." Among the men, no relationship was found between socioeconomic variables and treatment outcomes; findings for the women, however, were directly in line with the insularity hypothesis. Females who did not complete high school, had low-status occupations, and upper-lower or lower social status as measured by the McGuire-White Index of Value Orientation had a higher rate of abstinence.[87]

Data were available in my research to test four other insular positions to see if being labeled had a greater impact on those in such positions. The positions of race and housewife had to be dropped from the analysis due to the small number of cases in the sample. Two of the three measures used to test socioeconomic status, education and income, showed the expected relationships: (1) Those who were labeled alcoholics had higher self-esteem if they had a lower education level (see table A.16); (2) those who were heavy drinkers had a higher self-esteem if they had a higher level of education. The difference of means for education was not very large but was at least suggestive. When income was controlled, the difference of means was greater and in the predicted direction. As income increased through three categories (low, medium, and high), self-esteem among alcoholics dropped, and self-esteem among heavy drinkers increased (see table A.18). Findings using occupational prestige did not corroborate results from other socioeconomic measures (see table A.17), but only forty-eight alcoholics indicated that they were employed. It seemed reasonable to assume that those who had lost their job due to drinking would have even lower Self-Regard scores than those currently employed.

Marital status was the fourth insular position tested. It was predicted that those who were married would be in a more insular position and therefore have lower self-esteem if labeled than those who were single. Married male alcoholics had slightly higher self-esteem than single male alcoholics; however, the difference of means between alcoholics and heavy drinkers was in the predicted direction (see table A.19). In an attempt to verify Durkheim's prediction that marriage benefits men more than women,[88] gender was controlled (see table A.20). The difference of means of females showed almost no differences between married and single in the categories of alcoholics and heavy drinkers. Males, however, showed a greater difference in the predicted direction than appeared without controlling for gender. There was a greater difference of means for married men in self-esteem for alcoholics and heavy drinkers than single men. Although this difference was not large, it was enough to consider the findings at least suggestive.

Interpretation and Theoretical Relevance

Much of the theoretical relevance of status insularity was indicated in the discussion of labeling theory in chapter 4, where it was noted that labeling theorists underplay the importance of the structural aspects of society. Although the labeling and stigmatization processes are critical to the study of deviance, the status position sets the parameters within which these interactional processes occur. Status insularity does not explain why someone deviates, but it does attempt to explain why certain positions shield their occupants from labeling while other positions render them susceptible. In this chapter, I look at how status insularity relates to other theoretical formulations, examine the implications of the effects of status insularity on female alcoholics, and expand the discussion to include other types of deviance.

Theoretical Convergence

Some aspects of the status insularity concept are evident in other theoretical formulations of deviance. In discussing role engulfment, Schur says that "individuals have socially patterned, or categoric, variations in their susceptibility and resistance to engulfment in deviant roles."[1] Schur questions what kind of information acquired by others is likely to precipitate engulfment. While the literature he reviews does not indicate an answer to this question, several other theorists do offer some insights relevant to status insularity.

Subculture Theories

Deviant subcultures, whether they represent an inversion of the norms of the law-abiding[2] or "back places" where the deviant can stop making a pretense at normality,[3] have an insulating function. One clear purpose of these subcultures is to protect the individual from negative imputations against his or her self-concept: "The subculture serves... a kind of 'defensive' or 'protective' function, shielding the individuals from the negative attitudes of outsiders, from the quite practical problems posed by 'outsiders' reactions (including legal ones), or from both."[4] However, the insulation provided by a deviant subculture does not effect initial labeling: A member of a deviant subculture has most likely been labeled, even if only by him- or herself. The deviant subculture is a means of protecting members from harassment by the nondeviant society,[5] or as a way of facilitating a particular form of deviance.[6]

All subcultures are not deviant; some also offer insulation against certain types of deviance. The integration and ambivalence theories in the alcoholism literature suggest the possible effects of different cultures and subcultures on drinking:

> In any group or society in which the drinking customs, values and sanctions—together with the attitudes of all segments of the group or society—are well established, known to and agreed upon by all, and are consistent with the rest of culture, the rate of alcoholism will be low.[7]

Numerous studies support this hypothesis.[8] Little or no pathologies show up in relation to alcohol, from hangovers to alcoholism, if guilt feelings are not associated with drinking and if the use of alcohol is well integrated into the fabric of society. In the Jewish culture, for example, the use of alcoholic beverages is prescribed[9] and ritualistic.[10] Special strictures apply to drinking and prevent utilitarian[11] or hedonistic[12] drinking. As religious affiliations move from Orthodox to Reform to Secular indicating a lessening of the strength of traditional values, Snyder found that alcohol pathologies increase. "By curtailing the development of primary-group ties with non-Jews, Orthodox Judaism insulates its adherents from out-group pressures to drink immoderately."[13] More recent research shows that other mechanisms have replaced strict religious affiliations to keep the alcoholism rate low among Jews.[14] Studies of various other ethnic groups, including the Cantonese,[15] Italians, and Italian-Americans,[16] show similar findings—social integration of alcohol and cohesiveness as a subgroup prevent problems with alcohol consumption.

The type of insulation members of religious and ethnic subgroups experience varies greatly from status insularity, and the protection afforded by subgroups of this type is much closer to cultural protection[17] (see chapter 2). Most of these subgroups are organized in such a way that they lessen the likelihood of heavy drinking but do not prevent someone in that status from being labeled if heavy drinking occurs. Members of these subgroups are generally less likely to be labeled because they are less likely to deviate in the first place.

Techniques of Neutralization

A delinquent uses certain "techniques of neutralization" to shield and protect him- or herself from the "force of his own internalized values and the reaction of conforming others."[18] By means of these techniques, the juvenile delinquent justifies his or her deviance and comes to see it as a valid form of behavior. The delinquent remains committed to the dominant normative systems while committing deviant acts and by means of these techniques, prevents serious damage to his or her self-image. Reiss has shown how norms within a particular peer group govern relationships with homosexuals in such a way that they "tend to insulate the boy from a homosexual definition. So long as he conforms to these expectations, his *'significant others' will not define him* as homosexual; and this is perhaps the most crucial factor in his own self-definition."[19]

Techniques of neutralization show how certain norms and definitions of reality can insulate an individual from the ability of others to label him or her. This type of insulation varies in at least two ways from status insularity. First of all, the techniques do not prevent delinquents or peers from being labeled by the straight society. These techniques are mainly used to justify actions within the group. It does not protect members from the usual labeling agents, but from self-criticism and criticism from significant others. Secondly, these techniques do not refer to a given status and the characteristics of that status, but to individuals. The process, as described, refers to how an individual uses certain techniques to insulate or protect his or her self-definition. It does not describe how a certain position or place in society helps insulate any member of that status from being labeled deviant.

Social Control Perspective

In her exposition of the social control perspective, Nanette Davis posits that "The severity of the sanction is related to the relative amount of resources held by the conflicting party, and to elites' perception of the degree to which the behavior constitutes a threat to the authority system."[20] The corollaries of this proposition state that penalties are severe, moderate, or token in direct proportion to the amount of a person's resources. High-resource people are discussed in terms of only deviance committed as part of highly regarded occupational activities; a token penalty would be imposed for a white-collar crime committed by a high-resource person. On the other hand, riots by poor blacks would be severely sanctioned. "Deviance is normalized for high-resource violators, tolerated for moderate-resource violators, and severely punished for low-resource persons and groups."[21]

This hypothesis does offer a potential explanation of white-collar crime, which cannot be accounted for by the simplified model presented for female alcoholics. For example, a wealthy, white businessman occupies an insular position, making it less likely that he will be labeled deviant. If he commits a crime related to his employment, he is much less likely to be labeled than a lower-class person committing a similar offense. However, if caught, contrary to the prediction made on the basis of observations of female alcoholics, in many instances, he is also much less likely to be severely stigmatized.[22] The hypothesis about a high-resource person deviating from highly regarded occupational activities gives a possible explanation. Perhaps if crimes are of a certain type, expected within that class and not perceived as a great threat to the system, then they are not severely penalized.

Despite this potential insight, however, the social control argument is over-simplified and adds little to our understanding of the labeling process. It ignores the possibility of deviance committed by people in different status categories other than those stereotypically associated with a particular class. It envisions members of the lower classes committing crimes against property, and members of the upper classes committing only white-collar crimes. Certainly, the way deviant acts are defined and the degree to which they are perceived as threatening does depend partly on the group committing the offense. However, other crimes are perpetrated that do not fit our stereotypes. Wealthy people commit murder, poor people defraud the government, and middle-class people rob. Advocates of the social control perspective objected strongly to the reification of deviance in the other perspectives; however, the social control perspective also seems guilty of reification. The society it describes is rigid and stereotypical, allowing no room for changes in the structure of deviance due to human intervention and interaction.

Status and Opportunity Variables

An assumption common to labeling theorists is that groups with high resources are more likely to be able to resist negative labeling and impose their rules than those with low resources.[23] Schur expands this observation by discussing the "probability of acting" as another variable. He reaches two interesting conclusions; first, susceptibility to labeling varies with the type of deviation being considered. An individual possesses different combinations of personal characteristics and to some degree they determine his or her opportunities to deviate. "A youth may thus appear to have a relatively high probability of vagrancy and high susceptibility to labeling as a 'vagrant' yet relatively low probability of committing forgery and being labeled as a forger."[24] However, status characteristics do not always work in the same way. Blacks may be more likely than whites to engage in, and be labeled for, armed robbery but no more likely than whites to engage in, or be labeled for, homosexuality. What factors are salient depends on the particular type of deviance.

Secondly, Schur points out that a particular variable may not work in the same direction for likelihood of deviance and likelihood of being labeled. "Status characteristics of the individual tend to operate in one direction in determining the probability of specific deviation and the susceptibility to negative labeling, whereas opportunity factors tend to operate in opposite directions in determining the two aspects."[25]

If these two propositions were applied to alcoholics, it would be argued that men (status) are more likely to engage in heavy drinking and more likely to be labeled. And, conversely, women (status) are less likely to engage in heavy drinking and less likely to be labeled. Using a particular structural feature, the position of the housewife, Schur's predictions about opportunity also seem accurate. The housewife may be more likely to engage in heavy drinking (opportunity) and less likely to be labeled. Although this situation seems to be changing with the increasing presence of women in the work force, earlier research tended to support this proposition.[26]

Opportunity would appear to be what I have termed a structural feature of social organization. However, it is clear from Schur's examples that opportunity, although a structural feature, is not related to the likelihood of being labeled but to the likelihood of deviating. The youth in Schur's example is not just as likely to be a vagrant as a check forger even though he is unlikely to be labeled a forger. He is, in fact, more likely to commit the one act than the other in the first place and therefore less likely to be labeled.

"The Hidden Alcoholic"

Earl Rubington's article on "The Hidden Alcoholic"[27] discusses hypotheses similar to some of the status insularity predictions. Though there is theoretical overlap, many crucial differences exist between our studies. The first part of one of Rubington's general propositions is similar to status insularity in terms of the predictions it makes: "The higher the social status of the alcoholic, the more slowly will the label alcoholic be affixed to the person (and correlatively the later the assignment to the alcoholic role) and the stronger the displeasure of intimate others."[28] Thus Rubington describes someone in a high social status position just as I described someone in an insular position: The more insular the position (high social status being one example of a highly insular position), the less likely the person is to be labeled. Rubington also says that the higher the social position, the greater the displeasure of intimate others or in my account, the greater the stigmatization.

However, Rubington goes on to claim that "The higher the social status of the alcoholic the less exposed he is as an alcoholic to the eyes of others and consequently the less severe the public sanctions brought against him (in contrast to the severity of the private sanctions)."[29] This is the opposite of what was posited in the discussion of status insularity. Rubington claims that the higher the social status, the lower the public sanctions. This part of his proposition appears to be based purely on visibility and as such is far from clear. If those of high social status are able to hide from others, they are not labeled, and , of course, the severity of public sanctions are less because there are none. If, however, Rubington means that when their deviance is discovered, there are still less severe public sanctions, then his own examples contradict his proposition:

> the on-the-job sanctions for alcoholic behavior visited against relatively low-ranking workers are mild compared to both sentiments against and *actions taken against* supervisors when their alcoholism becomes known and its damages clearly seen.[30]

> persons of relatively high social status are expected to be alcoholics in private rather than public. Otherwise awareness of their behavior and its consequences for others real or imagined, would evoke *very strong societal reactions* paralleling the costly damages such high-ranking alcoholics might well inflict on others.[31]

Since his own examples and other statements indicate the higher the social status, the greater the stigmatization if labeled, it can only be assumed that Rubington either (1) stated the obvious—someone whose deviance is not seen by the public is not criticized by the public—or (2) routinely followed the traditional labeling view. Apparently, despite what he observed about people's reactions to alcoholics, he stated, in keeping with labeling theory, that those with more power are subject to fewer reprisals. It should be noted that this appears to be true in some forms of deviation, such as white-collar crime, but may not hold true for alcoholism.

There are other major differences between my analysis and Rubington's. His concept deals only with alcoholics. After reviewing the research on alcoholics, Rubington reached certain conclusions about how rank affects alcoholics. However, no attempt was made to generalize these findings to other forms of deviation.

The concept of social status that Rubington presents appears to be limited to the power dimension. Exactly what is meant by high or low status is never explicitly defined, but the examples all indicate that those of high social status have more money, better jobs, and are white. Although there are different problems facing male and female alcoholics, Rubington never mentions male-female disparities, thereby limiting his analysis even within the alcoholic population.

Although completely ignoring social evaluations based on cultural definitions (and therefore gender) as a source of status, Rubington does discuss the effects of structural features of social organization. However, instead of being a separate factor affecting a person's status, the social conditions he discusses are generally extensions of the power dimension.

In the home situation, Rubington simply indicates that those of a higher status are less likely to call the police to their home. He overlooks the fact that the home offers a chance for women to drink undetected. For the poor, how-

ever, it may afford little privacy if living conditions are so crowded that they
expose even what occurs in the home to scrutiny by neighbors.[32]

At work, executives have greater control over those who will or will not be
given access to them, whereas, as Rubington argues, the general worker is
forced to interact with a large number of people. Differently structured work
environments are a valid structural consideration, but there may not be a
one-to-one correlation between high status and the opportunity to manipulate work environments to cover up deviation. Door-to-door salesmen or
janitors may be better able to hide their drinking from those at work who
would label them than many executives.

In a discussion of what takes place on the street, Rubington again refers
strictly to the power dimension and ignores other structural considerations.
He gives an example of how policemen "hide" a judge who is drunk and dis-
orderly in public, then goes on to show that those of low status are not
accorded similar treatment. Women, as noted in chapter 2, may also be
treated leniently, and therefore police behavior may not simply depend on
the alcoholic's high socioeconomic status. Rubington's analysis tells little
about structural aspects of the street: The behavior he describes could and
does occur anywhere. Structural features related to the street include the fact
that police expect and look for trouble in certain areas of the city[33] and in
general, members of the lower classes are forced, because of cramped living
conditions, to use the street for many forms of behavior. As Chambliss and
Seidman note,

> The lower-class adolescent... if he drinks, must do so in an alley; when
> he gambles, he is not protected by the security of his parents' home;
> indeed, with the urban lower-class adolescent even so private a behavior as
> the sexual act is likely to be carried out in relatively more public arenas
> than is the case with the middle-class adolescent, who has the privacy of at
> least his car.[34]

Rubington's discussion of all three structural conditions is less a serious look
at structural features than an attempt to show three different places in which
higher and lower class individuals receive different treatment.

Rubington's rationale for why those of high social status are unlikely to be
labeled concentrates on the actions of the deviants: "Status commits a person
to a stake in the social order, and the higher the status, the higher the stakes.
Given this, it stands to reason that persons of high status would strive for low
visibility."[35]

Although there is no reason to question the validity of this position, it does
seem that a further explanation is necessary to understand fully why the
high-status deviator is less likely to be labeled. Even when the deviation of a
person in a highly insular position is known, he or she is less likely to be

labeled, and this fact cannot be explained simply by the lack of visibility. One of the main points of labeling theory is that deviation is not a result of individual wrongdoing, but a matter of social definition and interaction with labeling agents. Rubington's argument ignores this aspect of deviance. His explanation is incomplete without an explanation of why it is more difficult to label high-status individuals.

Status Insularity and Labeling Female Alcoholics

Status insularity was defined as the property of a social position that decreases the likelihood that an occupant of that status will be labeled deviant. It was hypothesized that once occupants of status insular positions were labeled, they would be more severely stigmatized and as a result, subject to lower self-esteem and greater secondary deviation.

Chapter 2 presented data to support the contention that women who drink excessively are less likely to be labeled alcoholic than men who drink excessively. The data is organized and presented in a discussion of the traditional roles, which, it is argued, protect women through the mechanisms of social evaluations based on cultural definitions and structural features of social organization. Although women's status insularity may be declining (see chapter 3), the available data lend strong support to the hypothesis that women still possess a certain amount of status insularity when the deviance is alcoholism.

The greater stigmatization of women is also supported by observations of experts and firsthand accounts (see chapter 4). Quantitative evidence is presented to show the inaccessibility of treatment facilities and the fact that women are more likely to be solitary drinkers. Although these findings are not proof that a negative attitude exists toward female alcoholics, they may reflect such an attitude, as many theorists claim. Despite the lack of direct quantitative evidence to support such a belief, there seems to be a general consensus among those who deal with female alcoholics that they are subject to greater stigmatization. In my own research, the findings were mixed. The alcohol practitioner's responses to the questionnaire could be seen as supportive. In observing the men and women whom they counseled, these experts perceived other patients as more critical of female alcoholics and female alcoholics as having lower self-esteem. As reported in chapter 2, the respondents in my sample did say they believed that others were more critical of female heavy drinkers. This was true for all categories of respondents. However, the subgroup with the highest percentage of people who felt this way were alcoholic females, 81 percent of whom believed others were more critical of women. It was expected that when asked if they felt it were worse for a woman to be an alcoholic, they would not admit to such a prejudice. This turned out to be the case. It is possible, however, that they answered honestly, and there is less criticism of women than initially believed. The three short-answer questions used to test directly the degree of stigmatization (how critical spouse, friends, and relatives were of their drinking) showed no marked differences between males and females. Although plausible explanations were provided and similar findings from other research were presented to explain these findings, it is also possible that they are accurate. A great deal more direct support, as opposed to the post hoc arguments of the unavailability of treatment facilities and solitary drinking patterns, is necessary to substantiate the hypothesis that women are more severely stigmatized.

That there is greater secondary deviation among female alcoholics has some support in the evidence presented on telescoped development and greater pathology in chapter 5. The most difficult part of analyzing what are at times contradictory findings is the argument that women are more disturbed to begin with, and that is why they drink heavily. My research provides some grounds for questioning this claim. The control sample drank heavily and by some definitions excessively; yet the Self-Regard scores of female and male heavy drinkers were much higher than the female and male alcoholic samples and higher than the normal population to which the test is standardized.

The alteration of self-concept, which is seen as a necessary part of the secondary deviation process, has been reported in numerous observations of alcoholics (chapter 6). As noted in chapter 6, there is evidence that alcoholics, both male and female, have lower self-esteem than nonalcoholics, and my findings agree with such findings, some of which use the POI. In using a heavy-drinking control sample, my research also gives some indication that it is the labeling, not the alcohol, that precipitates the low self-esteem. However, it must be remembered that the difference between the means are not for the same people at two different times. There could be other explanations for the lower self-esteem of those labeled, but the data are sufficient to give some indication of the possible importance of being labeled.

There is a great deal less quantitative research showing that female alcoholics have lower self-esteem than male alcoholics: One study shows no differences, and one shows female alcoholics with lower self-esteem than male alcoholics. My research showed very slight differences that tended to increase with a decrease in the number of A.A. meetings attended. The findings are not very supportive of the hypothesis that predicted a lower self-esteem in female alcoholics.

The same hypothesis for other insular positions had greater support. Marital status showed slight support. Those labeled alcoholics who were married did show slightly lower Self-Regard scores than those who were single. This difference increased when just male alcoholics were considered.

Of the three separate measures of socioeconomic status, two showed fairly good support for the insularity hypothesis. Occupational prestige, the third

to exist in all stages of the implementation of the law, from the police
gation to the trial.[52]

of Chambliss and Seidman's propositions summarize the findings
ast amounts of research:

here laws are so stated that people of all classes are equally likely to
te them, the lower the social position of an offender, the greater the
hood that sanctions will be imposed on him.

en sanctions are imposed, the most severe sanctions will be imposed
sons in the lowest classes.[53]

ose in the upper classes are less likely to be labeled and less likely to
y stigmatized once labeled.

onclusions of the criminal justice literature on stigmatization are
more detailed analysis than those of labeling theory, but their view-
parallel. Labeling theorists speak of deviance instead of crime, but
claim that those without power are the ones labeled deviant.[54]

ated by research in the field, it is reasonable to argue that status
and stigmatizaion varied as predicted for female alcoholics and
olics with relatively more income and education and possibly for
were married. However, the well-supported conclusion in studies
llar crime and the general area of criminal justice questions
ese two variables always operate in this way. It is clear that the
f being labeled and degree of stigmatization do not vary in the
on for all forms of deviance as they do for alcoholism. To the con
uld appear that generally the likelihood of being labeled and
gmatization vary together in a positive direction, as indicated by
eviance research, and opposite to the negative direction eviden
dies.
e of stigmatization is not part of the definition of status insu
re two separate variables related in one way in my research an
way in other areas, such as criminal justice. What determine
ip between the two variables is of particular theoretical interes
table can be used to represent how the two variables may
ble 7.1).

Sources of Insularity

tatus insularity must lie in society's norms. A status position
t of norms clustered around a recurrent social identity. Wha

measure, was not supportive, but these findings were questionable because
the number of people in the sample was halved due to those who were not
currently employed. It seemed reasonable to hypothesize that those without
current employment would have lower self-esteem than those who were still
employed. Education and income showed consistent and suggestive differences between those in insular and noninsular positions. Among the heavy
drinkers, as was expected, those with a higher educational level had a higher
Self-Regard score. Among the alcoholics, as predicted, those with a lower
educational level had a higher Self-Regard score. The third measure of socioeconomic status, income, also showed the predicted relationship. When
broken down into three categories (high, medium, and low), the difference
between the means was in the predicted direction and grew larger as the
status increased.

Status Insularity and Other Forms of Deviance

If status insularity is to be a meaningful concept, it should have application
outside of the field of alcoholism. And there are other serious challenges in
the deviance literature that necessitate a reevaluation of the hypothesis that
predicted greater stigmatization for those in insular positions once they are
labeled.

White-Collar Crime

Edwin H. Sutherland defined white-collar crime as "a crime committed by
a person of respectability and high social status in the course of his occupation."[36] In 1949, Sutherland investigated 70 large and respected corpora-
tions for this type of crime and found 890 criminal convictions.[37] A vast
amount of literature has expanded and and reconfirmed Sutherland's initial
analysis of white-collar crime, showing that weak penalties are generally
imposed on those who commit such crimes.[38] The concept has become generalized to include nonviolent crimes by upper- and middle-class people,
usually in connection with their occupation, such as embezzlement, bribery,
tax evasion, price fixing, and the like. Other research broadens the term even
more to include credit card violations, planned bankruptcies, and so forth.[39]
Although these crimes are nonviolent, they are not without serious cost.
Property and white-collar crimes were compared for annual cost by the
President's Commission on Law Enforcement and the Administration of
Justice,[40] and it was found that the cost of *reported* white-collar crime was
three times as large as property crimes.

Dinitz, Dynes, and Clarke have effectively argued that white-collar crime
is a very serious matter:

Criminologists agree that white collar crime is by far the most damaging of all violations and deviations. Not only is it more costly than any other form of deviation, but it also undermines trust in our basic economic arrangements; none of us can adequately protect ourselves from it.[41]

With the cost of white-collar crime so high, it is interesting how mildly (if at all) the criminals are punished. In a 1961 case, a federal court convicted several highly paid prestigious corporate executives of conspiracy in restraint of trade.[42] It was argued they did not need a stay in prison because they were such upstanding citizens and needed no deterrence to prevent them from repeating the crime. Chambliss and Seidman have argued just as effectively, however: "On the other hand, the objectives of retribution and general deterrence arguably demanded a substantial jail sentence, indeed precisely because the defendants were pillars of the community, the aim of general deterrence would seem to require a greater penalty."[43]

Herbert Edlehertz makes a similar comment based on his research on white-collar crime:

> In the abuse of trust and business crimes categories, the crimes are only possible because the violators are given the opportunity to commit crimes, by society, because they have presumably shown themselves worthy. Under these circumstances white-collar violations may well be more reprehensible, and more deserving of punishment if punishment is the sole criterion, than common crimes such as burglary.[44]

These arguments are similar to my contention that since greater forces have to be mustered to label people in such positions, we would expect them to be more heavily stigmatized once labeled.

Such, however, is not the outcome of most white-collar cases. As Kenkel and Voland note, "The person who commits a white collar crime usually does not think of himself as a criminal and is not so stigmatized by society."[45] The lack of serious punishment and of stigmatization is consistently shown by research on white-collar crime.[46] A deviant career model and secondary deviation, therefore, do not seem particularly relevant to the white-collar criminal. Even after conviction, white-collar criminals generally return to the community and are accepted as respectable citizens.

White-collar crime is a major exception to the hypothesis that those in insular positions are more heavily stigmatized if labeled. It does not challenge the basic concept of status insularity; however, it does call into question additional hypotheses founded on observations of female alcoholics. Not only is it difficult to fit white-collar crime into our model, it is questionable whether it makes much sense within the larger framework of labeling theory. The application of a label certainly does not "cause" white-collar deviancy, and a label is seldom imposed that leads to secondary deviation. Understanding why the

white-collar criminal is not treated as a crim
standing why these crimes are not considered
the majority of the population. How and wh
insulated against labeling to begin with wou
explanation.

Nanette Davis's social control perspectiv
white-collar crime. She states: "Token (or
with deviance committed by high-resour
regarded occupational activities (e.g., wh
government fraud) that sustain the existing

In part, white-collar criminals receive we
greater resources, which allow them to e
gested relationship between sanctions and
posited by labeling theorists. However, Da
sanction is tied to the "elites' perception
constitutes a threat to the authority system

This argument is contrary to my su
mustered to label someone deviant, then
It may take a great deal to label someo
due to their respected position and the
protect themselves. It may also be d
white-collar criminals, since what they
to the system by elites or others. Wh
collar crime is hardly what most peo
and rapes are easily seen as threat
bezzlement is not. Whether elites co
"moral entrepreneur,"[50] white-coll
trary, is not seen as a serious threat
not see themselves as the victim of
it costs all of us money.

The extent that an act threaten
definers appears to be a necessary
insularity functions.

Criminal Justice Literature

It is not my purpose to review
to discuss implications of the
general thrust of the fairly conc
to be punished for deviating th
generalizability of the hypothe
tion among female alcoholics

Table 7.1 Status insularity predictions

Likelihood of Being Labeled

Degree of stigmatization

	High	Low
High	Poor or black delinquent Cell 1	Female alcoholic Cell 2
Low	Lower-class brawler Cell 3	White-collar criminal Cell 4

it about the source of the norms associated with a particular status that make it unlikely for an occupant of that status to be labeled deviant even if he or she commits a deviant act?

As stated in the first chapter, three sources appear to be important: (1) power, (2) structural features of social organization, and (3) social evaluations based on cultural definitions.

Power

Those in positions of power, whether the source be economic, political, or prestige, clearly have influence over the labeling process.[55] As Howard Becker demonstrates in his "hierarchy of credibility" argument,[56] those at the top of the ranked system are assumed to have a more legitimate right to define reality. With this description, the labeling theorist makes an important contribution by challenging the assumption that deviance is universal and instead shows it to be part of a political process.

For example, psychiatrists in our society belong to a prestigious group. In the D.L. Rosenhan study discussed in the section on stigmatization in chapter 4, it was shown how eight sane people had themselves admitted to mental hospitals with a claim that they were hearing voices[57]. Once they were admitted they acted normally and yet one person was diagnosed as manic depressive and seven others as schizophrenic. They were not diagnosed on the basis of any existent "mental illness" but on the label applied when they entered the hospital. Psychiatrists in many situations can determine how a person will be labeled and what form of treatment he or she will receive. In short, they define reality for the patient. Erving Goffman makes a similar indictment in his work on mental asylums.[58] Chambliss and Seidman show the same type of process in relation to the importance of police discretion.[59]

Alvin Gouldner calls critiques by labeling theorists attacks of the "middleman" instead of serious challenges against the real power structure.[60] To some degree, this criticism is justified. Psychiatrists or the police do have some power based on their position; however, they are not the only source of power. They must answer to others—the middle- and upper-class public, those who head the institutions, or politicians who guarantee their funding.

Power has been defined as "the *chance* of carrying through the will of a person, or a group of persons, within a social relationship."[61] An example from the drug control area demonstrates that the real source of power may not be the police, who do not impose their own will. When drug use spread to the middle and upper classes, suburban parents requested police assistance in drug control. Chambliss and Seidman note:

> As it slowly became clear to the parents of these youths what the consequences of intervention by law enforcement agencies means in terms of prison sentences, jail sentences, interrupted education, etc.... law enforcement agencies have begun to feel the sting of community criticism for their processing of middle- and upper-class youthful law violators.[62]

Pressure from the community has made the police and prosecuting attorney withdraw from efforts to stop drug abuse in the wealthy areas: "The effort at drug control is, once again, being focused on the use of drugs in the slums, where arrests can be made and convictions obtained without creating the kind of organizational strains that have burgeoned with the arrest of middle- and upper-class youths."[63]

This is an excellent example of how sanctions depend on the elites' perception of how much the activity threatens the authority system.[64] Initially, elites perceived drugs to be a threat and therefore requested police involvement. Later, they realized that the police were more of a threat to their way of life.

Cells 1 and 4 in table 7.1 indicate examples of where deviance and the resultant stigmatization depend on power. The two cells correspond to our expectations if power were the sole source of insularity. The poor or a minority group are more likely to be labeled for a crime and more likely to be heavily stigmatized once labeled. The powerful and / or wealthy are less likely to be labeled, and if labeled, they are less heavily stigmatized. While these predictions are true in many cases, they do not exhaust the possibilities.

Structural Features of Social Organization

Structural features of social organization include physical and social distance patterns, ecological patterns, and the like, that differentially affect such variables as segregation, visibility, and subcultural growth.

Among the Mormons, for example, structural features of social organization may affect rule enforcement. As long as polygamy is practiced within

Mormon territory, a man will seldom be prosecuted, as is evidenced by the open espousal of polygamy in Salt Lake City. In parts of the country where the Mormon culture is not physically separated from the larger society, which consists of people holding different beliefs, the same law is much more likely to be enforced.

Lack of visibility is the primary way that structural features protect people from the scrutiny of rule enforcers. An example is the relatively low visibility of the middle or upper classes in comparison to the lower classes because of housing patterns. It was noted earlier that the poor are more likely to be labeled simply because crowded living conditions lead them to do many things (for example, gamble) in more public settings.[65] Rubington discussed the structural environment of the high status alcoholic. He claimed that those who came in contact with the alcoholic could be controlled, thus insulating the person and protecting him or her from being labeled. The housewife's role was also structured to protect her from labeling if she indulged in alcohol or drugs.

There may be many different structural features of social organization that protect deviants (from the way their work reduces their interaction with others to belonging to a sect that has little contact with the majority of the population), but the primary way they all provide protection is through lack of visibility. If the rule enforcers are not able to see their deviance, they are not likely to be labeled. Even if people know others are deviating but are not forced to confront it, they are less likely to feel any need to label the deviant person (e.g. polygamy among the Mormons or homosexuality). It is when the deviance is held up to the public as a flagrant violation of acceptable norms and values that labeling and stigmatization result.

Cell 1 in table 7.1 shows that the lack of insularity, accentuated by high visibility, may play a role in increasing the likelihood of being labeled. Cells 2 and 4 are examples of how structural features of social organization may protect the deviant. Female alcoholics have tended to have a low visibility in the past due to their role as housewives and their drinking patterns, which made them less likely to drink in public places. As noted, this low visibility is declining as more women move into the labor force. White-collar criminals are also protected from labeling by the way in which their work is structured: Their deviancy is not visible to most people with whom they work.

Social Evaluations Based on Cultural Definitions

When speaking of social evaluations based on cultural definitions as a source of insularity I am referring to entrenched norms that are part of our society. According to Davis, "Norms, values, and beliefs provide the context out of which societal reactions to labeling emerge."[66] They do not always coincide with the ranking system based on power.

Cell 2 in table 7.1 represents insularity brought about by cultural definitions. The person is less likely to be labeled, but once labeled, he or she is
more likely to be stigmatized. In my example of female alcoholics, the power
associated with the status of female does not lessen the likelihood of women
being labeled, but the norms that define femaleness cannot be made to mesh
with those we associate with drunkenness and alcoholism. It is possible, since
it was not considered appropriate (and here we may go back to power as the
initial "cause") for women to drink, that the norms have not yet caught up
with changing female roles. It may also be that the roles of mother and wife,
which put the female at the center of the American family, preclude a vision
of her as an alcoholic.

Other positions that offer their occupants high regard based on cultural definitions, such as the clergy, seem to provide similar status insularity. Cultural
definitions are such that the clergy is unlikely to be labeled for many forms of
deviance (for example, alcoholism or homosexuality), but if labeled, we
would expect its members to be more heavily stigmatized than those in less
protected statuses.

Clearly, these three sources of insularity cannot be completely isolated
from each other. Conflict and labeling theorists would agree that all three are
ultimately based on power. However, as the present research has shown,
power may not be the only important variable. Most statuses are likely to
include some combination of these sources of insularity. Female alcoholics, for
example, are insulated by both cultural definitions and structural features of
social organization; in addition, other positions they hold are bound to have
an effect. Females also hold a high or low socioeconomic status, a high or low
political status, and belong to various ethnic groups. Every status position
which a person holds will have some effect on the likelihood of the person
being labeled and / or stigmatized. However, there is something special about
being female (ignoring all other statuses) that has implications for secondary
deviation among alcoholics. It is also possible to separate economic position,
educational status, and marital status to show the independent effects of
labeling for each of these variables.

Conclusion

Whatever the possibility of being labeled, there exist variations in the kind
of sanctions imposed once the person is labeled. While it may require a wide
base of support and mustering large forces to label someone in a high-status
position, once labeled, there is wide variation in the sanctions that are
applied. For example, female alcoholics have greater sanctions imposed (cell
2), while white-collar criminals have slight sanctions imposed, given the
severity of their crimes (cell 4).

While a complete discussion of how status insularity functions is beyond the realm of the present research, some attempt has to be made to explain the existence of so many cases in cell 4 in the table 7.1, which contradict my hypothesis that those who are less likely to be labeled should, once labeled, be more heavily stigmatized.

As discussed earlier, whether the deviation threatens the authority system is important in explaining the severity of the sanctions. There is some agreement that the more tension and strain put on a system by deviance, the more likely that deviance is to be severely sanctioned.[67] White-collar criminals, for example, are not seen as a threat to the authority system, so they are not severely penalized despite the effort necessary to label them. Alcoholic women, on the other hand, are a great threat to a status system based on their moral superiority.

Secondly, legal versus nonlegal sanctions play a part in distinguishing the two groups. Alcoholics in insulated positions (those who are female, married, and occupy a higher socioeconomic status) suffer lower self-esteem. Apparently, less severe sanctions are applied to those in less-insulated positions (those who are male, single, and occupy a lower socioeconomic status); this is true even though individuals with a higher socioeconomic status are in a more powerful position. Alcoholism is a deviance that generally warrants nonlegal sanctions, such as criticism, disdain, or rehabilitative treatment.[68] If the deviance is such that legal sanctions are likely to be imposed, then the relationship seems to be reversed: Those in insulated positions (especially those backed by power) are less likely to receive criminal penalties (for example, white-collar criminals). This was the same relationship found among female alcoholics, who were also less likely to receive legal sanctions, even though they were more heavily criticized. While they may not receive formal sanctions, they may receive equal or greater informal sanctions, such as criticism, and therefore still be subject to secondary deviation.[69]

The legal versus nonlegal distinction appears to be a better predictor for status insularity than the private versus public dichotomy. Rubington's examples showed that high-status male alcoholics would be more severely criticized than low-status male alcoholics by both people close to the alcoholic (private sanctions) as well as by those who were not close (public sanctions). However, if a high-status male were caught speeding or shoplifting, it is less likely that legal action would be taken against him than against a low-status male. Politicians who get in trouble are severely criticized, both publicly and privately, but few if any legal sanctions are imposed. And in the long run, they are frequently allowed to return to careers as lawyers and even politicians and resume their previous place of distinction in the community.

Finally, where our hypotheses do hold true (cell 2) the main source of insularity is social evaluations based on cultural definitions and / or structural features of social organization. The female alcoholic is protected from labeling primarily by cultural definitions and secondarily by structural features of social organization. With deviant clergymen and polygamous Mormons (whom we would also expect to be in cell 2), the major source of insularity is the structural features of social organization. The main source of insularity for examples in cell 4 (white-collar criminals and other high socioeconomic status people who break the law) is power. It may well be that if there is enough power to back up the position, even though it takes a great deal of effort to label the person, the power will still protect the individual from strong sanctions. Imposing one's will on others includes getting away with breaking the rules. Protection received from cultural definitions or visibility, however, does not depend on the will of the person involved but on others. Because labeling undermines the source of insularity, nothing remains to protect the individual from heavy stigmatization.

One of these predictors of the severity of sanctions cannot be examined without regard to the other two. If they are all taken into account and the status of the person is known, fairly accurate predictions about the degree and kind of stigmatization are possible.

The chapter on labeling theory demonstrated the need for an increased focus on structural aspects of deviation. Status insularity provides one way of concentrating on the structural features of society while at the same time not ignoring labeling and its interactional nature. The data suggested that status insularity exists and functions as predicted for alcoholics, although socioeconomic status was shown to be a better predictor than gender. The discussion on the conceptualization of status insularity makes it clear that it can be dealt with at the theoretical level and has the potential for providing insights into why some people are labeled and others are not.

The concept of status insularity cannot answer all the critiques of labeling theory, and it cannot be used to investigate all structural features of deviance, but it is a step toward including some aspects of structure in labeling analysis and as such deserves further consideration.

Appendix
Report of Research on the Self-Esteem of Female Alcoholics

The concept of status insularity developed from the inability to explain available data on female alcoholics using the traditional perspective of labeling theory. Thus, theoretical support for the concept was based on research and observations that had already been completed.

Status insularity refers to the property of a social position that decreases the likelihood that an occupant of that status will be labeled deviant. Ample evidence exists and has been presented in the present text to suggest that women have traditionally been in such a status when the deviance to be labeled was alcoholism (see especially chapter 2).

It also appeared that once female alcoholics were labeled, they were more severely stigmatized. This is not necessarily part of the definition of status insularity but an hypothesis that was postulated on the basis of existing data and supported with a great deal of evidence, which is presented in the body of the text (see especially chapter 5).

By far the weakest support for my view of how the labeling process is effected by status insularity among female alcoholics is data showing that women who are labeled alcoholics have lower self-esteem than male alcoholics. In an effort to obtain a better understanding of the effect of status insularity on the self-esteem of female alcoholics, I conducted my own research, geared mostly to this particular aspect of the process.

References to various parts of this research are made throughout the text without specifying how the data were gathered. This appendix gives an overview of the research with greater attention to the technical aspects and a report of some of the most relevant findings. A much more detailed analysis of the results, other findings, copies of questionnaires I constructed for the research, and critical arguments pro and con on the use of a standardized test, such as that used to measure self-esteem, are presented in depth in my dissertation and can be referred to if more detail is desired. [1]

The main effort of the research was focused on a background questionnaire and the POI , a standardized psychological test that has a measure for self-esteem, which were administered to a sample of heavy drinkers and labeled alcoholics.

Sampling

Purposive nonprobability sampling was used to choose the alcoholic sample. Twelve halfway houses and hospital clinics were chosen because they guaranteed that (1) others had already labeled the resident an alcoholic; (2) the alcoholics would not be "recovered" alcoholics who had not been drinking for a long time, as found in many A.A. groups (3) the study would involve people from different socioeconomic groups (in general, halfway houses have lower socioeconomic groups, while hospital programs have higher ones); (4) they offered geographical variety, including residents from at least two states (New York and Ohio) and people from small towns and midsized and large cities; and (5) these have male and female alcoholics.

Although most statistics technically require a random sample, this is seldom achieved within the social sciences. The question is to what extent results are generalizable. With the kind of sampling done in this research, the findings could not justifiably be generalized to all alcoholics. However, given the diversified sample, the findings are more generalizable than most studies conducted on small groups of alcoholics (usually an A.A. sample). The total size of the sample was 152, with 73 male and 79 female alcoholics.

The control sample of heavy drinkers who were not labeled was a convenience sample drawn from bars, civic groups, and colleges. Participants were asked not to fill out the questionnaire unless they drank at least several glasses of alcoholic beverages every day. When the background questionnaires were coded, those who scored a total of less than six on questions 19 and 20 were discarded.

19. How frequently do you drink?

    0 Never _____
    1 Once a month _____
    2 Once every few weeks _____
    3 Once a week _____
    4 Several times a week _____
    5 Everyday _____

20. When you do drink, how many glasses of beer, wine, or liquor do you usually drink at one sitting?

    0 Less than two glasses _____
    1 2 or 3 glasses _____
    2 4 or 5 glasses _____
    3 6 or 7 glasses _____
    4 8 or more glasses _____

The numbers on the left were used for coding and defining a heavy drinker and did not appear on the questionnaire. Any combination of the code numbers totaling six or more qualified the person as a heavy drinker. For example, if someone drank several times a week (4), he or she would have to drink at least four or five glasses at one sitting (2) to be considered a heavy drinker (4+2=6).

Studies indicate that only a very small percentage of the population, 8 percent in Mulford[2] and 12 percent in Cahalan and others,[3] drink enough to be called heavy drinkers under these conditions.

The size of the sample of heavy drinkers was 122, with 62 females and 60 males. Twenty-six other questionnaires were turned in (sixteen female and ten male) whose drinking scores did not total six or more, and they were not used in analysis.

Measuring Instruments

The interactionists, with whom I concur, view the self as emergent in social acts, yet any standardized self-esteem measure can only treat the self as static.

> [The] essentially static nature of conventional quantitative analysis and measurement in the social sciences... [yields] descriptions of states not processes... No standard self-concept or self-esteem measures deal directly with the self as process. Participant observation and evaluative therapy techniques emphasizing observation of the self in situ are the only approaches which purport to do otherwise.[4]

However, one way of studying a process is to look at the results or products of that process. Although an excellent case can be made for the use of quantitative techniques, it is important to be fully aware of the methodological implications for generalizing from data gathered by such techniques. Quantitative data indicate what has taken place in the process, but they can never fully describe the process. Such data should be used as guideposts to direct our thinking about how the process of self-development actually does occur.

The Personal Orientation Inventory

The Personal Orientation Inventory was created as a standardized test of Abraham Maslow's theory of self-actualization. Maslow[5] outlines the normal development for healthy human growth by describing the basic needs that must be met for a person to reach his or her full potential. As one set of needs is gratified, a new set of needs arises. A person moves from a concern with physical needs to safety needs, then to belonging and love needs, esteem needs, and finally the need for self-actualization, which "refers to a man's

desire for self-fulfillment, namely to the tendency for him to become actual-
ized in what he is potentially... to become everything that one is capable of
becoming."[6]

Maslow argues that deductive reasoning supported the existence of a need
for self-actualization (that is, people acted so that their behavior could be
explained only in terms of the existence of such a need). Clinical evidence
and personal observation reinforced his belief in such a need.[7]

Recently, Everett L. Shostrom[8] developed an instrument designed to
quantitatively measure personal self-fulfillment by using self-actualizing concepts. Maslow applauded increase in empirical research brought about by
such a standardized measure. He felt confident that the test accurately
measured what he meant by self-actualization: "Self-actualization can now
be defined quite operationally, as intelligence used to be defined, i.e., self-
actualization is what the test tests. It correlates well with external variables
of various kinds and keeps on accumulating additional correlational
meanings."[9]

For most sociologists, particularly the interactionists, the self is reflexive.
The individual's experiences constitute the self, not the body or mind: "The
'self' involves only that portion of the personality which consists of reflexive or
self-conscious cognitions and behaviors."[10] Deviating from other theoretical
schools of thought, the self-actualization literature treats the self not as reflexive behavior but as individual potentialities. This critical distinction[11]
would seem to exclude the use of Maslow's concepts for research that maintains the self is reflexive in nature. The processes of labeling and secondary
deviation are centered around people's ability to respond to their environment. However, through the process of operationalizing self-actualization,
Shostrom's indicators from necessity become as reflexive as those in other
standardized tests. The "150, two-choice, comparative value and behavior
judgments,"[12] which comprise the POI are not phrased in terms of what you
will potentially become. Instead they are an appraisal of how a person feels
or acts under various conditions. The questions are based on the belief that
the person taking the test can treat his or her self as an object.

The POI is an "orthodox self-esteem measure"[13] because it is operationalized in such a way that it is standardized, objective, and quantitative. It
uses verbal self-reports and is subject to most criticisms leveled against such
objective measures. However, the common complaint that most self-esteem
measures are designed and used for only a specific instance and then fall into
disuse does not apply to the POI, which already has a rich history of research.[14]

The POI is a 150-item, single-stimulus rating scale. Subjects are asked to
choose the statement that is true or mostly true from a series of paired oppo-
sites. The items are scored twice: once for the two major scales of Time Competence (twenty-three items) and Inner-Directed (127 items) and then again

for ten subscales that purport to measure some element of self-actualization. Although not the central focus of my research, the Time Competence and Inner-Directed scales were compared, since they are considered the best predictors within the POI and their scores include the total 150 questions. Shostrom has argued that the Time Competence and Inner-Directed scales can be used alone when a quick estimate of self-actualization is needed.[15] Later studies with varying samples confirmed this conclusion.[16]

Time Competence "reflects the degree to which the individual lives in the present rather than the past or future; while Inner-Directed "persons are guided primarily by internalized principles and motivations."[17]

The Self-Regard (S_r) subscale "measures affirmation of self because of worth or strength. A low score indicates low self-worth."[18] The Self-Regard scale is composed of sixteen items scattered throughout the 150-question test.

The twelve POI scales can be plotted on a profile sheet that has standardized test scores to a "normal" population. When raw scores are plotted, they are automatically converted into standard scores by their placement. The self-actualized individual is expected to score above the norm mean on most scales but not by much more than one standard score range. The non-self-actualized person will score below the mean on most scales, usually not falling much below the standard score range.

The POI is in booklet form with directions on the front page. The answer sheet is a one-page form with several background questions(age, sex, and so forth) and 150 spaces with lines to be blackened in for either a or b. Both booklets and answer sheet are published and distributed by Educational and Industrial Testing Service (EdITS).

The POI was chosen primarily because the way in which it defines Self-Regard is close to the meaning of self-esteem as described by myself and others who have conducted research on female alcoholics. Many of the questions mesh well with a common sense understanding of what it means to have high or low self-esteem. The subjective interpretation of the researcher or extensive coding are not relied on as in other measurement techniques.[19] All the individual questions that make up the Self-Regard score make sense.

A great deal of material has been collected to support the validity of the concepts defined in the POI. These studies are dealt with at length in other sources.[20] However, it is important to note that what is so impressive about the testing done using the POI is not the result in one area of research, but in the number and variety of findings which support its validity. The POI does correlate reasonably well with other measures of mental health and negatively with measures of mental illness. It has been used effectively to separate nominated samples. The POI is plausible because the results empirically support many aspects of Maslow's theory from which it was derived. It also has practical applications, as evidenced by how well it has correlated with task-specific evaluations, "known groups," and facilitated changes in an alcoholic sample.[21] The POI is supported by an impressive amount of research, which builds confidence in the measure. Although individual studies may be criticized, the overall impact of the entire body of research is very persuasive.

The POI also rates reasonably high on reliability[22] despite a disclaimer stating that a concern with reliability may be inappropriate when discussing measures to tap "concepts of dynamic traits of personality."[23] Different investigators using different subjects have reported a fairly consistent profile for several groups.[24]

It is also important that various studies have found there are few significant sex differences in scoring on the POI. Females score slightly higher than males, which would make a finding that females scored lower even more persuasive. None of the studies reported in summaries of work on the POI[25] show significant gender differences on the S_r subscale. For the present research, it was crucial to have minimal sex differences to begin with in order to draw conclusions about the different effects of being labeled alcoholic on males and females.

It was also necessary to have a test that effectively separated the alcoholic from the nonalcoholic sample. Previous research has shown that the POI is sensitive enough to distinguish between labeled alcoholics and the normal samples on Self-Regard and most other subscales. In three reports on a study of seventy alcoholics in an alcoholism treatment program,[26] alcoholics were shown to score significantly lower than a clinically nominated, normal adult sample, as measured by Shostrom and used in determining standard scores for the POI.[27] Other findings on a sample of alcoholics from Wilmar State Hospital produce a similar profile.[28] "The typical alcoholic POI profile is low, generally about one standard deviation below the 'normal' adult mean."[29]

Finally, there was the humanistic attraction of the POI. Although I did not use the self-actualization model in my theory development, the attempt by Maslow and his disciples to avoid a pathological model was appealing. The POI researchers claim to pay more attention to positive growth rather than illness: "A major thrust of the POI research in alcoholic treatment involves the orientation toward positive concepts of personal growth rather than employment of a pathological frame of reference."[30] This approach is very much in tune with labeling theory. It is not that deviants are so different from other people (deviation is a continuum) but that they have been labeled.

Background Questionnaires

Questionnaires were developed to gather as much information as was reasonably possible to help control for factors other than gender that might affect the POI. They were composed of three sections, the first two of which were the same for alcoholics and heavy drinkers. The third section differed.

Section 1 asked if the respondent thought other people criticized men or women more for drinking and if the respondent considered it worse for one sex or the other to drink. The purpose of these questions was to see if people really are more critical of female alcoholics, as the literature insists.

Section 2 asked sixteen general background questions, such as size of the town the respondent came from, parents' religion, age at first drink, drinking habits of parents and siblings, and the like. These variables have been related to drinking problems in various studies.

Section 3, for heavy drinkers, was used to obtain information about the current family situation (occupation, income, and children),[31] drinking patterns (how much, how frequently, and with whom), other's responses to the respondent's drinking (criticism by friends, relatives, and spouse). This section was composed of fifteen questions.

The third section of the questionnaire for alcoholics tried to obtain much the same information by assessing the family situation (occupation, income, and children). It also indicated some drinking patterns (effects of alcohol and whether the respondent drinks socially or alone); respondents were also asked how many A.A. meetings they had attended. The remainder of the questions were similar to those for the heavy drinkers—how others responded to their drinking (friends, relatives, and spouse). There were thirteen questions in Section 3 for alcoholics. Whenever possible, these were exactly the same as questions in the third section for heavy drinkers so these two sets could be compared.

Selected Findings from the Background Questionnaires

Criticism of Female Alcoholics

With the progress made in the 1970s toward equality of the sexes, it seemed reasonable to assume that respondents in my research, both male and female, would not want to admit they considered it worse for a woman to be a heavy drinker or an alcoholic. That would be tantamount to saying they were prejudiced. Therefore, two separate questions were asked—what they believed others thought of women drinking heavily and what they themselves thought of females being alcoholics. The more extreme case of women being alcoholics was asked of respondents so that if they denied thinking it were worse, it would be an even more emphatic denial of prejudice.

The hypothesis that males and females, alcoholic and nonalcoholic, will say that *others* criticize women more is strongly supported by the data (table A.1).

Table A.1
How critical those in the sample say *others* are of women
drinking heavily

Who is Criticized More?

	Men	Women	No Difference	
Female alcoholics	4 5.1%	64 81.0%	11 13.9%	79
Male alcoholics	13 18.6%	42 60.0%	15 21.4%	70
Female heavy drinkers	5 8.1%	48 77.4%	9 14.5%	62
Male heavy drinkers	5 8.6%	40 69.0%	13 22.4%	58
	27	194	48	269

As predicted, males and females, both labeled alcoholic and nonlabeled heavy drinkers, said that *others* criticize women more than men for drinking heavily; 72.1 percent of the entire sample responding ($N=269$) believed that others criticize women more for drinking heavily. A higher percentage of women (79.4 percent) believed this than men (64.1 percent). Only a small percentage of the total sample (10 percent) believed men were more heavily criticized. Those who believe most strongly that others criticize women more are female alcoholics (81.0 percent), indicating they do feel others are more critical of them. The largest percentage of people who believe others criticize men more are male alcoholics (18.6 percent). Overall, this is still a very small percentage of how male alcoholics think others feel. Sixty percent think women are criticized more and 21.4 percent think there is no difference.

When asked whether they considered it worse for man or a woman to be an alcoholic, it was predicted that few people would admit to such a prejudice, the data strongly support this hypothesis (table A.2).

There was an impressive shift in the predicted direction especially among the heavy drinkers. Only 34.2 percent of the female alcoholics, 38.8 percent of the male alcoholics, 9.7 percent of the female heavy drinkers, and 16.7 percent of the male heavy drinkers admitted to thinking it was worse for a woman than a man to be an alcoholic. The largest percentage of the sample (63.3 percent of the female alcoholics, 52.9 percent of the male alcoholics, 90.3 percent of the female heavy drinkers, and 78.3 percent of the male heavy drinkers) feel there is no difference.

It is possible that most of the respondents in this research were not prejudiced against female alcoholics and were honestly giving their opinions.

Table A.2
Whether they consider it worse for a man or a woman to be an alcoholic

For Whom Is It Worse to Be an Alcoholic?

	Men	Women	No Difference	
Female alcoholics	2 2.5%	27 34.2%	50 63.3%	79
Male alcoholics	6 8.6%	27 38.8%	37 52.9%	70
Female heavy drinkers	0 0%	6 9.7%	56 90.3%	62
Male heavy drinkers	3 5.0%	10 16.7%	47 78.3%	60
	11 4.1%	70 25.8%	190 70.1%	271

However, a switch of this magnitude in all of the sample's categories does not make this explanation plausible. This change occurred despite some different interpretations of the question, which made it even more likely that some people would say they thought it was worse for a woman to be an alcoholic. By worse some of those sampled meant it was harder on a woman because she was open to abuse or she could hide it better and therefore would suffer longer before being discovered. However, this was only a small part of the entire sample ($N=3$).

Solitary versus Social Drinking

Solitary drinking is considered an indicator of alcoholism among male and female heavy drinkers. I expected to find that those labeled alcoholics were much more likely than the heavy drinkers in my sample to drink alone. The data supported this prediction (table A.3).

Table A.3
Solitary versus social drinking of alcoholics and heavy drinkers

How You Usually Drink

	Alone	Socially	
Alcoholics	70 56%	55 44%	125
Heavy drinkers	5 4.3%	111 95.7%	116
	75	166	241

Almost all of the heavy drinkers usually drink socially, while over half of the alcoholics usually drink alone.

When the table is further broken down into subsamples, it is interesting to see that female alcoholics are even more likely than male alcoholics to drink alone (table A.4).

Table A.4
Solitary versus social drinking of alcoholics and heavy drinkers,
broken down by gender

How You Usually Drink

	Alone	Socially	
Female alcoholics	40 60.6%	26 39.4%	66
Male alcoholics	30 50.8%	29 49.2%	59
Female heavy drinkers	4 6.8%	55 93.2%	59
Male heavy drinkers	1 1.8%	56 98.2%	57
	75	166	241

Female alcoholics are 10 percent more likely to drink alone than male alcoholics. The numbers are too small to generalize about heavy drinkers, but females do slightly outnumber males who drink alone.

Reaction of Significant Others to Alcoholic's Drinking Problems

Three short-answer questions were included in the background question-naire for alcoholics to test the greater stigmatization hypothesis. Respondents were asked how critical their spouse, relatives, and friends were of their drinking problems. This was believed to give some indication of how much censure they had experienced at the hands of significant others. Given the other available information, female alcoholics were expected to say that their spouse, relatives, and friends were more critical of them than of male alcoholics.

However data did not support these three hypotheses. There is no indication the women's husbands are less sympathetic than are the wives of male alcoholics (table A.5).

The one interesting finding from those who chose to elaborate on their answer is the number of female alcoholics who had heavy drinking or alco-

Table A.5
Reaction of spouses to drinking problem of male and female alcoholics

Alcoholics	Sympathetic	Not Sympathetic	
Female	26 45.6%	31 54.4%	57
Male	17 40.5%	25 59.5%	42
	43	56	99

holic husbands. Only one male mentioned that his wife was also an alcoholic. Twelve women said their husbands were alcoholics, which, they suggested, was one reason they were sympathetic. Most of the sample did not explain their answer, so it was not possible to determine it female alcoholics in this sample were more likely than male alcoholics to have a spouse with a drinking problem or simply more likely to mention it.

Criticism by relatives also showed little differentiation by gender (table A.6).

Table A.6
Criticism of male and female alcoholics by relatives

Alcoholics	Very Critical	Mildly Critical	Not Critical	Very Helpful	
Female	23 31.1%	15 20.3%	10 13.5%	26 35.1%	74
Male	20 32.3%	14 22.5%	14 22.6%	14 22.6%	62
	43	29	24	40	136

A lack of gender differences was also evident in alcoholics' opinion of how critical their friends were of their drinking problem (table A.7).

Table A.7
Criticism of male and female alcoholics by friends

Alcoholics	Very Critical	Mildly Critical	Not Critical	Very Helpful	
Female	12 17.7%	15 21.4%	17 24.3%	26 37.1%	70
Male	12 18.8%	16 25.0%	18 28.1%	18 28.1%	64
	24	31	35	44	134

It is interesting to note that among those who elaborated on their answer to this question, male and female respondents alike tended to indicate that their friends were not critical because "they drank heavily also." Thus friends tended to minimize the seriousness of the alcoholic's drinking problem or to . be unaware of it.

Marital Status

As noted in the text, previous research has shown that alcoholics have a higher divorce rate than the general population. Data gathered in my research indicated this disparity also exists among labeled alcoholics and heavy drinkers (table A.8).

Table A.8
Marital status of alcoholics and heavy drinkers

	Married	Separated or Divorced	
Alcoholics	60 63.8%	34 36.2%	94
Heavy drinkers	86 94.5%	5 5.5%	91
	146	39	185

Female alcoholics were expected to have a higher divorce rate than male alcoholics. The data did show a slightly higher rate for female alcoholics, but the difference (3.9 percent) was not large enough to indicate support for the prediction (table A.9).

Table A.9
Marital status of male and female alcoholics

Alcoholics	Married	Separated or Divorced	
Female	31 62.0%	19 38.0%	50
Male	29 65.9%	15 34.1%	44
	60	34	94

Selected Findings from the Personal Orientation Inventory

Alcoholic and the Heavy-Drinker Profiles

For a better understanding of how male and female alcoholics and non-labeled heavy drinkers compare, it is helpful to look at how they ranked on their overall self-actualization on the POI profile sheet.

The profile for female heavy drinkers is close to that for a normal population. The profile for the male heavy drinker is lower than expected on some variables and somewhat erratic. As predicted, male and female alcoholics in this sample have a profile below the normal population but not so consistently low as that found by other researchers.[32] As can be seen in figure A.1, Self-Regard was one of the scales that effectively differentiated alcoholics from the heavy drinkers.

Self-Regard Scores

All of the data in the following discussion were first analyzed in their longest form. Recoding was conducted if and when it did not obscure relationships existing in the data and if it were compatible with the theoretical model.

For most hypotheses, POI scores were eventually recoded into high and low categories with no significant changes in the interpretation of the findings. Theoretically, the high and low categories made the most sense. The POI is comprised of standard scores. The standard Self-Regard score for a normal population is approximately twelve. Technically, those above twelve are self-actualizing, and those below are non-self-actualizing. In looking at the POI profile sheet in figure A.1, it can be seen that the POI claims to be a very sensitive measure: A 2.5 difference in Self-Regard scores is the difference between a non-self-actualized and a normal person or a normal and a self-actualized person. Relatively small differences in S_r scores, therefore, may be important. A difference as small as one point could be considered suggestive.

Self-Regard for the present research was recoded, with one through twelve constituting low and thirteen through the highest score constituting high, to match the standard scores. In comparisons, there was seldom a reason to divide the scores, into high, medium, and low (with twelve as medium), since there were exactly twenty-one alcoholics and twenty-one heavy drinkers who scored twelve. When this comparison made a difference, the medium categories were kept and analyzed. When comparing the means difference, the POI scores were not recoded.

There was no emphasis on tests of significance or association measures, since assumption of independent random sampling could not be met. The

Figure A.1.
POI Profiles for Male and Female Heavy Drinkers and Alcoholics
(Reproduced by permission of Educational & Industrial Testing Service, San Diego,
California, copyright © 1963, 1965)

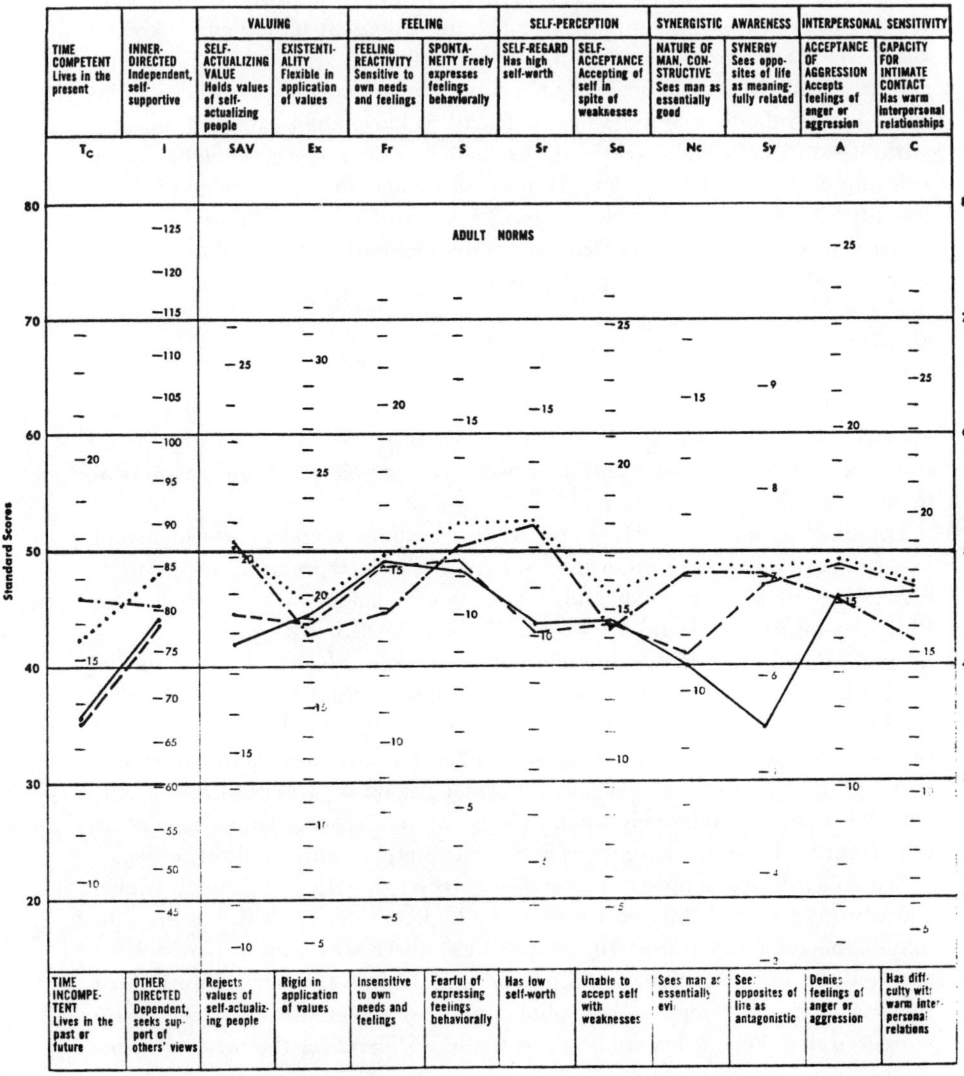

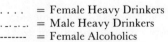

. . . .   = Female Heavy Drinkers
. _ . _ _.   = Male Heavy Drinkers
------   = Female Alcoholics
————   = Male Alcoholics

findings were used as indicating possible relationships and suggesting areas that needed further research.

I predicted the alcoholics in my sample would have lower self-esteem than the sample of nonlabeled alcoholics (table A.10).

Table A.10
Self-Regard scores of alcoholics and heavy drinkers

	Low	High	
Alcoholics	111 73.0%	41 27.0%	152
Heavy drinkers	49 40.2%	73 59.8%	122
	160	114	274

Seventy-three percent of the alcoholics had low Self-Regard scores as compared to only 40 percent of the heavy drinkers. Despite the large amount of drinking done by the comparison sample, it is clearly not true that people who need to drink have a lower self-esteem. The findings support the conclusion that the effects of labeling lower the individual's self-esteem.

Small or no differences were expected between male and female heavy drinkers on the Self-Regard measure. The data supported this hypothesis (table A.11).

Table A.11
Self-Regard scores of male and female heavy drinkers, divided into
high and low

Heavy drinkers	Low	High	
Female	27 43.5%	35 56.5%	62
Male	22 36.7%	38 63.3%	60
	49	73	122

As table A.11 indicates, S_r differences were very slight between male and female heavy drinkers. If twelve were used as a medium instead of a low score, differences would be even slighter. The same number (fourteen) and almost the same percentage of men (23.3 percent) and women (22.6 percent) have low Self-Regard. Women are a little more likely to have a medium

Self-Regard score, and men are more likely than women (by a slight margin) to have a high Self-Regard.

Female alcoholics were expected to have a lower Self-Regard score than male alcoholics. An initial look at the data did not support this prediction (table A.12).

Table A.12
Self-Regard scores of male and female alcoholics, divided
into high and low

Alcoholics	Self-Regard Scores		
	Low	High	
Female	58 73.4%	21 26.6%	79
Male	53 72.6%	20 27.4%	73
	111	41	152

Table A.12 indicates that both male and female alcoholics tended to have low Self-Regard scores but there was very little difference between them. If divided into three categories, the relationship does not change much, although it does show a very slight tendency for women to have a low Self-Regard score (see table A.13).

Table A.13
Self-Regard scores of male and female alcoholics, divided
into high, medium, and low

Alcoholics	Self-Regard Scores			
	Low	Medium	High	
Female	49 62.0%	9 11.4%	21 26.6%	79
Male	41 56.2%	12 16.4%	20 27.4%	73
	90	21	41	152

It seemed likely that one of the reasons we did not find a great difference between male and female alcoholics on Self-Regard scores is that despite an attempt to sample men and women who were not long-time A.A. members, some of the respondents had attended quite a number of A.A. meetings. Research has shown that Alcoholics Anonymous is particularly effective in raising the self-esteem of those who attend. In a study of fifty alcoholics, twenty-four of whom were practicing alcoholics and twenty-six of whom were A.A. members, one researcher found all the POI scores, with the exception of the Nature of Man, were significantly higher for A.A. members.[33] The A.A. members were in the self-actualized range for most of the scales.

Using this logic, the number of A.A. meetings was controlled to see if this affected the Self-Regard score of the alcoholics in my sample. The sample was divided into two groups, those who had attended eight or fewer A.A. meetings and those who had attended nine or more meetings (table A.14).

Table A.14
Self-Regard scores for male and female alcoholics who have attended eight or fewer A.A. meetings and those who have attended nine or more

A.A. Meetings Attended

	8 or Less				9 or More		
	Self-Regard Scores				Self-Regard Scores		
	Low	High			Low	High	
Female	28	5	33	Female	30	16	46
	84.8%	15.2%			65.2%	34.8%	
Male	35	9	44	Male	18	11	29
	79.8%	20.5%			62.1%	37.9%	
	63	14	77		48	27	75

As expected, Self-Regard scores for alcoholics are more likely to be higher if the person has attended more A.A. meetings. There are clear differences in Self-Regard scores for those who have attended eight or fewer meetings (18 percent had high Self-Regard scores) and those who have attended more (36 percent had high Self-Regard scores). Also as expected, the difference in Self-Regard scores between male and female alcoholics is slightly greater among those who had attended eight or fewer meetings. There were too few people who had attended less than eight meetings to lower the cutoff point. We would expect greater differences by gender if we had tested people who had attended a few A.A. meetings or none at all.

The differences in mean scores, although still slight, show up more clearly for both males and females who have attended up to eight meetings or those who have attended more (table A.15).

Table A.15
Mean scores for alcoholics by number of A.A. meetings attended

A.A. Meetings Attended

Alcoholics	8 or Less	9 or More	
Female	$X = 9.423$ $N = 33$	$X = 10.444$ $N = 45$	78
Male	$X = 10.093$ $N = 43$	$X = 10.370$ $N = 27$	70
	76	72	148

A person who has attended more than nine A.A. meetings, is more likely to have a higher Self-Regard score. Alcoholics Anonymous seems to have an especially beneficial effect on the self-esteem of female alcoholics, with a 1.02 difference in means between the two groups. Table A.15 indicates that females who have attended eight or fewer meetings have lower self-esteem than males, while females who have attended more than nine meetings have higher Self-Regard.

Overall, male and female differences in Self-Regard as measured by the POI were disappointing. However, though not impressively large, these were enough to suggest that further research, controlling for A.A. meetings attended, might show greater self-esteem differences for male and female alcoholics.

Six additional hypotheses related to insular positions were tested. Two positions, those of race and housewife, were dropped from the analysis due to the small number of cases in the sample: There were only twenty-one black alcoholics and eight black heavy drinkers, and only eight women in the entire sample listed themselves as housewives. These samples would be too small to permit drawing conclusions.

The important differences for the remaining hypotheses were between heavy drinkers and alcoholics in each subcategory of the variables: education, occupational prestige, income, and marital status. It was predicted that those labeled alcoholic who had more education, and therefore were in a more status insular position, would have proportionately lower Self-Regard scores. Table A.16 suggests this may be true.

Table A.16
Self-Regard scores for alcoholics and heavy drinkers, controlling
for education

	Education [a]		
	1-12	Higher than 12	
Alcoholics	$X = 10.250$ $N = 100$	$X = 9.684$ $N = 38$	138
Heavy drinkers	$X = 12.388$ $N = 49$	$X = 13.055$ $N = 72$	121
	149	110	259

[a] Education, measured by number of years of school attended.

The difference in means for table A.16 are

Low Education		High Education	
Heavy drinkers	(12.88)	Heavy drinkers	(13.055)
− Alcoholics	(10.250)	− Alcoholics	(9.684)
	2.138		3.371

There tends to be an increase in Self-Regard scores among heavy drinkers as their education increases, while alcoholics tend show a decrease in Self-Regard scores as education increases.

The same kind of relationship was expected to exist for occupational prestige: Among alcoholics, those with high occupational prestige would have lower Self-Regard scores than those with low occupational prestige. Table A. 17 shows that data does not support this contention.

Table A.17
Self-Regard scores for alcoholics and heavy drinkers, controlling
for occupational prestige

	Occupational Prestige [a]		
	Low	High	
Alcoholics	$X = 9.778$ $N = 36$	$X = 10.667$ $N = 12$	48
Heavy drinkers	$X = 12.378$ $N = 53$	$X = 13.000$ $N = 35$	88
	89	47	136

[a] Low, 12–49 on the occupational prestige ranking of the 1972 NORC codebook; high, 50-76 on the occupational prestige ranking of the 1972 NORC codebook. [34]

Both alcoholics and heavy drinkers who had a job with low occupational prestige had slightly lower Self-Regard scores when compared to those whose job had high occupational prestige. There tends to be an increase in Self-Regard scores as occupational prestige increases, and this is true among alcoholics and heavy drinkers.

Low Occupational Prestige		High Occupational Prestige	
Heavy drinkers	(12.378)	Heavy drinkers	(13.000)
− Alcoholics	(9.778)	− Alcoholics	(10.667)
	2.600		2.333

Although these findings do not support the predictions made on the basis of status insularity, it should be noted that only forty-eight alcoholics listed themselves as currently having a job that could be ranked for occupational prestige. Apparently, many more alcoholics are unemployed than heavy drinkers. It seems logical to assume that those who have lost high-prestige jobs due to drinking would be likely to have a lower Self-Regard score than those who are currently employed.

One measure of socioeconomic status, education, showed the relationship we expected to find, and another one, occupation, showed no relationship. Looking at the third measure of socioeconomic status, income, allows us to see if it is reasonable to speculate that a relationship exists despite contradictory findings on occupational prestige.

It was predicted that those alcoholics with a relatively high income would have proportionately lower Self-Regard scores than those with relatively lower income. Table A.18 suggests support for this hypothesis across a three-category breakdown.

Table A.18
Self-Regard scores for alcoholics and heavy drinkers, controlling for income

	Income [a]			
	Low	Medium	High	
Alcoholics	$X=10.351$ $N=74$	$X=10.125$ $N=41$	$X=9.750$ $N=12$	127
Heavy drinkers	$X=12.221$ $N=28$	$X=12.928$ $N=84$	$X=13.222$ $N=9$	121
	102	125	21	248

[a] Low income, $0–$10,000; medium income, $10,001–$25,000; high income, $25,001 and up.

The difference in means showed a consistent increase as the amount of income rose.

Low Income			Medium Income	
Heavy drinkers	(12.221)		Heavy drinkers	(12.928)
– Alcoholics	(10.351)		– Alcoholics	(10.125)
	1.870			2.803

High Income	
Heavy drinkers	(13.222)
– Alcoholics	(9.750)
	3.472

Not only are there proportionately lower Self-Regard scores for alcoholics with a high income, there are actual declines in Self-Regard scores as income increases. For heavy drinkers, the relationship is reversed. It appears being labeled has the greatest impact on those with the highest education.

Those who were married were also seen as being in an insulated status. It was predicted that those married and labeled alcoholic would have proportionately lower Self-Regard scores than those who were single (see table A. 19).

Table A.19
Self-Regard scores for alcoholics and heavy drinkers, controlling
for marital status

	Marital Status		
	Married	Single	
Alcoholics	$X=10.339$ $N=59$	$X=10.155$ $N=71$	130
Heavy drinkers	$X=12.896$ $N=86$	$X=12.514$ $N=35$	121
	145	106	251

The findings are in the predicted direction as shown by the difference in means; however, the differences are very slight (0.198).

Married			Single	
Heavy drinkers	(12.896)		Heavy drinkers	(12.514)
– Alcoholics	(10.339)		– Alcoholics	(10.155)
	2.557			2.359

If gender is controlled, the differences are slightly more apparent (see table A.20).

Tabel A.20
Self-Regard scores for male and female alcoholics and heavy
drinkers, controlling for marital status

	Marital Status		
	Married	Single	
Female alcoholics	$X=10.161$ $N=31$	$X=10.176$ $N=34$	65
Male alcoholics	$X=10.536$ $N=28$	$X=10.135$ $N=37$	65
Female heavy drinkers	$X=12.725$ $N=40$	$X=12.864$ $N=22$	62
Male heavy drinkers	$X=13.043$ $N=46$	$X=11.923$ $N=13$	59
	145	106	251

The differences in means for males only, are:

Married		Single	
Heavy drinkers	(13.043)	Heavy drinkers	(11.923)
− Alcoholics	(10.536)	− Alcoholics	(10.135)
	2.507		1.788

It appears that as Durkheim predicted, marriage benefits the man more than the woman.[35] Women tend to have a higher Self-Regard score if they are single whether they are labeled alcoholic or not. Male heavy drinkers, on the other hand, show a marked increase in Self-Regard scores if they are married. Labeled alcoholics show a proportionately lower Self-Regard score if they are married (2.507) than if they are single (1.788).

These findings for the socioeconomic variables are in line with research cited earlier that found female alcoholics with less than a high school education, lower occupation and lower social status more likely to be abstinent.[36] We would expect a person with lower self-esteem to have less success in the rehabilitation process and therefore be less likely to remain abstinent. These relationships did not hold true for males in previous research, however, the relationships held for both males and females in the present study. Socioeconomic factors appear to be better predictors of status insularity and warrant further research.

Professionals Who Work with Alcoholics

Although the main effort of my research was directed at the sample of labeled alcoholics and nonlabeled heavy drinkers, additional research was conducted by means of a questionnaire for those who worked with alcoholics in clinics and halfway houses.

This additional research was conducted with the belief that data from disparate sources would supplement the findings from the POI to give a more complete picture of female alcoholics. Details of this study are reported elsewhere,[37] but a description of the research and a few of the results are presented here, since findings from this investigation have been interspersed throughout the study.

The opinions of those who work with alcoholics in the clinics and halfway houses from which the sample was drawn were of particular interest, inasmuch as they had a chance to observe the labeled alcoholics whom I sampled. Since I dealt with many of the clinics by mail and telephone, a questionnaire was developed. Its substance was based on findings suggested in the literature review, lengthy conversations with a few directors, and the framework of the theoretical model. To make certain that the questions were properly understood, the test was first administered verbally to one director.

The questions were both closed-and open-ended. If asked for a *yes* or *no*, respondents were also given the opportunity to explain their answer.

Concepts referring to alcoholics and people's reaction to them, such as self-esteem, difficult, and critical were not explained but treated as part of a common sense vocabulary. After all questions calling for some kind of judgment on the part of the practitioner, a what or why question was asked that gave respondents an opportunity to explain their answers further. Responses on the open-ended part of the questionnaire indicated there was little or no misinterpretation.

At least one response from a professional affiliated with each group was received from all except two of the locations in which sampling was conducted. A total of eleven questionnaires were filled out, with another person responding to several of the questions in person, making a total of twelve on some questions.

The questions were designed to provide those who work with alcoholics a chance to generalize on the basis of their experience about differences among alcoholics they would attribute to gender. The hypotheses based on these questions were not formal in the sense that they did not present independent and dependent variables. Respondents were simply asked to answer questions based on their own expert observations. It provided a way of seeing if practitioners working with the sampled alcoholics generally agreed with the opinions of those experts reported in the literature and what we learned about male and female alcoholics from the POI and background questionnaires.

Each practitioner was sent or given a two-page description of the research, which included a simplified statement of the problem. Included in this summary was a sentence that read, "Those who work with alcoholics have argued that females are more heavily stigmatized for their heavy drinking than men." It is possible that respondents would attempt to assist my research by giving answers I anticipated or wanted in order to create a favorable impression, but it seems doubtful. The respondents were appealed to as experts, and they obviously regarded themselves as professionals and their opinions as valid.

Because the sample is so small and therefore clearly not generalizable, the results are not presented in tables.

Selected Findings from Professionals Who Work with Alcoholics

Those who work with alcoholics believed, by a ratio of two to one (eight yes, four no), that female alcoholics have lower self-esteem than male alcoholics. One practiconer who responded negatively said that even though women do not have lower self-esteem, they think they do. Believing one has low self-esteem could be expected to have some effect on behavior.

Professionals who said women have lower self-esteem attribute this to women's historical and traditional roles, which make it is less socially acceptable for them to be alcoholics (especially if they have children) and / or because there is a double standard for sexual conduct.

The professionals, with a greater than two to one ratio (eight said they were, three said they were not), said they felt women were more subject to criticism by other patients than males. The reasons were diverse. One expert indicated it was female behavior patterns, such as dependency that infuriated men. However, most experts claimed it was due to the double standard for men and women. Several of them commented that men were not only less inclined to accept the female alcoholic, but other women were too. One expert did comment that men seemed to like having female alcoholics around. This was the only positive expression about the reactions of male alcoholics to their female counterparts.

Four of the professionals who work with alcoholics said women are more difficult to treat than men; six that they are no more difficult to treat; and one that they are easier. Those who responded that women were more difficult to treat indicated this was so because women have more problems since they are looked down on by society. Women also tend to be further along in their alcoholism since their addiction is hidden. Not a single response indicated the traditional view that women were more difficult to work with or had more initial psychological problems than men. One response stated that women needed more continuing support than men and another that they were protected from the consequences of their drinking. These were the only two comments which came close to insinuating that women are really more difficult to treat than men in rehabilitative settings.

As expected, those who work with alcoholics generally said there is no differnce in the success rate of male and female alcoholics. Out of four who said there is a difference, three indicate that women are more likely to be successful. The myth of the maladjusted female alcoholic with little chance for successful recovery was not substantiated by the rehabilitative settings in my sample.

Conclusion

Status insularity was defined as a property of a social position that decreases the likelihood that an occupant of that status will be labeled deviant. It was hypothesized that once occupants of status insular positions were labeled, they would be more severely stigmatized and as a result subject to greater secondary deviation. The findings presented in the appendix a do provide some support for these hypotheses.

Responses by professionals who work with alcoholics to the questionnaire supported the main insularity hypotheses. In observing the men and women whom they counseled, these experts perceived other patients to be more critical of female alcoholics and female alcoholics to have a lower self-esteem.

Responses by alcoholics and heavy drinkers on the POI were generally supportive. Although the major portion of the differences in means for insulated versus noninsulated positions was explained by whether the person was a labeled alcoholic or a heavy drinker, differences within status insular positions suggested a process similar to the one described.

The predicted differences between Self-Regard scores for male and female alcoholics were very slightly in the predicted direction. When the number of A.A. meetings was controlled, however, a greater difference between males and females was found if they had attended eight or fewer meetings. If they had attended more than eight meetings, the Self-Regard scores of all alcoholics were higher; this was even more so for females by a small margin. The differences in means between those who had attended eight or fewer or nine or more A.A. meetings was greater for females than for males. Although still of too small a magnitude to permit drawing conclusions, it would be reasonable to hypothesize that females may enter Alcoholics Anonymous with lower self-esteem and Alcoholics Anonymous is effective in raising it.[38] To test this hypothesis, sampling would have to include men and women who had not attended A.A. meetings.

Three separate measures of socioeconomic status were considered— education, occupational prestige, and income. The differences in means for education clearly indicates that among men and women labeled alcoholic, those with more education (higher status insularity) are more likely to have lower Self-Regard scores. Among heavy drinkers, as was expected, those with more education had a higher Self-Regard score. The differences in means between heavy drinkers with more education and labeled alcoholics with more education was over three points. A difference of this magnitude on the POI subscale of Self-Regard is greater than the difference between a non-self-actualized person and a normal person or a normal person and a self-actualized person. These findings support the contention that those with more education (high insularity) experience more damage to their Self-Regard than those with less education (low insularity).

Occupational prestige did not show the expected relationship. There was more of a difference between labeled alcoholics with low-prestige jobs and heavy drinkers with low-prestige jobs than between those with high-prestige jobs. As noted, however, there were only forty-eight labeled alcoholics who listed an occupation. It could be hypothesized that those without current employment would have lower self-esteem than those who still are employed.

The third measure of socioeconomic status, income, also showed the predicted relationship. When broken down into three categories (high, medium, and low), the differences in means was in the predicted direction and grew larger as the status increased. There was only a moderate difference between heavy drinking and alcoholic samples for those who had a low income. Those who had a medium income showed a greater difference in means. The high-income samples evidenced a large difference (more than a one-and-a-half standard score difference). Although the sample is small, this is a considerable difference on the Self-Regard subscale. It would appear that those with a high income are more strongly affected by the labeling process.

Data on marital status showed slight differences in the predicted direction. There was a larger difference between alcoholics who were married and heavy drinkers who were married than for the single group. When further broken down by sex, males showed a greater difference in means than females. Perhaps this suggests support for early sociological work which argued that marriage was more important for "protecting" males than females.[39] Measurement of two additional insular positions (housewives and blacks) were dropped because of the very small sample.

Overall, data from the three types of research used in this analysis are supportive, or at least suggestive, of the insularity hypotheses. It is especially interesting to note that two of the measures of socioeconomic status (education and income) show the largest differences in means. As speculated in chapter 1, a more consistent status, such as socioeconomic status, is a better predictor of status insularity. The data confirm this supposition and indicate that further research on status insularity should focus more on socioeconomic variables.

Notes

Chapter 1. The Insulated Status of the Female Alcoholic

1. This is an estimate by Dr. Jean Kirkpatrick, the founder of Women for Sobriety, in a 1976 publication ("Women for Sobriety," [Quakertown, Penn.: Women for Sobriety, Inc., 1976]). During the Senate Subcommittee Hearing on Alcohol Abuse among Women in September 1976, LeClair Bissel, M.D., claimed the rate was at least three or four million (U.S. Senate Subcommittee on Alcoholism and Narcotics of the Committee on Labor and Public Welfare, 94th Congress, *Alcohol Abuse among Women: Special Problems and Unmet Needs*, [Washington, D.C.: U.S. Government Printing Office, 1976]). A conservative estimate according to Sister Mary Leo Kammier in her work *Alcoholism the Common Denominator: More Evidence on the Male Female Question* (Center City, Minn.: Hazelden, 1977) is at least 1.8 million. Regardless of the figure accepted, there appears to be a large number of female alcoholics.

2. Marc A. Schuckit, "The Alcoholic Woman: A Literature Review," *Psychiatry in Medicine* 3, no. 1(1972):37–43. There were a number of important articles (see, for example, Marilyn W. Johnson, "Physicians Views on Alcoholism: With Special Reference to Alcoholism in Women," *Nebraska State Medical Journal* 50, no. 7(1965):343–47; Barry A. Kinsey, "Psychological Factors in Alcoholic Women from a State Hospital Sample," *American Journal of Psychiatry* 124(1968):1463–66; and several articles by Joan Curlee (only one was cited), of which Dr. Schuckit was apparently unaware, but his main point does not suffer from this. He was accurate when he stated that "the literature on alcoholism deals primarily with male populations yielding data of questionable significance when applied to the female alcoholic" (Schuckit, "The Alcoholic Woman," 37.)

3. *Quarterly Journal of Studies on Alcohol (QJSA)*, the major alcohol journal, began publication in 1942. In the year Dr. Schuckit wrote this article (1972), the March issue of *QJSA* listed 334 articles in the documentation section. Of these, seventy-six definitely referred to only males and thirty-nine mentioned women. Frequently, women comprised only a small portion of the sample (one or two). It was not possible to classify many of the articles as pertaining to only males, since not enough was specified to determine if they did exclude women. Only four articles dealt specifically with women: One was on fetal alcohol syndrome, and the other three related to experimental work using alcohol on women who were undergoing surgery. The documentation section is published four times a year. If over the forty-seven years since its inception, the *QJSA* listed each time only one hundred articles on male alcoholics (an underestimate), that would total 16,800 articles about male alcoholics listed in this one source.

4. See, for example, Linda J. Beckman, "Women Alcoholics: A Review of Social and Psychological Studies," *Journal of Studies on Alcohol* 36, no.7 (1975):797–824; Vera L.Lindbeck, "The Woman Alcoholic: A Review of the Literature," *International Journal of Addictions* 7, no.3 (1972):567–80.

5. Susan J. Christenson and Alice Q. Swanson, "Women and Drug Use: An An-

notated Bibliography," *Journal of Psychedelic Drugs*, 16, no.4 (1974):371–414.

6. H. Paul Chalfant and Brent S. Roper, *Social and Behavioral Aspects of Female Alcoholism: An Annotated Bibliography*, (Westport, Conn.: Greenwood Press, 1980).

7. See, for example, Patricia Kent, *An American Woman and Alcohol* (New York: Holt, Rinehart, and Winston, 1967); Bonnie-Jean Kimball, *The Alcoholic Woman's Mad, Mad World of Denial and Mind Games* (Center City, Minn.: Hazelden, 1978); Jean Kirkpatrick, *Turnabout: Help for a New Life* (Garden City, N.Y.: Doubleday, 1978); or Evelyn Leite, *To Be Somebody*, (Center City, Minn.: Hazelden, 1979).

8. Women for Sobriety has its headquarters at 344 Franklin St., Quakertown, Penn. 18951.

9. See, for example, Giorgio Lolli, *Social Drinking: The Effects of Alcohol*, (New York: Collier, 1961); Mark Keller and Vera Efron, "The Prevalence of Alcoholism," *Quarterly Journal of Studies on Alcohol* 16, no.4 (1955):623, 631–33; and Mark Keller and Vera Efron, " The Rate of Alcoholism in the U.S.A. 1954–1956," *QJSA* 19, no.2 (1955):317, 319; and Elvin M. Jellineck, *The Disease Concept of Alcoholism*, (Highland Park, N.J.: Hillhouse Press, 1960).

10. Mary Cover Jones, "Personality Antecedents and Correlates of Drinking Patterns in Women," *Journal of Consulting and Clinical Psychology* 36 (1971):61–69.

11. Nils I. Bateman and David M. Peterson, "Factors Related to Outcome of Treatment for Hospital White Male and Female Alcoholics," *Journal of Drug Issues* 2 (1972):66–74.

12. Marvin A. Block, "Alcoholism: The Physician's Duty," *General Practitioner* 6, no. 3 (1952):55–58 or Lindbeck, "The Woman Alcoholic."

13. U.S. Senate Subcommitte on Alcoholism and Narcotics, *Alcohol Abuse among Women*, 47.

14. Ibid., Ruth Fox, M.D., 341; and Jean Kirkpatrick, 370.

15. *Journal of Studies on Alcohol* 43, no.6: (1982) section B.

16. Dr. Jean Kirkpatrick, "Women for Sobriety" (Quakertown, Penn.: Women for Sobriety, Inc., 1976).

17. Ibid.

18. See, for example, Robert W. Jones, "Changing Patterns and Attitudes toward Use of Alcoholic Beverages in the U.S., 1900–1963," *Interpreting Current Knowledge about Alcohol and Alcoholism to a College Audience*, Proceedings of conference held in Albany, N.Y., 28–30 May 1963, New York State Department of Mental Hygiene, 9–20; Mark Keller, "The Definition of Alcoholism and the Estimation of its Prevalence,"in David J. Pittman and Charles R. Synder (eds.), *Society, Culture, and Drinking Patterns*, (New York: Wiley, 1962); Keller and Efron, "Alcoholism; Barry A. Kinsey, *The Female Alcoholic: A Social-Psychological Study*, (Springfield, Ill.: Charles C. Thomas, 1966); Edith S. Lisansky, "The Woman Alcoholic," *Annals of the American Academy of Political and Social Science* 325 (1958):73–81; Lolli, *Social Drinking*; Robert O'Brien and Morris Chavetz, *The Encyclopedia of Alcoholism*, (New York: Facts on File Publications, 1982); and Secretary of Health, Education, and Welfare, "Extent and Patterns of Use and Abuse of Alcohol," in Mark Keller, ed., *The First Special Report to the U.S. Congress on Alcohol and Health* (Washington, D.C.: National Institute on Alcohol Abuse and Alcoholism, 1971).

19. See, for example, Joan Curlee, "Alcoholic Women: Some Considerations for Further Research," *Bulletin of the Menninger Clinic* 31 (1967):154–63; Lindbeck, "The Woman Alcoholic", O'Brien and Chavetz, *Encyclopedia*; Jim Orford, Seta Waller, and Julian Peto, "Drinking Behavior and Attitudes and Their Correlates among University Students in England: I—Principle Components Domain. II—Personality and Social Influences. III—Sex Differences," *QJSA* 35 (1974):1316–74.

20. See, for example, Joseph Hirsh, "Women and Alcoholism," in William C. Bier ed., *Alcoholism and Narcotics* (New York: Fordham University Press, 1962); Keller, "Definition of Alcoholism" Kent, *An American Woman*; Kinsey, *Female Alcoholic*; Jacob Levine, "Sexual Adjustment of Alcoholics: A Clinical Study of a Selected Sample," *QJSA* 16, no.4 (1955):675–78; Edith Lisansky, "The Woman Alcoholic"; Lolli, *Social Drinking*; and Joseph Mayer, David J. Myerson, Merrill A. Needham, and Marion M. Fox, "The Treatment of the Female Alcoholic: The Former Prisoner," *American Journal of Orthopsychiatry* 36 (1966):248–49.

21. U.S. Bureau of Census, *Statistical Abstract of the United States*, (Washington, D.C.: Government Printing Office, 1970).

22. Ibid.

23. Ibid., 1950.

24. Ibid., 1960.

25. Ibid., 1970.

26. Ibid., 1982.

27. Ibid., 1970.

28. Ibid., 1982.

29. See James H. Wall, "A Study of Alcoholism in Women," *American Journal of Psychiatry* 93, no.4 (1937):941–55; and Benjamin Karpman, *The Woman Alcoholic* (Washington, D.C. Lincare Press, 1948).

30. See, for example, the second chapter of Marian Sandmaier, *The Invisible Alcoholics: Women and Alcohol Abuse in America* (New York: McGraw-Hill, 1980); or the introduction to Edith Lynn Hornick, *The Drinking Woman* (New York: Association Press, 1977).

31. These are terms used by Edwin M. Lemert, *Human Deviance, Social Problems, and Social Control*, (Englewood Cliffs, N.J.: Prentice-Hall, 1967), 41–42.

32. The term used by Alvin W. Gouldner in "The Sociologist as Partisan: Sociology and the Welfare State," *American Sociologist* (May 1968):103-16.

33. Edwin Schur, for example, argues that susceptibility to labeling is "based largely on the individual's pre-existing power resources" and that "women's vulnerability to stigmatization rests on their general subordination" [Edwin Schur, *Labeling Women Deviant: Gender Stigma and Social Control* (New York: Random House, 1984), 8].

34. See, for example, Edwin M. Schur, 1971, *Labeling Deviant Behavior: Its Sociological Implications*, (New York: Harper and Row, 1971).

35. A label may also be positive. Deviance theorists usually concentrate on the negative effects of labeling, since applying the label deviant to a person is generally considered a form of censure. For example, labeling someone in a subculture deviant may be a positive status symbol within that subculture. The assumption in this study is that the label alcoholic is negative and does lead to stigmatization.

36. Lemert, Human Deviance,

37. Ibid., 41.

38. See, for example, the critiques of labeling theory by Nanette J. Davis, *Sociological Constructions of Deviance*, (Dubuque, Iowa: Wm. C. Brown, 1975); Gouldner, "The Sociologist as Partisan"; and Ian Taylor, Paul Walton and Jack Young, *The New Criminology: For A Social Theory of Deviance* (New York: Harper and Row, 1973).

39. Lemert, *Human Deviance*, 53.

40. See especially the work on homosexuality by Ronald A. Farrell and James F. Nelson, "A Causal Model of Secondary Deviance: The Case of Homosexuality," *Sociological Quarterly* 17 (Winter 1976): 109–20; and Sue Kiefer Hammersmith and Martin S. Weinberg "Homosexual Identity: Commitment, Adjustment, and Significant Others," *Sociometry* 36, no.1 (1973):56–79. Farrell and Nelson found that among

homosexuals, societal rejection does lead to increased association with a deviant subgroup but not to incorporating homosexual stereotypes into one's self-definition. In a large sample of 2,497 males, Hammersmith and Weinberg found a strong positive relationship between commitment to a deviant identity and psychological adjustment as well as a negative relationship with maladjustment. However, these data do not show the expected relationship between adjustment and support from significant others. Such studies as these make it clear that even though the concepts of primary and secondary deviation have been helpful tools in investigating and explaining deviance, we are far from understanding exactly how the process works.

41. See, for example, Erving Goffman, *Stigma: Notes on the Management of Spoiled Identity*, (Englewood Cliffs, N.J.: Prentice-Hall, 1963); or Gresham M. Sykes and David Matza, "Techniques of Neutralization: A Theory of Delinquency," *American Sociological Review* 22 (December 1957):664–70; or Albert J. Reiss, Jr., "The Social Integration of Queers and Peers," *Social Problems* 13 (Spring 1961):102-20.

42. See, for example, Albert K. Cohen, *Delinquent Boys: The Culture of the Gang*, (New York: Free Press, 1955).

43. However, this is only in the eyes of his peers and still leads to problems of adapting to the larger society. There is some quantitative research indicating increased self-esteem with delinquent group identification that supports the qualitative and theoretical work. See, for example, Peter M. Hall, "Identification with Delinquent Subculture and Level of Self-Evaluation," *Sociometry* 29 (June 1966):146–58. In a study of emotionally disturbed children, Michael Schwartz, Gordon F. Fearn, and Sheldon Stryker in "A Note on Self-conception and the Emotionally Disturbed Role," *Sociometry* 29 (September 1966):300–305 tested the self-evaluations of those who are committed and those who are not committed to the disturbed role. Although they found only slight and statistically nonsignificant differences on self-evaluation, they did find that those who are most committed show the least variability in their self-evaluations and are most likely to share self-definitions with significant others in their lives.

44. See Hammersmith and Weinberg, "Homosexual Identity."

45. Lewis A. Coser and Bernard Rosenberg, *Sociological Theory: A Book of Readings*, 5th ed. (New York, Macmillan, 1982), 263–64.

46. Robert K. Merton, *Social Theory and Social Structure* (Glencoe, Ill.: Free Press, 1957).

47. Coser and Rosenberg, *Sociological Theory*, 264.

48. Ephraim H. Mizruchi and Robert Perrucci, "Prescription, Proscription, and Permissiveness: Aspects of Norms and Deviant Drinking Behavior," in Mark Lefton, James K. Skipper, Jr., and Charles H. McCaghy, eds., *Approaches to Deviance* (New York: Appleton-Century-Crofts, 1968).

Chapter 2. Alcohol and the Traditional Roles of Women in Society

1. Sex throughout the literature, from Ralph Linton *The Study of Man* (New York: Appleton-Century-Crofts, 1936), to more current textbooks on sociology (for example, Coser and Rosenberg, *Sociological Theory*) to *International Encyclopedia of the Social Sciences*, has been considered an ascribed status. "Characteristics such as skin color ... sex and ethnicity may come to be differentially evaluated in society. We can think of these characteristics independently of the particular actors who possess them and analyze the properties of this abstracted status structure" [Morris Zeldich, Jr., "Status, Social," in *International Encyclopedia of the Social Sciences* (New York: Macmillan and Free Press, 1968)].

2. Inge K. Broverman, Donald M. Broverman, Frank E. Clarkson, Paul S. Rosenkranz, and Susan R. Vogel, "Sex-Role Stereotypes and Clinical Judgments of Mental Health," *Journal of Consulting and Clinical Psychology* 34, no.1 (1970):1–7.

3. Ibid., 4–5.

4. See Joann Gardner, "Sexist Counseling Must Stop," *Personnel and Guidance Journal* 49 (1971):705–14; and Carol Wesley, "The Woman's Movement and Psychotherapy," *Social Work* 20 (1975):120–24.

5. See, for example, Philip M. Kitay, "A Comparison of the Sexes in Their Attitude and Beliefs about Women," *Sociometry* 3, no. 4 (1940):399–407; D.B. Lynn, " A Note on Sex Differences in the Development of Masculine and Feminine Identification," *Psychological Review* 64 (1959):356–63; Elanor Emmons Maccoby and Carol Nagy Jacklin, *The Psychology of Sex Differences*, (Stanford: Stanford University Press, 1974); John O. McKee and Alex C. Sherriffs, "Men's and Women's Beliefs, Ideals, and Self-Concepts," *American Journal of Sociology* 64, no.4 (1959)):356–63; H.N. Mischel, "Professional Sex Bias and Sex Role Stereotypes in the U.S. and Israel," corrected draft, 1972; Lynn Monahan, Deanna Kuhn, and P. Shaver, "Intrapsychic versus Cultural Explanations of the 'Fear of Success' Motive," *Journal of Personality and Social Psychology* 29 (1974):60–64; Paul S. Rosenkrantz, Susan Vogel, H. Bee, Inge K. Broverman. "Sex Role Stereotypes and Self-Concepts in College Students," *Journal of Consulting and Clinical Psychology* 32 (1968): 287–95; Alex C. Sherriffs and John P. McKee, "Sex Differences in Attitudes about Sex Differences," *Journal of Psychology* 35 (1953): 161–68; and Alex C. Sherriffs and John P. Mckee, "Quantitative Aspects of Beliefs about Men and Women," *Journal of Personality* 25 1957: 451–64; Lynn Townsend White, *Educating Our Daughters* (New York: Harper, 1950).

6. See John P. Garske, 1975, "Role Variation as a Determinant of Attributed Masculinity and Femininity," *Journal of Psychology* 91 (1975):31–37, for support of this position.

7. Seymor J. Friedland, Walter Crockett, and James D. Laird, "The Effects of Role and Sex on the Perception of Others," *Journal of Social Psychology* 91 (1973):273–83.

8. See, for example, Judy Fraser, "The Female Alcoholic," *Addictions* 20 (1973): 371 –414 (reprinted 1974, Toronto: Addiction Research Foundation, 1–16); Albert D, Ullman, *To Know the Difference* (New York: St. Martin's Press; 1960); and John Langone and Doris Nobrega Langone, *Women Who Drink* (Reading, Mass.: Addison-Wesley, 1960).

9. Walter C. Clark, "Sex Roles and Alcoholic Beverage Usage," working paper no. 16, Mental Research Institute Drinking Practices Study, 1967. In an interesting study, John P. McKee and Alex C. Sherriffs, "The Differential Evaluations of Males and Females," *Journal of Personality* 25 (1957): 356–71, found that women believe men are even more restrictive in their views of women than is true. Women not only conform more than men but also more than men would require of them.

10. Clark, "Sex Roles."

11. See, for example, Iradj Siass, Guido Crocetti, and Herzl R. Spino, "Drinking Patterns and Alcoholism in a Blue-Collar Population," *QJSA* 34, no.3 (1973):916–26; and Henry Wechsler, Harold W. Demone, Jr., and Nell Gottlieb, "Drinking Patterns of Greater Boston Adults," *Journal of Studies on Alcohol* 39, no.7 (1978): 1158–65.

12. Genevieve Knupfer, "Female Drinking Patterns," in *Selected Papers Presented at the Fifteenth Annual Meeting of the North American Association of Alcoholism Programs* (Washington, D.C.: NAAAP, 1964), 140–60.

13. Ibid., 153.

14. Joseph J. Lawrence and Milton A. Maxwell, "Drinking and Socioeconomic Status," in David J. Pittman and Charles R. Snyder, eds., *Society, Culture, and Drinking Patterns* (New York: Wiley, 1962).

15. Muriel W. Sterne and David J. Pittman, *Drinking Patterns in the Ghetto*, vol. 2 (St. Louis: Social Science Institute, Washington University, 1972).

16. These two questions were contained in section 1 of the background questionnaire, as explained in the appendix.

17. See, for example, arguments by Genevieve Knupfer, "Female Drinking."

18. Joseph Hirsh, "Women and Alcoholism," in William C. Bier, ed., *Problems in Addiction* (New York: Fordham University Press, 1962);

19. U.S. Senate Subcommittee on Alcoholism and Narcotics, *Alcohol Abuse among Women*, 15.

20. See the excellent review of this history by Sandmaier, *The Invisible Alcoholics*, in which she traces how women who drink were treated throughout Western civilization from the ancient Greeks and Romans to the temperance movement and current times.

21. Ibid., 28–29.

22. Knupfer, "Female Drinking Patterns," 157.

23. Barbara Tamasi, *I'll Stop Tomorrow* (Orleans, Mass.: Paraclete Press, 1982).

24. U.S. Senate Subcommittee on Alcoholism and Narcotics, *Alcohol Abuse Among Women*, 18.

25. U.S. Senate Subcommitte on Alcoholism and Narcotics, *Alcohol Abuse Among Women*, 206.

26. Ibid., 208.

27. See, for example, Wall, "Alcoholism in Women."

28. See, for example, Karpman, *The Alcoholic Woman*; or Norm Southerby and Alexandra Southerby, *Twelve Young Women* (Long Beach, Calif.: Norm Southerby and Associates, 1975).

29. Marc A. Schuckit, "Sexual Disturbance in the Woman Alcoholic," *Medical Aspects of Human Sexuality* 6, no.9 (1972):44–65.

30. See, for example, Myron L. Belfer, Richard I. Shrader, Mary Carroll, and Jerold Harmatz, "Alcoholism in Women," *Archives of General Psychiatry* 25(December 1971):540–44; Schuckit, "The Alcoholic Woman"; and the work of George Winokur and his colleagues (for example, John Rimmer, Ferris N. Pitts, Theodore Reich, and George Winokur, "Alcoholism III. Diagnosis and Familial Psychiatric Illness in 259 Alcoholic Probands," *Archives of General Psychiatry* 23, no.2 (1971):104-11. All of these studies suggest that the sociopathic female alcoholic constitutes a very tiny part of the overall female alcoholic population.

31. M.M. Glatt, "Drinking Habits of English (Middle-Class) Alcoholics," *Acta Psychiatrica Scandinavica* 37 (1961):88–113; Kinsey, "Psychological Factors," 157–60; "The Sexual Adjustment of Alcoholics"; Mary Jane Sherfey, "Psychopathology and Character Structure in Chronic Alcoholism," in Oskar Diethelm, ed., *Etiology of Chronic Alcoholism* (Springfield, Ill.: Charles C. Thomas, 1955); and Howard P. Wood and Edward L. Duffy, "Psychological Factors in Alcoholic Women," *American Journal of Psychiatry* 123, no.3 (1966):341–45. All of these studies reported a decrease in libido in female alcoholics.

32. Inhibition and / or poor sexual adjustment is reported in many sources, including Howard T. Blane, *The Personality of the Alcoholic: Guises of Dependency* (New York: Harper and Row, 1968); Frank J. Curran, "Personality Studies in Alcoholic Women," *Journal of Nervous and Mental Disease* 86, no.6 (1937): 643–67; Levine, "Sexual Adjustment of Alcoholics"; Schuckit, "The Alcoholic Woman"; and Wall, "Alcoholism in Women."

33. Schuckit, "The Alcoholic Woman," 44.

34. Knupfer, "Female Drinking Patterns."

35. Proscriptive and prescriptive norms were used by Mizruchi and Perrucci,

"Prescription, Proscrtiption, and Permissiveness," to explain deviant drinking behavior. Although their analysis focused on the distinction between the drinking behaviors of Jews, ascetic protestants, and Mormons, it is no less applicable to male and female differences.

36. Robert Straus and Seldon D. Bacon, *Drinking in College*, (New Haven, Conn.: Yale University Press, 1954), 144.

37. Lawrence Galton, "Alcoholism in Women: The Hidden Epidemic," *Syracuse Herald-American Parade*, (5 February) 1978, 10.

38. See, for example, George M. Anderson, "Women Drinking: Stigma and Sickness," *America* (December): 434–37; Fraser, "The Female Alcoholic"; or Galton, "Alcoholism in Women."

39. Anderson, "Women Drinking."

40. Jack Nero, *If Only My Wife Could Drink Like a Lady* (Minneapolis, Minn.: Comp Care Publications, 1977), 10.

41. Fraser, "The Female Alcoholic, 8."

42. See Joan Curlee, "Women Alcoholics," *Federal Probation* 32, no.1 (1968): 16–20; and unsigned, "Alcoholism in Women," *Journal of the American Medical Association* 225 (20 August 1973): 988.

43. Jane E. James, "Symptoms of Alcoholism in Women: A Preliminary Survey of A.A. Members," *Journal of Studies on Alcohol* 36, no.11 (1975):1564–69.

44. Sandmaier, *The Invisible Alcoholics*, 208.

45. Keith M. Kilty, "Attitudes toward Alcohol and Alcoholism among Professionals and Nonprofessionals," *QJSA* 36, no.3 (1975): 327.

46. David J. Pittman and Muriel J. Sterne, "Analysis of Various Community Approaches to the Problem of Alcoholism in the U.S.," in David J. Pittman, ed., *Alcoholism* (New York: Harper and Row, 1967), 208. Similar results were found by S.J. Levy and C.M. Doyle, "Attitudes toward Women in a Drug Abuse Treatment Program," *Journal of Drug Issues* 4 (1974): 428–34, in reasearch on a drug abuse treatment program. Women were seen by staff as being "more emotional, more sensitive, limited by their biology, needing to please men and implicitly 'sicker' than men" (430).

47. See, for example, Kenneth A. Wallston, Barbara S. Wallston, and Brenda M. Devellis, "Effect of Negative Stereotype on Nurses' Attitudes toward an Alcoholic Patient," *Journal of Studies on Alcohol* 37, no.5 (1976): 659–65.

48. Johnson, "Physicians Views of Alcoholism."

49. Robert W. Jones and Alice R. Helrich, "Treatment of Alcoholism by Physicians in Private Practice: A National Survey," *QJSA* 33, no.1 (1972): 117–31.

50. U.S. Senate Subcommittee on Alcoholism and Narcotics, *Alcohol Abuse Among Women*, 40.

51. Jones and Helrich, "A National Survey," table 4.

52. Galton, " Alcoholism in Women," 10.

53. Harry S. Abram and William F. McCourt, "Interaction of Physicians with Emergency Ward Alcoholic Patients," *QJSA* 25 (1964): 679–88.

54. Joan Curlee, "A Comparison of Male and Female Patients at an Alcoholism Treatment Center," *Journal of Psychology* 74 (January 1970): 239–47, makes this suggestion. The findings of Luis M. Schwartz and Stanton Fjeld, "The Alcoholic Patient in the Psychiatric Hospital Emergency Room," *QJSA* 30, no.1 (1969): 104–11, could be interpreted as support of this position.

55. Cara, "Women and Alcohol: A Close-up," in Vasanti Burtle, ed., *Women Who Drink. Alcoholic Experience and Psychotherapy* (Springfield, Ill.: Charles C. Thomas, 1979).

56. Sandmaier, *The Invisible Alcoholics*, p. 45.

57. New York Narcotic Addiction Control Commission, *Differential Drug Use within the New York State Labor Force*, (Albany, N.Y.. NYNACC, 1971).

58. Dean I. Manheimer, Glenn D. Mellinger, and Mitchell B. Balter, "Psychotherapeutic Drugs: Use among Adults in California," *California Medicine* 109 (1968): 445–51.

59. Hugh J. Parry, Mitchell B. Balter, Glen D. Mellinger, Ira H. Cissin, and Dean I. Manheimer, "National Patterns of Psychoterapeutic Drug Use," *Archives of General Psychiatry* 28 (1973): 769–83. See also Joan Curlee, "Sex Differences in Patient Attitudes towards Alcoholism," *QJSA* 32 (1971): 643–50; and N.H. Rathod and I.G. Thompson, "Women Alcoholics: A Clinical Study," *QJSA* 32 (1971): 45–52.

60. Kimball, Mind Games.

61. U.S. Senate Subcommittee on Alcoholism and Narcotics, *Alcohol* Abuse Among Women, 38.

62. Eileen M. Corrigan, *Alcoholic Women in Treatment* (New York: Oxford University Press, 1980).

63. O'Brien and Chavetz, *Encyclopedia*.

64. Ibid.

65. Nero, *Drink Like a Lady*.

66. Cara, "A Close-up," 21.

67. Elmer A. Johnson, *Crime, Correction, and Society* (Homewood, Ill.: Dorsey Press, 1964), 80.

68. Ibid., 80.

69. Ibid.

70. See, for example, Paul Anthony Pastor, Jr., "The Control of Public Drunkenness: A Comparison of the Legal and Medical Models," Ph. D. diss., Yale University, 1975; and Orford, Waller, and Petro, "Drinking Behavior."

71. Cited in Fraser, "The Female Alcoholic," 4–5.

72. See, for example, John Rimmer, Ferris N. Pitts, Theodore Reich, and George Winokur, "Alcoholism II: Sex, Socioeconomic Status, and Race in Two Hospitalized Samples," *QJSA* 32, no.4 (1971): 942–52.

73. Fraser, "The Female Alcoholic."

74. Ibid., 7.

75. U.S. National Highway Traffic Safety Administration, *Factors Influencing Alcohol Safety Action Project Police Officers' DWI Arrests* (Washington, D.C.: Department of Transportation, 1974).

76. Galton, "Alcoholism in Women."

77. Milton Angeriou and Donna Paulino, "Women Arrested for Drunken Driving in Boston: Social Characteristics and Circumstances of Arrest," *Journal of Studies on Alcohol* 373, no.5 (1976): 648–58.

78. Ibid., 649.

79. See, for example, Gerald R. Garret and Howard M. Bahr, "Comparison of Self-Rating and Quantity Frequency Measures of Drinking," *QJSA* 35 (1974): 1294–1306; John L. Horn and Kenneth N. Wanberg, "Females Are Different: On the Diagnosis of Alcoholism in Women," in Morris Chavetz, ed., *Proceedings of the First Annual Alcoholism Conference* (Washington, D.C.: Department of H.E.W., 1973) 332–54; Marilyn W. Johnson, Johanna C. Devries, and Mary I. Houghton, "The Female Alcoholic," *Nursing Research* 15, no.4 (1966): 343–47; Lisansky, "The Woman Alcoholic"; Lawrence A. Senseman, "The Housewife's Secret Illness: How to Recognize the Female Alcoholic," *Rhode Island Journal of Medicine* 49, no.1 (1966): 40–42; James H. Wall, "Alcoholism in Women"; Kenneth N. Wanberg and John L. Horn,

"Alcoholism Syndromes Related to Sociological Classifications," *International Journal of Addictions* 8 (1973):99–120; and Kenneth N. Wanberg and John Knapp, "Differences in Drinking Symptoms and Behavior of Men and Women Alcoholics," *British Journal of Addiction* 64 (1970): 347–55.

80. Fraser, "The Female Alcoholic," 9.

81. Ibid., 2.

82. See, for example, Hirsh, "Women and Alcoholism"; Massam, "Female Drinking"; and Wanberg and Horn, "Females Are Different."

83. Langone and Langone, *Women Who Drink*, 7.

84. Ibid., 5–6.

85. See comments by Hirsh, "Women and Alcoholism"; Clark, "Sex Roles"; Andre G. Jacob and Camil Lavoie, "A Study of Some of the Characteristics of a Group of Women Alcoholics," in Ruth Brock, ed., *Selected Papers Presented at the General Sessions Twenty-Second Annual Meeting, September 12–17, 1971, Hartford, Connecticut* (Washington, D.C.: Alcohol and Drug Problems Association of North America, 1971), 25–32; and Jan Moore, "The Drinking Woman: Where Does She Go for Help?" *Syracuse Herald American*, 29 May 1978.

86. See, for example, Marvin A. Block, *Alcoholism: Its Facets and Phases* (New York: John Day Company, 1965).

87. See Keller and Efron, "Alcoholism," for a discussion of the rates in various settings. For an updated and comprehensive discussion, see Marc. A. Schuckit and Elizabeth R. Morrissey, "Alcoholism in Women: Some Clinical and Social Perspectives with an Emphasis on Possible Subtypes," in Milton Greenblat and Marc A Schuckit, eds., *Alcoholism Problems in Women and Children* (New York: Grune and Stratton, 1976).

88. Jones, "Personality Antecedents."

89. See, for example, Sidney Cahn, *The Treatment of Alcoholics: An Evaluative Study* (New York: Oxford University Press, 1970); Curran, "Alcoholic Women"; or Seymour L. Zelen, Jack Fox, Edward Gould, and Ray W. Olson, "Sex-Contingent Differences between Male and Female Alcoholics," *Journal of Clinical Psychology* 22 (1966): 160–65.

90. Rimmer et al., " Alcoholism II."

91. Block, "Physician's Duty"; Lindbeck, "The Woman Alcoholic"; and Jones and Helrich, "A National Survey."

92. See, for example, Kimball's *Mind Games* for an account of denial in which alcoholic women and all those who deal with them conspire.

Chapter 3. Declining Insularity

1. John W. Riley and Charles F. Marden, "The Social Pattern of Alcoholic Drinking," *QJS Alcohol* 8, no.2 (1947): 265.

2. Margaret Mead, *Sex and Temperament in Three Primitive Societies* (New York: William Morrow and Company, 1935).

3. Ibid., 145.

4. Ibid., 225.

5. Ibid.

6. See, for example Gayle Fad, ed., *Woman's Role in Aboriginal Society*, Australian Aboriginal Studies, no. 36 (Canberra: Australian National Institute of Aboriginal Studies, 1970); or Patricia Draper, "!Kung Women: Contrasts in Sexual Egalitarianism in Foraging and Sedentary Contexts," in Rayna R. Reiter, ed., *Toward an Anthropology*

of Women, (New York: Monthly Review Press, 1975), 77–109.

7. Juanita H. Williams, *Psychology of Women: Behavior in a Biosocial Context*, (New York: W.W. Norton and Company, 1983), 83.

8. See, for example, Karen Sacks, *Sisters and Wives: The Past and Future of Sexual Equality*, (Chicago: University of Illinois Press, 1982).

9. See, for example, Hirsch, "Women and Alcoholism" Lolli, *Social Drinking*; and Fredrick Parker, "Sex Role Adjustment in Women Alcoholics," *QJSA* 33, no.3 (1972): 647–57.

10. See, for example, Wall, "Alcoholism in Women"; Karpman, *The Alcoholic Woman*; Sherfey, "Psychopathology"; Kinsey, *The Female Alcoholic*; Vladimir Pishkin and Frederick C. Thorne, "A Factorial Structure of the Dimensions of Femininity in Alcoholic, Schizophrenic, and Normal Populations," *Journal of Clinical Psychology* 33, no.1 (1977):10–17; or see Wood and Duffy, "Psychological Factors."

11. See Sharon C. Wilsnak's work, including "Femininity in the Bottle," *Psychology Today* 6, no.11 (1973):39–102; "The Needs of the Female Drinker: Dependency, Power, or What?" in Morris Chavetz, ed., *Proceedings of the Second Annual Conference of the NIAAA* (Washington, D.C.: Department of H.E.W., 1973); and "Sex Role Identification in Female Alcoholism," *Journal of Abnormal Psychology* 82, no.2 (1973): 253–61. The most complete and clearest presentation of Wilsnak's argument appears in a more recent article, "The Impact of Sex Roles on Women's Alcohol Use and Abuse," in Milton Greenblatt and Marc A. Schuckit, eds., *Alcoholism Problems in Women and Children* (New York: Grune and Stratton, 1976).

12. See, for example, Helen S. Astin, *The Woman Doctorate in America* (Hartford, Conn.: Russell Sage Foundation, 1969); Louise M. Bachtold and Emmy E. Werner "Personality Profiles of Gifted Women: Psychologists," *American Psychologist* 25 (1970): 234–43; Lillian Kaufman Cartwright, "Women in Medical School," Ph.D. diss., University of California, Berkeley, 1970; Eli Ginzberg, *Life Styles of Educated Women* (New York: Columbia University Press, 1966); and Sandra Schwartz Tangri, "Determinants of Occupational Role Innovation among College Women," *Journal of Social Issues* 28, no.2 (1972): 177–99.

13. See, for example, Donald Hoyt and Carroll Kennedy, "Interest and Personality Correlates of Career-Motivated College Women," *Journal of Counseling Psychology* 5(1958):44–48; and Nevitt Sanford, ed., "Personality Development during the College Years," *Journal of Social Issues* 12, no.4 (1956): 3–12.

14. Edwin C. Lewis, *Developing Woman's Potential*, (Ames: Iowa State University Press, 1968).

15. Ravenna Helson, "The Changing Image of the Career Woman," *Journal of Social Issues* 28, no.2 (1972): 40.

16. Ibid, 41.

17. Mead, *Sex and Temperament*, 308.

18. Merton, *Social Theory*, 162.

19. Mizruchi and Perrucci, "Prescription, Proscription, and Permissiveness," 162.

20. Wilsnak, "Dependency, Power, or What?" 259.

21. Wilsnak, "The Impact of Sex Roles," 39.

22. It is interesting to note that one of the main theories of why men become alcoholics states that they drink from a need for dependency, which is generally considered a feminine trait in our society. See, for example, the classic work by William McCord and Joan McCord, *Origins of Alcoholism*, (Stanford: Stanford University Press, 1960). If the dependency theory for men is accurate, it could also be an example of the sex role confusion theory: Men suffering from incomplete masculine identification (i.e. their unconscious need is for dependency which traditionally has

been a feminine trait in our society) are prone to alcoholism.

23. Quoted in Maria Riccardi, "Drinking Women: Women for Sobriety's Self-Help Program Recognizing Why They Become Alcoholics," *Rochester Democrat and Chronicle*, 19 September 1981, 12B.

24. Schuckit and Morrisey, "Alcoholism in Women."

25. Ibid., 13.

26. Ibid., 18.

27. Thomas J. Keil, "Sex Role Variations and Women's Drinking: Results from a Household Survey in Pennsylvania," *Journal of Studies on Alcohol* 39, no.5 (1978): 859–68.

28. P.B. Johnson, "Working Women and Alcohol Use: Preliminary National Data," paper presented at symposium, Psychological Issues Related to Women's Employment, American Psychological Association Convention, Toronto, August 1978.

29. Garske, "Role Variation," 31–37.

30. Friedland, Crockett, and Laird, "The Effects of Role and Sex."

31. O'Brien and Chavetz, *Encyclopedia*.

32. See, for example, Grace M. Barnes and Marcia Russel, "Drinking Patterns in Western New York State: Comparison with National Data," *Journal of Studies on Alcohol* 39, no.7 (1978): 1148–57; or Henry Wechsler, Harold W. Demone, and Nell Gottlieb, "Drinking Patterns of Greater Boston Adults: Subgroup Differences on the QFV Index," *Journal of Studies on Alcohol* 39, no.7 (1978): 1158–65.

33. O'Brien and Chavetz, *Encyclopedia*.

34. Edith S. Lisansky, "Alcoholism in Women: Social and Psychological Concomitants. Social History Data," *QJSA* 18 (Dec. 1958): 589.

35. See arguments by Keller and Efron, "Alcoholism." See also Kinsey, *The Female Alcoholic*.

36. See Johnson, "Physicians' Views."

37. See, for example, Jan E. E. de Lint, "Alcoholism, Birth Rank, and Parental Deprivation," *American Journal of Psychiatry* 120 (1964): 1062–65; or D.A. Pemberton, "A Comparison of the Outcome of Treatment in Female and Male Alcoholics," *British Journal of Psychiatry* 113, no.497 (1967): 367–73.

38. Betty Ford, *The Times of My Life*, (New York: Harper and Row and the Reader's Digest, 1978).

39. U.S. Bureau of Census, *Statistical Abstract*, 1941 and 1982.

Chapter 4. Labeling Theory and Stigmatization

1. These questions were investigated by Howard S. Becker, *Outsiders: Studies in the Sociology of Deviance*, (New York: Free Press, 1963).

2. Ibid., 9; emphasis by Becker.

3. Schur, *Labeling Deviant Behavior*, 4.

4. William Edward Hartpole Lecky, 1877 reprint, *History of European Morals from Augustus to Charlemagne*, vol. 2, (New York: Arno Press, 1975), 285.

5. D.L. Rosenhan, 1973, "On Being Sane in Insane Places," *Science* 179, no. 4070 (1973): 250–58.

6. See, for example, Theodore R. Sarbin and James C. Mancuso, "Failure of Amoral Enterprise; Attitudes of the Public toward Mental Illness," *Journal of Consulting and Clinical Psychology* 35 (1970): 159–73; or Jim C. Nunnally, Jr., *Popular Conceptions of Mental Health*, (New York: Holt, Rinehart, and Winston, 1961).

7. Rosenhan, "On Being Sane," 257.

8. Edwin M. Lemert, *Human Deviance*, 42.

9. As can be seen in the case of alcoholism, labels do not always have this function and can at times assist in recovering, as is evidenced by Alcoholics Anonymous's first step, which insists that the individual acknowledge his or her powerlessness over alcohol.

10. See Becker, *Outsiders*, 124.

11. See the strong critique of the labeling perspective from an empirical standpoint in Walter R. Gove, ed., *The Labelling of Deviance: Evaluating a Perspective*, 2d ed. (Beverly Hills, Calif.: Sage Publications, 1980).

12. Schur, *Labeling Deviant Behavior*, 33.

13. As indicated in their articles at the end of Gove's book, John I. Kitsuse, "The 'New Conception of Deviance' and Its Critics," in Walter R. Gove, ed., *The Labelling of Deviance: Evaluating a Perspective*, 2d ed. (Beverly Hills, Calif.: Sage Publications, 1980), 381–92, and Edwin M. Schur, "Comments," in Walter R. Gove, ed., *The Labelling of Deviance: Evaluating a Perspective*, 2d ed. (Beverly Hills, Calif.: Sage Publications, 1980), 393–402, do not accept Gove's contention that he has successfully isolated the basic tenets of labeling theory.

14. Schur, "Comments," 401.

15. The labeling section in Allen E. Liska, *Perspectives on Deviance* (Englewood Cliffs, N.J.: Prentice–Hall, 1981), provides a much less biased and more persuasive review of studies that support and fail to support the labeling perspective.

16. Richard D. Swartz and Jerome H. Skolnick, "Two Studies of Legal Stigma," *Social Problems* 10 (1962): 133–42.

17. Wouter Buikhuisen and Fokke P.H. Dijksterhuis, "Delinquency and Stigmatisation," *British Journal of Criminology* 11, no.2 (1971):185–87.

18. Ibid., 186.

19. Kitsuse, "New Conception."

20. Lee N. Robins, "Alcoholism and Labelling Theory," in Walter R. Gove, ed., *The Labelling of Deviance: Evaluating a Perspective*, 2d. ed. (Beverly Hills, Calif.: Sage Publications, 1980), 43.

21. Gwynn Nettler effectively makes this point in his criticism of labeling theory in *Explaining Crime*, (New York: McGraw-Hill, 1974): "On the level of social concerns, the labeling hypothesis does not answer the perennial questions about crime" (211).

22. Milton Mankoff, "Societal Reaction and Career Deviance: A Critical Analysis," *Sociological Quarterly* 12 (Spring 1971): 211.

23. Gwynn Nettler, *Explaining Crime*, 211.

24. Davis, *Deviance*, 173.

25. Gouldner, "The Sociologist as Partisan," 106.

26. Edwin M. Lemert, "Beyond Mead: The Societal Reaction to Deviance," *Social Problems* 21 (April 1974): 459.

27. Ibid., 460.

28. Harrison M. Trice and Paul Michael Roman, "Delabeling, Relabeling, and Alcoholics Anonymous," *Social Problems* 17 (Spring 1970): 123–43.

29. George Lowe and H. Eugene Hodges, "Race and Treatment of Alcoholism in a Southern State," *Social Problems* 20 (Fall 1972): 240–52.

30. Taylor, Walton, and Young, *The New Criminology*.

31. See Davis, *Deviance*, 166.

32. Ibid., 181.

33. Gouldner, "The Sociologist as Partisan," 111.

34. Kitsuse, "New Conception."

35. Jack P. Gibbs, "Conceptions of Deviant Behavior: The Old and the New," in Mark Lefton, James K. Skipper, Jr., and Charles H. McCaghy, eds., *Approaches to Deviance: Theories, Concepts, and Research Findings* (New York: Appleton-Century-Croft, 1968).

36. Schur,"Comments."

37. Schur, *Labeling Deviant Behavior.*

38. Barry Glassner, "Labeling Theory," in M. Michael Rosenberg, Robert A. Stebbins, and Allan Turowetz, eds., *The Sociology of Deviance* (New York: St. Martin's Press, 1982).

39. Thomas J. Scheff, "The Labeling of Mental Illness," *American Sociological Review* 39 (1974): 444–52.

40. See, for example, Gibbs, "Deviant Behavior"; Nettler, *Explaining Crime*; or Laurie Taylor and Paul Walton, "Industrial Sabotage: Motives and Meanings," in Stanley Cohen, ed., *Images of Deviance* (Harmondworth, England: Penguin, 1971).

41. Schur, *Labeling Deviant Behavior,* 21.

42. See, for example, the excellent critiques of Davis, *Deviance*; Gibbs, "Deviant Behavior"; Nettler, *Explaining Crime*; or Taylor, Walton, and Young, *The New Criminology.*

43. See, for example, the excellent work on labeling by Schur, *Labeling Deviant Behavior.*

44. Ibid., 12–13.

45. Ibid., 13.

46. Ibid., 29.

47. Ibid., 31.

48. Ibid., 58.

49. Ibid., 34.

50. Lemert, "Beyond Mead," 458.

Chapter 5. The Societal Reaction to Female Alcoholics

1. Fraser, "The Female Alcoholic," quotation is from 1974 reprint, 4.

2. This holds true in very diverse sources; see, for example, Curlee, "Alcoholic Women"; and Curlee, "Women Alcoholics"; Hirsh, "Women and Alcoholism"; Hornik, *The Drinking Woman*; Langone and Langone, *Women Who Drink*; Lisansky, "The Woman Alcoholic"; Lolli, *Social Drinking*; Sandmaier, *The Invisible Alcoholics*; Senseman, "The Housewife's Secret Illness"; and Geraldine Youcha, *A Dangerous Pleasure,* (New York: Hawthorn Books, 1978).

3. See, for example, Anderson, "Women Drinking"; Galton, "Alcoholism in Women"; or Jan Moore, "The Drinking Woman: Where Does She Go for Help?" *Syracuse Herald-Journal*, 30 May 1978.

4. See, for example, Kilty, "Attitudes toward Alcohol," and Pittman and Sterne, "Alcoholism in the U.S."

5. There was some research by Jim C. Nunnally, Jr., "What the Mass Media Present," in Thomas J. Scheff, ed., *Mental Illness and Social Process,* (New York: Harper and Row, 1967) that indicated the media stereotyped mental illness more than the public. The research reported on was conducted twenty-nine to thirty years ago. While this may be of great interest historically, its applicablility today is questionable.

6. See, for example, statements by Jan Clayton and Susan B. Anthony before the U.S. Senate Subcommittee on Alcoholism and Narcotics Alcohol Abuse among Women; Kent, *An American Woman*; Langone and Langone, Women Who Drink;

Sandmaier, The Invisible Alcoholics; and Barbara Tamasi, *I'll Stop Tomorrow*, (Orleans, Mass.: Paraclete Press, 1982).

7. James, "Symptoms of Alcoholism in Women."

8. Corrigan, *Alcoholic Women in Treatment*.

9. Ibid., 66–67.

10. See Eleanor Emmons Maccoby and Carol Jacklin Nagy, *The Psychology of Sex Differences*, (Stanford: Stanford University Press, 1974) for an extensive review of the literature.

11. Albert Bandura, "Influence of Models' Reinforcement Contingencies on the Acquisition of Imitative Responses," *Journal of Personality and Social Psychology* 1 (1965): 589–95.

12. Eleanor Emmons Maccoby and Wayne C. Wilson, "Identification and Observational Learning from Films," *Journal of Abnormal and Social Psychology* 55 (1957): 76–87.

13. Marv Moore, "Aggression Themes in a Binocular Rivalry Situation," *Journal of Personality and Social Psychology* 3 (1966): 685–88.

14. Jerome Kagan and Howard A. Moss, *Birth and Maturity: A Study in Psychological Development*, (New York: Wiley, 1962).

15. William J. McGuire, "Personality and Susceptibility to Social Influence," in Edgar F. Borgatta and William W. Lambert, eds., *The Handbook of Personality Theory and Research*, (Chicago: Rand McNally, 1968).

16. Dana Braumal, Quoted in Elizabeth Nel, Robert Helmreich, and Elliot Aronson, "Opinion Change in the Advocate as a Function of the Personality of the Audience: A Clarification of the Meaning of Dissonance," *Journal of Personality and Social Psychology* 12 (1969): 117–24.

17. Howard F. Taylor, 1970, *Balance in Small Groups*, (New York: Van Nostrand-Reinhold, 1970), 48.

18. Horace English and Eva C. English, *A Comprehensive Dictionary of Psychological and Psychoanalytic Terms*, (New York: Logmans, Green, 1958).

19. Jean Kirkpatrick, "Women and Alcohol," in Cristen C. Eddy and John L. Ford, eds., *Alcoholism in Women*, (Dubuque, Iowa: Kendall / Hunt Publishing, 1980), 172.

20. Horn and Wanberg, "Females Are Different:" Similar findings emerged from a study by John S. Tamerin, Alexander Tolor, and Betsy Harrington, "Sex Differences in Alcoholics: A Comparison of Male and Female Alcoholics' Self and Spouse Perceptions," *American Journal of Drug and Alcohol Abuse* 3, no.3 (1976): 457–72: "the female alcoholics more frequently endorsed all three items on the Guilt-Shaw Factor of the Mood Scale" 461. They found no such factor with male alcoholics: "While it might be inferred that he is depressed, the alcoholic male does not conciously experience feelings of guilt, shame, or depression" 470. Observations by Penny Clemmons in her practice as a psychologist also confirmed that guilt is one of the most prominent aspects of the female alcoholic's personality. See Penny Clemmons, "A Comprehensive Psychoanalytic Approach to Alcoholism Treatment," in Vasanti Burtle, ed., *Women Who Drink: Alcoholic Experience and Psychotherapy*, (Springfield, Ill.: Chareles C. Thomas, 1979), 217–28.

21. See, for example, the discussion by Linda J. Beckman, "Women Alcoholics," 799.

22. See, for example, Selden D. Bacon, "Excessive Drinking and the Institution of the Family," in Yale University Center of Alcohol Studies, ed., *Alcohol, Science, and Society*, (Westport, Conn.: Greenwood Press, 1972); Margaret B. Bailey, "Alcoholism and Marriage: A Review of Research and Progressional Literature," QJSA 22 (1961): 81–97; Don Cahalan, Ira H. Cissin, and Helen M. Crossley, *American Drinking*

Practices: A National Study of Drinking Behavior and Attitudes, (New Brunswick, N.J.: Rutgers Center of Alcohol Studies 1969); Ruth Fox, "The Alcoholic Spouse," in Victor W. Einstein ed., *Neurotic Interaction in Marriage*, (New York: Basic Books, 1956); Joan K. Jackson, "Alcoholism and the Family," in David J. Pittman and Charles R. Snyder, eds., *Society, Culture, and Drinking Patterns*, (New York: Wiley, 1962). Elvin M. Jellinek, "The Phases of Alcohol Addiction," *QJSA* 13 (1952): 673–84; Harrison Trice, *Alcoholism in America*, (New York: McGraw-Hill, 1966); or Woodruff, Jr., Guze, and Clayton, "Psychiatric Out-patients."

23. U.S. Bureau of Census, *Statistical Abstract*, 1980.

24. See, for example, Penny Clemmons, "Issues in Marriage and the Family and Child Counseling in Alcoholism," in Vasanti Burtle, ed., *Women Who Drink: Alcoholic Experience and Psychotherapy* (Springfield, Ill.: Charles C. Thomas, 1979); Joan Curlee, "A Comparison of Male and Female Patients"; M.M. Glatt, "A Treatment Center for Alcoholics in a Public Mental Hospital: Its Establishment and Working," *British Journal of Addiction* 52 (1955): 55–92; Glatt, "Drinking Habits"; O'Brien and Chavetz, *Encyclopedia*; and Kenneth W. Wanberg and John L. Horn, "Alcoholism Symptom Patterns of Men and Women," *Quarterly Journal of Studies on Alcohol* 31 (1970): 40–61.

25. See, for example, Fraser, "The Female Alcoholic"; or Sandmaier, *The Invisible Alcoholics*.

26. Vernelle Fox, "Clinical Experiences in Working with Women with Alcoholism," in Vasanti Burtle, ed., *Women Who Drink: Alcoholic Experience and Psychotherapy* (Springfield, Ill.: Charles C. Thomas, 1979), 123.

27. Ibid., 124.

28. See, for example, George M. Anderson, "Women Drinking"; and Ruth Maxwell, *The Booze Battle*, (New York: Praeger, 1976).

29. Nero, *Drink Like a Lady*, 162.

30. See, for example, Corrigan, *Alcoholic Women*; Edith S. Lisansky, "Alcoholism in Women: Social and Psychological Concomitants. I. Social History Data," *QJSA* 18, no.4 (December 1957): 588–662; A. Balfour Sclare, "The Female Alcoholic," *Journal of Addictions* 65, no.2 (1970): 99–127; or Antonia Regina Tavarone, *The Role of Family Members in the Treatment of Women Alcoholics*, Ph. D. diss., Syracuse University, 1983.

31. Schuckit and Morrissey, "Alcoholism in Women," 17.

32. See, for example, Glatt, "A Treatment Center"; or "Drinking Habits"; Rathod and Thompson, "Women Alcoholics," 45–52.

33. Maxwell, *The Booze Battle*, 72.

34. See the review of this research in Patricia Edwards, Cheryl Harvey, and Paul C. Whitehead, "Wives of Alcoholics: A Critical Review and Analysis," *QJSA* 34 (1973): 112–32. Quotation is from p.128. See also more current reviews by Linda J. Beckman, "Alcoholism Problems and Women: An Overview," in Milton Greenblatt and Marc A. Schuckit, eds., *Alcoholism Problems in Women and Children*, (New York: Grune and Stratton, 1976); and Edith S. Gomberg, "Women and Alcoholism," in Violet Franks and Vasanti Burtle, eds., *Women in Therapy: New Psychotherapies for a Changing Society*, (New York: Brumer / Mazel, 1974). This view of wives of alcoholic men did not cease in 1959 but still persists in some of the literature; see, for example, Joseph C. Reingold, *The Fear of Being a Woman: A Theory of Maternal Destruction*, (New York: Grune and Stratton, 1964).

35. See, for example, Samuel Futterman, "Personality Trends in Wives of Alcoholics," *Journal of Psychiatric Social Work* 23 (1953): 37–41.

36. Edwards, Harvey, and Whitehead, "Wives of Alcoholics."

37. See, for example, Kate L. Kogan and Joan K. Jackson, "Stress, Personality, and Emotional Disturbance in Wives of Alcoholics," *QJSA* 26, no.3 (1965): 486–95.

38. Gomberg, "Women and Alcoholism," 185.

39. See, for example Gomberg, "Women and Alcoholism"; and Beckman, "Women Alcoholics."

40. Chalfant and Roper, *Annotated Bibliography*,

41. Maxwell, *The Booze Battle*, 78–79.

42. Kirkpatrick, "Women and Alcohol," 172. Similar problems with the availability of treatment for the female alcoholic were found in research on Canada; See Virginia Carver, "The Female Alcoholic in Treatment," *Canadian Psychological Review* 18, no.1 (1977): 96–103.

43. U.S. Department of Health and Human Services, "Tailoring Alcoholism Therapy to Client Needs" (Washington, D.C.: Government Printing Office, 1981).

44. Sandmaier, *The Invisible Alcoholics*, 72ff.

45. See, for example, Fraser, "The Female Alcoholic"; or Kent, *An American Woman.*

46. Johnson, "Physicians Views."

47. Richard A. Mackey, "Views of Caregiving and Mental-health Groups about Alcoholics," *QJSA* 39 no.3 (1969): 665–71.

48. Schwartz and Fjeld, "The Alcoholic Patient," (1969).

49. Sandmaier, *The Invisible Alcoholics*, 217.

50. Cristenson and Swanson, "Women and Drug Use."

51. See, for example, Anderson, "Women Drinking"; Curlee, "Alcoholic Women," and Joseph C. Kern, William Schmelter, and Michael Fanelli, "A Comparison of Three Alcoholism Treatment Populations," *Journal of Studies on Alcohol* 39, no.5 (1978): 785–92.

52. Bateman and Peterson, "White Male and Female Alcoholics."

53. Ardelle M. Schultz, "Radical Feminism: A Treatment Modality for the Addicted Woman," in Edward C. Senay, Vernon Shorty, and Harold Alksae, eds., *Developments in the the Field of Drug Abuse*, (Cambridge, Mass.: Schenkman, 1975).

54. See, for example, Bateman and Peterson, "White Male and Female Alcoholics;" John F. Burnum. "Outlook for Treating Patients with Self-Destructive Habits," *Annals of Internal Medicine* 81, no.3 (1974): 387–93; Curlee, "A Comparison of Male and Female Patients"; Anne F. Davidson, "Evaluation of the Treatment and Aftercare of a Hundred Alcoholics," *British Journal of Addiction* 71 (1976): 217–24; Harold W. Demone, Jr., "Experiments in Referral to Alcoholism Clinics," *QJSA* 24 (1963): 495–502; Curtis H. Ebbe and Charles E. McKeown, "An Evaluation of the Use of Tetraethylthiuram Disulfide in the Treatment of 560 Cases of Alcohol Addiction," *American Journal of Psychiatry* 109 (1953): 670–73; Glatt, "A Treatment Center"; M.M. Glatt, "Treatment Results in an English Mental Hospital Unit," *Acta Psychiatrica Scandinavica* 37 (1961): 143–67; and Pemberton, "Female and Male Alcoholics."

55. Some research reports no differences. See, for example, Eileen M. Corrigan, *Problem Drinkers Seeking Treatment* (New Brunswick, N.J.: Rutgers Center of Alcohol Studies, 1974); Bernard J. Fitzgerald, Richard A. Pasework and Robert Clark, "Four-year Follow-up of Alcoholics Treated at a Rural State Hospital," *QJSA* 32 (1971): 636 42; D.L. Davies, Michael Sheperd, and Edgar Myers, "The Two-Year Prognosis of Fifty Alcohol Addicts after Treatment in Hospital," *QJSA* 17 (1956): 485 –502; and Donald L. Gerard and Gerhart Sanger, *Outpatient Treatment of Alcoholism*, Brookside monograph no.4, (Toronto: University of Toronto Press, 1966). Other research indicates that women have a higher rate of success: R.J. Crawford, "Treatment Success in Alcoholism," *New Zealand Medical Journal* 84, no.569 (1976): 93–96; Harry Grayson Davis, "Variables Associated with Recovery in Male and Female Alcoholics Following Hospitalization," Ph. D. diss., Texas Technological College, 1966, Vernelle Fox and Marguerite A. Smith, "Evaluation of a Chemopsycho-

therapeutic Program for the Rehabilitation of Alcoholics: Observations over a Two-Year Period," *QJSA* 20 (1959): 767–80; Marvin R. Godfried, "Prediction of Improvement in an Alcoholism Outpatient Clinic," QJSA 30 (1969): 129–39; National Institute of Alcohol Abuse and Alcoholism, *Women in Treatment for Alcoholism: A Profile* (Rockville, Md.: NIAAA, 1977); and Walter L. Voegtlin and William R. Broz, "The Conditioned Reflex Treatment of Chronic Alcoholism. X. An Analysis of 3,125 Admissions over a Period of Ten-and-a-Half Years," *Annals of Internal Medicine* 30 (1949): 580–97. Other research indicates that success rates for women can be greatly increased with a change in treatment: Fox, "Clinical Experiences"; and Schultz, "Radical Feminism."

56. Edwin M. Lemert, *Social Pathology* (New York: McGraw-Hill, 1951), 370.

57. Ibid., 371.

58. Ibid.

59. Lemert, *Human Deviance*, 17.

60. See, for example, Bateman and Peterson, "White Male and "Female Alcoholics"; Curlee, "A Comparison of Male and Female Patients"; de Lint, "Alcoholism"; Demone, Jr., "Alcoholism Clinics"; Glatt, "A Treatment Center"; Glatt, "Drinking Habit"; Glatt, "Treatment Results"; Johnson, "Physicans' Views"; Johnson, DeVries, and Houghton, "The Female Alcoholic"; Karpman, The Woman Alcoholic; Pemberton, "Female and Male Alcoholics"; Rathod and Thompson, "Women Alcoholics"; Rimmer, Pitts, Reich, and Winokur, "Alcoholism II"; Schuckit, "Alcoholic Woman"; Marc A. Schuckit, "Depression and Alcoholism in Women," *Proceedings of the First Annual Alcoholism Conference of the National Institute on Alcohol Abuse and Alcoholism, June 1971* (Washington, D.C.: Department of Health, Education, and Welfare, 1973); A. Balfour Sclare, "The Female Alcoholic," *Journal of Addictions* 65, no.2 (1970): 99–127; Marc Schuckit, Ferris N. Pitts, Jr., Theodore Reich, Luch J. King, and George Winokur, "Alcoholism: I. Two types of Alcoholism in Women," *Archives of General Psychiatry* 20 (1969): 301–6; David M. Spain, "Portal Cirrhosis of the Liver: A Review of Two Hundred Fifty Necropsies with Reference to Sex Differences," *American Journal of Clinical Pathology* 15 (1945): 215–18; Sidney Vogel, "Psychiatric Treatment of Alcoholism," *Annals of the American Academy of Political and Social Sciences* 315 (1968): 99–107; S. Waller and B. Lorch, "Social and Psychological Characteristics of Alcoholics: A Male-Female Comparison," *International Journal of Addictions* 13 (1978): 201–12; P. Wilkinson, J.N. Santamaria, and J.G. Rankin, "Epidemiology of Alcoholic Cirrhosis," *Australas. Ann. Med.* 18 (1969): 222–26; P. Wilkinson, J.N. Santamaria, and J.G. Rankin, "Epidemiology of Alcoholism: Social Data and Drinking Patterns of a Sample of Australian Alcoholics," *Medical Journal of Austrailia* 1 (1969): 1020–25; J.C. Windseth and J. Mayer, "Drinking Behavior and Attitudes toward Delinquent Girls," *International Journal of Addictions* 6 (1971): 453–61; George Winokur and Paula Clayton, "Family History Studies. II. Sex Differences and Alcoholism in Primary Affective Illness," *British Journal of Psychiatry* 113, no.500 (1967): 973–79; George Winokur and Paula Clayton, "Family History Studies. IV. Comparison of Male and Female Alcoholics," *QJSA* 29, no.3 (1968): 885–91; and World Health Organization Expert Committee on Mental Health, Alcoholism Subcommittee, 2nd report, *Technical Report Series No.48* (Geneva: World Health Organization, 1952).

61. See, for example, B. Barraclough, J. Bunch, B. Nelson, and P. Sainsbury, "A Hundred Cases of Suicide; Clinical Aspects," *British Journal of Psychiatry* 125 (1974): 355–73; Horn and Wanberg, "Females are Different"; Parker, "Sex-Role Adjustment"; Rimmer, Pitts, Reich, and Winokur, "Alcoholism II"; John Rimmer, Theodore Reich, and George Winokur, "Alcoholism V. Diagnosis and Clinical

Variations among Alcoholics," *QJSA* 33, no.3 (1972): 658–66; and Wolfgang Schmidt and Jan de Lint, "Mortality Experiences of Male and Female Alcoholic Patients," *QJSA* 30, no.1 (1969): 112–18; and Vogel, "Alcoholism." Some of the studies listed in notes 60 and 61 show results that indicate that women are more pathological in some aspects and men in others.

62. See, for example, the findings of E. Mogar, Wayne Wilson, and Stanley T. Helm, "Personality Subtypes of Male and Female Alcoholic Patients," *International Journal of Addictions* 5, no.1 (1970): 99–113, which show that men were more often ranked in the moderate or severe categories of personality disturbance on the Minnesota Multiphasic Personality Inventory.

63. Lisansky, "The Woman Alcoholic."

64. Lisansky, "Alcoholism in Women."

65. See, for example, John D. Armstrong, "The Search for the Alcoholic Personality," *Annals of the American Academy of Political and Social Sciences* 315 (1958): 40–47; or Jellinek, *Alcoholism,*

66. Jellinek, *Alcoholism,* 35.

67. Most notable are reviews by Beckman "Women Alcoholics"; and Beckman, "Alcoholism Problems."

68. Twila Fort and Ausin L. Porterfield, "Some Backgrounds and Types of Alcoholism among Women," *Journal of Health and Human Behavior* 2, no.1 (1961): 283–92.

69. Rimmer, Reich, and Winokur, "Alcoholism V"; Schuckit, "Depression"; Schuckit, Pitts, Reich, and Winokur, "Alcoholism I"; and Marc A. Schuckit and George Winokur, "A Short-Term Follow-up of Women Alcoholics," *Diseases of the Nervous System* 33 (1972): 672–78.

70. See, for example, Mary Jane Cramer and Edward Blacker, "Social Class and Drinking Experiences of Female Drunkenness Offenders," *Journal of Health and Human Behavior* 7 (1966): 276–83; Barry A. Kinsey, "Psychological Factors in Alcoholic Women from a State Hospital Sample," *American Journal of Psychiatry* 124 (April 1978): 157–60; Lisansky, "Alcoholism in Women"; Lisansky, "The Woman Alcoholic"; and Mayer, Myerson, Needham, and Fox, "The Former Prisoner."

71. John S. Tamerin, P. Neumann, and M.H. Marshall, "The Upper-Class Alcoholic: A Syndrome in Itself ?" *Psychometrics* 12 (1971): 200–204.

72. See, for example, Schmidt and de Lint, "Mortality Experiences."

73. Other research supports this position. See, for example, Kitay, "Beliefs about Women"; Lynn, "Feminine Identification"; McKee and Sherriffs, "The Differential Evaluations"; Rosenkrantz, Vogel, Gee, Broverman, and Broverman, "Sex-Role Stereotypes"; and White, *Educating Our Daughters,*

74. World Health Organization Expert Committee on Mental Health, *Technical Report.*

75. See, for example, Mary J. Ashley, Jack S. Olin, W. Harding le Riche, Alex Kornaczewski, Wolfgang Schmidt, and James G. Rankin, "Morbidity in Alcoholics. Evidence for Accelerated Development of Physical Disease in Women," *Archives of Internal Medicine,* 137, no.7 (1977): 883–87; Bateman and Peterson, "White Male and Female Alcoholics"; Cramer and Blacker, "Social Class"; L. Dahlgreen, "Female Alcoholics. III. Development and Pattern of Problem Drinking," *Acta Psychiatrica Scandinavica* 57 (1978): 325–35; Vera Efron, Mark Keller, and Carol Guriolo, *Statistics on Consumption of Alcohol and on Alcoholism,* (New Brunswick, N.J.: Rutgers Center of Alcohol Studies, 1974); Thomas C. Elder, "Alcoholism and Its Onset in a Population of Admitted Alcoholics (An AA Study)," *British Journal of Addiction* 68 (1973): 291–94; Fort and Porterfield, "Alcoholism among Women"; Glatt, "Drinking Habits"; Jacob and Lavoie, "Women Alcoholics"; Jellinek, "Alcohol Adddiction"; Kinsey, "Psy-

chological Factors"; Lisansky, "Alcoholism in Women"; Rathod and Thompson, "Women Alcoholics"; Schuckit, "Alcoholic Woman"; A. Balfour Sclare, "The Female Alcoholic"; Southerby and Southerby, *Twelve Young Women*; Wanberg and Knapp, "Men and Women Alcoholics"; Wilkinson, Santamaria, Rankin, and Martin, "Epidemiology of Alcoholism," 1020–25; and George Winokur, Theodore Reich, John Rimmer, and Ferris Pitts, "Alcoholism III. Diagnosis and Familial Psychiatric Illness in 259 Alcoholic Probands," *Archives of General Psychiatry* 23, no.2 (1970): 104–11.

76. M.M. Glatt, "Drinking Habits," 179.

Chapter 6. Self-Esteem and the Status Insularity of Female Alcoholics

1. See, for example, Renate G. Armstrong and David B. Hoyt, "Personality Structure of Male Alcoholics as Reflected in the IES Test," *QJSA* 24 (1963): 239–48; Norman L. Berg, "Effects of Alcohol Intoxication on Self-Concept: Studies of Alcoholics and Controls in Laboratory Conditions," *QJSA* 32 (1971): 442–53; Cahn, *The Treatment of Alcoholics*, Howard J. Clinebell, *Understanding and Counseling the Alcoholic through Religion and Psychology* (New York: Abingdon Press, 1968); Otto Fenchinel, *The Psychoanalytic Theory of Neurosis* (New York: Norton, 1945); William H. Fitts, J. Arney, and W. Patton, *A Self-Concept Study of Alcoholic Patients*, Research Monograph no.6, (Nashville, Tenn.: Dede Wallace Center, 1973); Robert Fleming, "Medical Treatment of the Inebriate," in Yale University, Center of Alcohol Studies, eds., *Alcohol, Science, and Society* (Westport, Conn.: Greenwood Press, 1972); William F. Gross and Linda O. Alder, "Aspects of Alcoholics' Self-Concepts as Measured by the Tennessee Self-Concept Scale," *Psychological Reports* 27(1970): 431–34; James A. Vanderpool, "Alcoholism and Self-Concept," *QJSA* 30 (1969): 59–77; and Vogel, "Alcoholism."

2. Fitts et al., *Alcoholic Patients*, 16.

3. See, for example, Linda J. Beckman, "Self-Esteem of Women Alcoholics," *Journal of Studies on Alcohol* 39, no.3 (1978): 491–98; Joan Curlee, "Alcoholism and the 'Empty Nest'," *Bulletin of the Menninger Clinic* 33, no.3 (1969): 165–71. Curran, "Alcoholic Women"; Stephan A. Karp, Dorothy C. Poster, and Allan Goodman, "Differentiation in Alcoholic Women," *Journal of Personality* 31(1963): 386–93; Karpman, *The Alcoholic Woman*; Kinsey, *The Female Alcoholic;* Kinsey, "Psychological Factors"; and Jan Moore, "Recovered Alcoholic: She Turned Her Life About," *Syracuse Hearald-American*, 28 May 1978.

4. See, for example, Anderson, "Women Drinking"; Blane, *Guises of Dependency*; Curlee, "Women Alcoholics"; and Hirsh, "Women and Alcoholism."

5. See, for example, Anderson, "Women Drinking"; Fraser, "The Female Alcoholic"; Langone and Langone, *Women Who Drink*; Moore, "Recovered Alcoholic"; and Moore, "Without Alcohol," *Syracuse Herald-Journal*, 29 May 1978.

6. L. Edward Wells and Gerald Marwell, *Self-Esteem: Its Conceptualization and Measurement*, (Beverly Hills, Calif.: Sage Publications, 1976), 7–8.

7. This section owes much to the expert analysis of Wells and Marwell, *Self-Esteem*, in their examination of how self-esteem has been conceptualized and measured.

8. See William James, *Principles of Psychology*, vol.1 (New York: Henry Holt, 1890).

9. Don Martindale, *The Nature and Types of Sociological Theory* (Boston: Houghton Mifflin, 1960), 347.

10. Charles Horton Cooley, *Human Nature and the Social Order* (New York: Charles Scribner's Sons, 1902), 151–52.

11. Martindale, *Sociological Theory*, 345.

12. Cooley stated,

A formal definition of self-feeling, or indeed any sort of feeling, must be as hollow as a formal definition of the taste of salt, or the color of red; we can expect to know what it is only by experiencing it. There can be no final test of self except the way we feel; it is that towards which we have the "my" attitude. *Human Nature*, 40.

13. See the analysis of this point by Sandra Peterson-Hardt, "The Relationship of Self-Esteem and Achievement Behavior among Low-Income Youth," Ph.D. diss., Syracuse University, 1976.

14. George Herbert Mead, *Mind, Self, and Society*, Charles W. Morris, ed., (Chicago: University of Chicago Press, 1967), 173.

15. Ibid., 158.

16. Ibid.

17. Ibid., 173, emphasis added.

18. Ibid., 178.

19. Ibid., 204.

20. Wells and Marwell, *Self-Esteem*.

21. Ibid., 17, italics in original.

22. Lemert, *Human Deviance*,

23. Wells and Marwell, *Self-Esteem*, 28.

24. Herbert Blumer, *Symbolic Interactionism: Perspective and Method*, (Englewood Cliffs, N.J.: Prentice-Hall, 1969).

25. David Matza, *Becoming Deviant*, (Englewood Cliffs, N.J.: Prentice Hall, 1969), 108, italics in original.

26. Mead, *Mind, Self, and Society*.

27. Blumer, *Symbolic Interactionism*.

28. Ibid., 2.

29. See, for example, S. Frank Miyamoto and Sanford M. Dornbush, "A Test of Interactionist Hypotheses of Self-Conception," *American Journal of Sociology* 61, no.5 (1956): 399–403.

30. See, for example, Walter C. Reckless, Simon Dinitz, and Ellen Murray, "Self-Concept as an Insulator against Delinquency," *American Sociological Review* 21 (1956): 744–46.

31. Wells and Marwell, *Self-Esteem*, 29.

32. See Barney G. Glaser and Anselm L. Strauss, *The Discovery of Grounded Theory: Strategies for Qualitative Research*, (Chicago: Aldine Press, 1967); or Arnold M. Rose ed., *Human Behavior and Social Process: an Interactionist Approach*, (Boston: Houghton Mifflin, 1962).

33. Glaser and Strauss, *The Discovery of Grounded Theory*, 18, italics in original.

34. Arnold M. Rose, "A Systematic Summary of Symbolic Interaction Theory," in Arnold M. Rose, ed., *Human Behavior and Social Process: An Interactionist Approach* (Chicago: Aldine Press, 1967), 3–19.

35. Blumer, *Symbolic Interactionism*, 18.

36. Rose, "A Systematic Summary," 13.

37. Rose, *Human Behavior and Social Process*.

38. Ibid., xii.

39. Arnold M. Rose, "A Social-Psychological Theory of Neurosis," in Arnold M. Rose, ed., *Human Behavior and Social Process: An Interactionist Perspective* (Chicago: Aldine Press, 1967), 3–19.

40. Blumer, *Symbolic Interactionism*, 40–42.

41. Much of the sociological literature on self-esteem and deviance that uses some

form of quantitative methods is guided by Mead's perspective. Such studies as Norman R. Jackman, Richard O'Toole, and Gilbert T. Geis, "The Self-Image of a Prostitute," *Sociological Quarterly* 4 (Spring 1963): 150–61; and Hall, "Self-Evaluation," see the self as created socially, stress the importance of significant others in self-evalution, and are concerned with process.

42. Detailed reviews of research leading to these conclusions can be found in Maccoby and Jacklin, *Sex Differences*; and Florence Ridlon, "Status Insularity and Stigmatization among Female Alcoholics," Ph. D. diss., Syracuse University, 1982.

43. In their summary of studies on self-esteem, Maccoby and Jacklin, *Sex Differences*, list six studies showing that males have higher self-esteem, nine showing women have higher self-esteem, and twenty-four showing no difference between the sexes. See their summary table, 152–53.

44. See the discussion by Maccoby and Jacklin, *Sex Differences*, 155–60.

45. With subjects over eighteen years of age, studies tend to show that men have more of an internal locus of control (See Alan A. Benton, Eric R. Gelber, Harold H. Kelley, and Barry A. Liebling, "Reactions to Various Degrees of Deceit in a Mixed-Motive Relationship," *Journal of Personality and Social Psychology* 12 (1969): 170–80; Gary G. Brannigan and Alexander Tolor, "Sex Differences in Adaptive Styles," *Journal of Genetic Psychology* 119 (1971): 143–49; and N.T. Feather, "Attribution of Responsibility and Valence of Outcomes in Relation to Initial Confidence and Task Performance," *Journal of Personality and Social Psychology* 13 (1969): 129–44. Maccoby and Jacklin, *Sex Differences*, conclude: "What is surprising is that the sex difference in this scale does not emerge earlier in life" (157). Closely related to the internal locus of control are the high scores that men receive on strength and potency on self-concept tests. Various studies of individuals from age six to seventy-nine show unanimously, with a qualification offered by only one of them—Allen M. Goss, "Estimated versus Actual Physical Strength in Three Ethnic Groups," *Child Development* 39 (1968): 283–90—that males have a greater sense of potency and strength. See, for example, Benton et al., "A Mixed-Motive Relationship"; Paul Cameron, "The Generation Gap: Which Generation Is Believed Powerful versus Generational Members' Self-Appraisals of Power," *Developmental Psychology* 3 (1970): 403–4; E.S. Fleming and R.G. Attonen, "Teacher Expectancy as Related to the Academic and Personal Growth of Primary-Age Children," *Monographs of Society for Research in Child Development* 36 (1971); Richard M. Kurtz, "Body Attitude and Self-Esteem," *Proceedings of the 79th Annual Convention of the APA* 8 (1971): 467–68; B.H. Long, E.H. Henderson, and R.C. Ziller, "Developmental Changes in Self-Concept during Middle Childhood," *Merrill-Palmer Quarterly* 13 (1967): 201–15; and Robert L. McDonald, "Effects of Sex, Race, and Class on Self, Ideal-Self, and Parental Ratings in Southern Adolescents," *Perceptual and Motor Skills*, 27: 15–25. Maccoby and Jacklin, *Sex Differences*, call the feeling of control over outcomes, confidence in task performance, and a greater sense of potency a male cluster (258) in self-concept among college students.

46. Jellinek, *Alcoholism*, 29.

47. Knupfer, "Female Drinking Patterns," 142. See Mizruchi and Perrucci "Pre-scription, Proscription and Permissiveness," for a discussion of the low alcoholism rates among Jews.

48. Rathod and Thomson, "Women Alcoholics," 50.

49. See, for example, Bateman and Petersen, "White Male and Female Alcoholics"; Rathod and Thomson, "Women Alcoholics"; Schuckit, "The Alcoholic Woman;" and Winokur and Clayton, "Family History Studies."

50. Wood and Duffy, "Psychological Factors."

51. Kinsey, *The Female Alcoholic*, and Kinsey, "Psychological Factors."

52. Kinsey, *The Female Alcoholic*, 65, footnote.

53. Curlee, "Alcoholism."

54. Southerby and Southerby, *Twelve Young Women*.

55. This research was cited in Fraser, "The Female Alcoholic," 15.

56. Richard A. Nazro, "Gestalt Therapy, Self-Esteem, and the Alcoholic Woman," in Vasanti Burtle, ed., *Women Who Drink*: *Alcoholic Experience and Psychotherapy* (Springfield, Ill.: Charles C. Thomas), 237.

57. Arlene La Fleur Hartson, "The Self Concept of the Alcoholic in-Patient before and after Treatment," master's thesis, University of California, Los Angeles, 1976.

58. Clemmons, "Alcoholism Treatment," 221.

59. Alan Krasanoff, "Self-Reported Attitudes toward Drinking among Alcoholics before and after Treatment," *QJSA* 34 (1973): 947–50.

60. Melvin L. Selzer, "Treatment-Related Factors in Alcoholic Populations," paper presented at American Psychiatric Association's 128th Annual Meeting, Anaheim, California (Rockville, Md.: *National Institute on Alcohol Abuse and Alcoholism*, 1975).

61. See William F. Gross, "Self-Concepts of Alcoholics before and after Treatment," *Journal of Clinical Psychology* (October 1971): 539–41; Ronald D. Page, "Prognosis of the Alcoholic as Indicated by the Tennessee Self-Concept Scale," master's thesis, Purdue University, 1971; and James A. Vanderpool, "Self-Concept Differences in the Alcoholic under Varying Conditions of Drinking and Sobriety, Ph. D. diss., Loyola University, 1966; and Vanderpool, "Alcoholism and Self-Concept."

62. Vasanti Burtle, Doris Whitlock, and Violet Franks, "Modification of Low Self-Esteem in Women Alcoholics: A Behavior Treatment Approach," *Psychotherapy*: *Theory, Research, and Practice* 11, no.1 (1974): 36–40.

63. Ibid., 38.

64. See H. Aronson and Anita Gilbert, "Preadolescent Sons of Male Alcoholics," *Archives of General Psychiatry* 8 (1963): 235–41; Berg, "Effects of Alcohol Intoxication on Self-Concept"; Cahn, *The Treatment of Alcoholics*; Fleming, "Medical Treatment"; David G. Jansen, 1974, reported in Robert R. Knapp, *Handbook for the POI*, (San Diego: EdITS Publishers, 1972); Vanderpool, "Alcoholism and Self-Concept"; Vogel, "Alcoholism"; William R. Weir, "The Use of a Measure of Self-Actualization in the Treatment of Alcoholics and Their Spouses in an Out-Patient Agency," master's thesis, University of North Dakota, 1965; William R. Weir and Eldon M. Gade, "An Approach to Counseling Alcoholics," *Rehabilitation Counseling Bulletin* 12 (June 1969): 227–30; and Joseph S. Zaccaria and William R. Weir, "A Comparison of Alcoholics and Selected Sample of Nonalcoholics in Terms of Positive Concept of Mental Health," *Journal of Social Psychology* 71 (1967): 151–57.

65. Curlee, "Alcoholism"; Curran, "Alcoholic Women"; Karp, Poster, and Goodman, "Alcoholic Women"; Karpman, *The Alcoholic Woman*; Kinsey, *The Female Alcoholic*; and Jan Moore, "Recovered Alcoholic: She Turned Her Life about," *Syracuse Herald-American*, 28 May 1978.

66. Note, for example, the emphasis placed on the problem by the excellent book by the Camberwell Council on Alcoholism, *Women and Alcohol* (London: Tavistock Publications, 1980). Three of the articles (half of the articles on the social or psychological aspects of alcoholism), and the introduction posit low self-esteem as one of the most important problems facing female alcoholics.

67. Many of these sources have been listed in previous notes. See, for example, Kent, *An American Woman*; Kirkpatrick, *Turnabout*, or Tamasi, *I'll Stop Tommorrow*.

68. Blane, *Guises of Dependency*, 112.

69. J.W. Bedell, "The Alcoholic Housewife in American Culture," abstracted in

Susan Issel, Andrae Mitchell, Patricia F. Shanks, and Holly J. Sherwood, *Women and Alcohol: A Selective Annotated Bibliography* (Berkeley, Calif.: State Office of Alcoholism, 1976).

70. Senate Subcommittee on Alcoholism and Narcotics, *Alcohol Abuse among Women*, 418.

71. See, for example, Vasanti Burtle, "Developmental / Learning Correlates of Alcoholism in Women," in Vasanti Burtle, ed., *Women Who Drink: Alcoholic Experience and Psychotherapy* (Springfield, Ill.: Charles C. Thomas, 1979), 170.

72. Langone and Langone, *Women Who Drink*, 65.

73. Tamerin, Tolor, and Harrington, "Sex Differences in Alcoholics."

74. Sandra K. Clarke, "Self-Esteem of Women Alcoholics," *QJSA* 35 (1974): 1380–81.

75. Beckman, "Women Alcoholics."

76. See appendix for details of the research.

77. See David G. Jansen, 1974, reported in Knapp, *Handbook for the POI*; Weir, "The Use of a Measure of Self-Actualization"; Weir and Gade, "Counseling Alcoholics"; and Zaccaria and Weir, "Mental Health."

78. As defined by Everett L. Shostrom, *Manual for the Personal Orientation Inventory*, (San Diego: EdITS / Educational and Industrial Testing Service, 1974). The profile sheet on which scores are plotted are standardized to this normal population.

79. M.A. Kremers, "A Comparison of Members of Alcoholics Anonymous with Practicing Alcoholics and Selected Samples of Nonalcoholics, in Terms of a Positive Concept of Mental Health," unpublished manuscript.

80. See, for example, the Burtle, Whitlock, and Franks, "A Behavior Treatment Approach."

81. E. Mansell Pattison, Ronald Coe, and Robert J. Rhodes, "Evaluation of Alcoholism Treatment," *Archives of General Psychiatry* 20 (1969): 478–88.

82. Mayer, Myerson, Needham, and Fox, "The Former Prisoner."

83. See, for example, Davies, Sheperd, and Myers, "The Two-Year Prognosis of Fifty Alcoholic Addicts"; or Sulammith Wolff and Lydia Holland, "A Questionnaire Follow-up of Alcohol Patients," *QJSA* 25 (1964): 108–19.

84. Cramer and Blacker, "Social Class."

85. Burtle, Whitlock, and Franks, "A Behavior Treatment Approach."

86. Bateman and Peterson, "White Male and Female Alcoholics."

87. Findings from the Burtle et al. and the Bateman and Peterson articles did not agree with Corrigan, *Alcoholic Women*. Corrigan found that professional women, women in the highest SES, and those who were white were significantly more likely to be totally abstinent. The meaning of results of studies on the effect of socioeconomic status on the rehabilitation of both men and women is far from clear at the present time.

88. Emile Durkheim, *Suicide* (Glencoe, Ill.: Free Press, 1951).

Chaper 7. Interpretation and Theoretical Relevance

1. Schur, *Labeling Deviant Behavior*, 70.

2. Cohen, *Delinquent Boys*.

3. Erving Goffman, *Stigma: Notes on the Management of Spoiled Identity*, (Englewood Cliffs, N.J.: Prentice-Hall, 1962).

4. Schur, *Labeling Deviant Behavior*, 77.

5. See, for example, Becker, *Outsiders*; or Earl Rubington, "Variations in Bottle-

Gang Controls," in Earl Rubington and Martin S. Wienberg, eds., *Deviance: The Inter-actionist Perspective*, (New York: MacMillan, 1963).

6. See, for example, Rubington, "Bottle-Gang Controls"; Edwin Schur, *Crimes without Victims*, (Englewood Cliffs, N.J.: Prentice-Hall, 1968); and Martin S. Wien-berg, "Sexual Modesty, Social Meanings, and the Nudist Camp," in Mark Lefton, James K. Skipper, Jr., and Charles H. McCaghy, eds., *Approaches to Deviance: Theories, Concepts, and Research Findings*, (New York: Appleton-Century-Crofts, 1968).

7. Albert D. Ullman, "Sociocultural Backgrounds of Alcoholism," *Annals of the American Academy of Politial and Social Sciences* 315 (1958):50.

8. See, for example, Ruth Bunzel, "The Role of Alcohol in Two Central American Cultures," *Psychiatry* 3 (August 1940): 220–37; Peter B. Field, "A New Cross-Cultural Study of Drunkenness," in David J. Pittman and Charles R. Snyder, eds., *Society, Culture, and Drinking Patterns*, (New York: Wiley, 1962); Dwight B. Heath, "Drinking Patterns in the Bolivian Camba," in David J. Pittman and Charles R. Snyder, eds., *Society, Culture, and Drinking Patterns* (New York: Wiley, 1962); Lemert, *Human Deviance*; William Mangin, "Drinking among Andean Indians," *QJSA* 18 (March 1957): 55–65; and Mizruchi and Perrucci, "Prescription, Proscription, and Permissiveness."

9. Mizruchi and Perrucci, "Prescription, Proscription, and Permissiveness."

10. Robert F. Bales, "Cultural Differences in Rates of Alcoholism," *Quarterly Journal of Studies on Alcohol* 6 (March 1946): 480–99.

11. As represented in Irish drinking practices. See, for example, Robert F. Bales, "Attitudes toward Drinking in the Irish Culture," in David J. Pittman and Charles R. Snyder, eds., *Society, Culture, and Drinking Patterns* (New York: Wiley, 1962).

12. Charles R. Snyder, "Culture and Jewish Sobriety: The In Group-out Group Factor," in David J. Pittman, and Charles R. Snyder, eds., *Society, Culture and Drinking Patterns* (New York: Wiley, 1962).

13. Ibid., 203.

14. Barry Glassner and Bruce Berg, "How Jews Avoid Alcohol Problems," *American Sociological Review* 45 (August 1980): 647–64.

15. Milton L. Barnett, "Alcoholism in the Cantonese of New York City: An Anthropological Study," in Oskar Diethelm, ed., *Etiology of Chronic Alcoholism*, (Springfield, Ill.: Charles C. Thomas, 1955).

16. Giorgio Lolli, Emidio Serrianni, Ferruccio Banissoni, Grace Golder, Aldo Mariani, Raymond G. McCarthy, and Mary Toner, "The Use of Wine and Other Alcoholic Beverages by a Group of Italians and Americans of Italian Extraction," *Quarterly Journal of Studies on Alcohol* 13 (March 1952): 27–48.

17. Knupfer, "Female Drinking Patterns."

18. Sykes and Matza, "Techniques of Neutralization," 669.

19. Reiss, Jr., "Queers and Peers," 381, italics in original.

20. Davis, *Deviance*, 219.

21. Ibid., 220.

22. See, for example, Swartz and Skolnick, "Legal Stigma."

23. See Schur, *Labeling Deviant Behavior*, 148–58.

24. Ibid., 157.

25. Ibid., 152.

26. See, for example, Block, "Physicians Duty"; Don Cahalan, Ira H. Cisin, and Helen M. Crossley, "American Drinking Practices: A National Study of Drinking Behavior and Attitudes," *Rutgers Center of Alcohol Studies, Monograph no. 6*, (New Brunswick, N.J.: Rutgers Center of Alcohol Studies, 1969); Cramer and Blacker, "Social Class"; Fraser, "The Female Alcoholic"; and Mayer, Myerson, Needham, and Fox, "The Former Prisoner."

27. Earl Rubington, "The Hidden Alcoholic," *QJSA*, 33 (1972): 667–683.

28. Ibid., 677.

29. Ibid., 677.

30. Rubington, "Bottle-Gang Controls" 667; emphasis added.

31. Ibid.

32. William J. Chambliss and Robert B. Seidman, *Law, Order, and Power*, (Reading, Mass.: Addison-Wesley, 1971), 333.

33. Aaron Circourel, *The Social Organization of Juvenile Justice* (New York: Wiley, 1968).

34. Chambliss and Seidman, *Law, Order, and Power*, 333.

35. Rubington, "The Hidden Alcoholic," 678.

36. Edwin H. Sutherland, *White Collar Crime*, (New York: Holt, Rinehart, and Winston, 1949), 9.

37. Ibid.

38. See, for example, Donald R. Cressey, "The Respectable Criminal," in James F. Short, Jr., ed., *Modern Criminals* (Chicago: Aldine, 1970); Gilbert Geis, ed., *White-Collar Criminal* (New York: Athernon, 1968); Ferdinand Lundberg, *The Rich and the Superrich* (New York: Bantam, 1969); and Donald J. Newman, "Public Attitudes toward a Form of White Collar Crime," *Social Problems* 4 (1957): 228–32.

39. Herbert Edlehertz, "The Nature, Impact, and Prosecution of White Collar Crime," in Simon Dinitz, Russell R. Dynes, and Alfred C. Clarke, eds., *Deviance: Studies in Definition, Management, and Treatment* (New York: Oxford University Press, 1975).

40. President's Commission on Law Enforcement and the Administration of Justice, *The Challenge of Crime in a Free Society* (Washington, D.C.: Government Printing Office, 1967).

41. Simon Dinitiz, Russell R. Dynes, and Alfred C. Clarke, *Deviance: Studies in Definition, Management, and Treatment* (New York: Oxford University Press, 1975), 111.

42. Chambliss and Siedman, *Law, Order, and Power*.

43. Ibid., 199.

44. Herbert Edlehertz, "White Collar Crime," 147.

45. William F. Kenkel and Ellen Voland, *Society in Action*, (San Francisco: Canfield Press, 1975), 520.

46. See, for example, Cressey, "The Respectable Criminal"; Dinitiz, Dynes, and Clarke, *Deviance*; Edlehertz, "White Collar Crime"; Gilbert Geis, *White-Collar Criminal*; Lundberg, *The Rich and the Superrich*; Newman, "Public Attitudes"; and Sutherland, *White Collar Crime*.

47. Davis, *Deviance*, 219.

48. Ibid.

49. Davis, *Deviance*.

50. Becker, *Outsiders*.

51. See, for example, Chambliss and Seidman, *Law, Order, and Power*; William Ryan, *Blaming the Victim*, (New York: Vintage, 1971); Bruce Wasserstein and Mark J. Green, eds., *Justice for Some*, (Boston: Beacon, 1972); and Marvin E. Wolfgang, *Crime and Race: Conceptions and Misconceptions*, (New York: Institute on Human Relations, 1964).

52. Chambliss and Seidman, *Law, Order, and Power*.

53. Ibid., 475.

54. See, for example, Milton L. Barron, *The Juvenile Delinquent in Society*, (New York: Alfred A. Knopf, 1956); Chambliss and Seidman, *Law, Order, and Power*; Lamar T. Empey and and Maynard L. Erickson, "Hidden Delinquency and Social Status,"

Social Forces 74, no.4 (1966): 546–54; Martin Gold, "Undetected Delinquent Behavior," *Journal of Research on Crime and Delinquency* 3 (1966): 44; William Kvaraceus, *What Research Says to the Teacher*: *Juvenile Delinquecny*, (Washington, D.C.: National Education Association, 1958); Clemet S. Mihanovich, "Who Is the Juvenile Delinquent?" *Social Science* 22 (1947): 45–50; Ivan F. Nye, James F. Short, and Virgil Olson, "Socioeconomic Status and Delinquent Behavior," *American Journal of Sociology* 63, no.3 (1957): 381–89; Irving Pivilian and Scott Briar, "Police Encounters with Juveniles," *American Journal of Sociology* 69 (September 1964): 206–14; Sophia M. Robinson, *Can Delinquency Be Measured?*, (New York: Columbia University Press, 1936); Edward Schwartz, "A Community Experiment in the Measurement of Juvenile Delinquency," in Marjorie Bell, ed., *National Probation Association Yearbook* (New York: National Probation Association, 1945); Jeremiah Shalloo, "Youth and Crime," *Annals of the American Academy of Political and Social Science* 194 (November 1937): 79–86; and Wasserstein and Green, eds., *Justice for Some*.

55. See the argument by Howard S. Becker in *Outsiders* and "Whose Side Are We on?" *Social Problems* 14 (Winter 1967): 239–47.

56. Becker, "Whose Side Are We on?" 242.

57. Rosenhan, "On Being Sane."

58. Erving Goffman, *Asylums*: *Essays on the Social Situation of Mental Patients and Other Inmates*, (Garden City, N.J.: Prentice-Hall, 1961).

59. Chambliss and Seidman, *Law, Order, and Power*.

60. Gouldner, "The Sociologist as Partisan."

61. Isidor Walliman, Howard Rosenbaum, Nicholas Tatsis, and George Zito, "Misreading Weber: The Concept of 'Macht', " *Sociology*: *The Journal of the British Sociological Association* 14, no.2 (1980): 266, italics in original.

62. Chambliss and Seidman, *Law, Order, and Power*, 341.

63. Ibid.

64. Davis, *Deviance*.

65. Chambliss and Seidman, *Law, Order, and Power*.

66. Davis, *Deviance* 176.

67. See Chambliss and Seidman, *Law, Order, and Power*; and Davis, *Deviance*.

68. Arrests occur, but these are in relation to other actions, such as vagrancy or driving while intoxicated, not for the act of drinking or alcoholism itself.

69. In some cases, those in powerful positions suffer few legal or nonlegal sanctions. As noted earlier in chapter 4, doctors who are sued for malpractice seem to suffer little from the labeling process.

Appendix: Report of Research on the Self-Esteem of Female Alcoholics

1. Ridlon, "Status Insularity and Stigmatization."

2. Harold A. Mulford, "Drinking and Deviant Drinking, U.S.A., 1963," *QJSA* 25 (1963): 634–50.

3. Don Cahalan, Ira H. Cisin, and Helen M. Crossley, *American Drinking Practices*: *A National Survey of Behavior and Attitudes Related to Alcoholic Beverages*, Social Science Group Report no.3 (Washington, D.C.: Washington University, 1967); or Cahalan, Cisin, and Crossley, *American Drinking Practices*.

4. Wells and Marwell, *Self-Esteem*, 48.

5. Abraham H. Maslow, *Toward a Psychology of Being*, (New York: Van Nostrand Reinhold, 1968).

6. Ibid., 46.

7. Abraham H. Maslow, *Motivation and Personality*, 2d ed. (New York: Harper and Row, 1970).

8. Everett L. Shostrom, *Personal Orientation Inventory: An Inventory for the Measurement of Self-Actualization*, (San Diego: Educational and Industrial Testing Service, 1974).

9. Abraham H. Maslow, *The Farther Reaches of Human Nature*, (New York: Viking, 1971).

10. Wells and Marwell, *Self-Esteem*, 39.

11. This distinction is elucidated by Wells and Marwell in *Self-Esteem*, 3.

12. Shostrom, *Personal Orientation Inventory*, 4.

13. Wells and Marwell, *Self-Esteem*, 78.

14. See reviews of research in Knapp, *Handbook for the POI*; or Ridlon, "Status Insularity and Stigmatization."

15. Shostrom, *Personal Orientation Inventory*, 6.

16. See, for example, Vernon J. Damm, "Overall Measures of Self-Actualization Derived from the Personal Orientation Inventory," *Educational and Psychological Measurement* 29 (1969): 977–81; or Vernon J. Damm, "Overall Measures of Self-Actualization Derived from the Personal Orientation Inventory: A Replication and Refinement Study," *Educational and Psychological Measurement* 32 (1972): 485–89; or Robert R. Knapp, "Relationship of a Measure of Self-Actualization to Neuroticism and Extraversion," *Journal of Consulting Psychology* 29 (1965): 168–72.

17. Knapp, *Handbook*, 5.

18. Shostrom, *Manual*, 17.

19. See, for example, the Twenty-Statements Test (TST) associated with Manford H. Kuhn, "Self-Attitudes by Sex and Professional Training," *Sociological Quarterly* 1 (1960): 39–55. It is an instrument "derived from and usually scored in accordance with symbolic interaction theory" (Stephen P. Spitzer, "Test Equivalence of Unstructured Self-Evaluation Instruments," *Sociological Quarterly* 10, no.2 [1969]: 204).

20. See the discussion by Knapp, *Handbook*, and Ridlon, "Status Insularity and Stigmatization," on the validity of the POI.

21. Weir and Gade, "Counseling Alcoholics."

22. See Ridlon, "Status Insularity and Stigmatization," 213–21.

23. Knapp, *Handbook*, 76.

24. Especially for alcoholics are Weir, "The Use of a Measure of Self-Actualization"; William R. Weir, research cited in Shostrom, *Personal Orientation Inventory*, 12; and Zaccaria and Weir, "Mental Health"; and for drug abusers, see A. G. Cyrns, "Personality Characteristics of Heroin Addicts in a Methadone Treatment Program: An Exploratory Study," *International Journal of Addictions* 9 (1974): 255–66; and Peter K. Kilmann, "Self-Actualization of Female Narcotic Drug Addicts," *Journal of Clinical Psychology* 30 (1974): 308–10.

25. See Knapp, *Handbook*; and Shostrom, *Personal Orientation Inventory*, for summaries of research that has been conducted using the POI.

26. See Weir, "The Use of a Measure of Self-Actualization"; William R. Weir, research cited in Shostrom, *Personal Orientation Inventory*; and Joseph S. Zaccaria and William R. Weir, "Mental Health."

27. Shostrom, *Personal Orientation Inventory*.

28. David G. Jansen, reported in Knapp, *Handbook*.

29. Knapp, *Handbook*, 63.

30. Ibid.

31. Marital status, education, and age were asked on the POI answer sheet.

32. See David G. Jansen, reported in Knapp, *Handbook*; Kremers, "A Comparison"; and Zaccaria and Weir, "Mental Health."

33. Kremers, "A Comparison."

34. James A. Davis, *National Data Program for the Social Sciences: Code Book for the Spring of 1972*, Chicago, Ill.: National Opinion Research Center.

35. Durkheim, *Suicide*.

36. Bateman and Peterson, "White Male and Female Alcoholics."

37. Ridlon, "Status Insularity and Stigmatization."

38. It should be noted that the differences in means is not between the same person at two different times; other factors could account for these differences. However, data are sufficient to suggest that the kind of process we expected to find may indeed be taking place.

39. See Durkheim, *Suicide*.

Bibliography

Abram, Harry S., and William F. McCourt. 1964. "Interaction of Physicians with Emergency Ward Alcoholic Patients." *Quarterly Journal of Studies on Alcohol* 25: 679–88.

Anderson, George M. 1977. "Women Drinking: Stigma and Sickness." *America* (December): 434–37.

Angeriou, Milton, and Donna Paulino. 1976. "Women Arrested for Drunken Driving in Boston: Social Characteristics and Circumstances of Arrest." *Journal of Studies on Alcohol* 373, no.5: 648–58.

Armstrong, John D. 1958. "The Search for the Alcoholic Personality." *Annals of the American Academy of Political and Social Sciences* 315: 40–47.

Armstrong, Renate G., and David B. Hoyt. 1963. "Personality Structure of Male Alcoholics as Reflected in the IES Test." *Quarterly Journal of Studies on Alcohol* 24: 239–48.

Aronson, H., and Anita Gilbert. 1963. "Preadolescent Sons of Male Alcoholics." *Archives of General Psychiatry* 8: 235–41.

Ashley, Mary J., Jack S. Olin, W. Harding le Riche, Alex Kornaczewski, Wolfgang Schmidt, and James G. Rankin. 1977. "Morbidity in Alcoholics. Evidence for Accelerated Development of Physical Disease in Women." *Archives of Internal Medicine* 137, no.7: 883–87.

Astin, Helen S. 1969. *The Woman Doctorate in America*. Hartford, Conn.: Russell Sage Foundation.

Bachtold, Louise M., and Emmy E. Werner. 1970. "Personality Profiles of Gifted Women: Psychologists." *American Psychologist* 25: 234–43.

Bacon, Selden D. 1972. "Excessive Drinking and the Institution of the Family." In *Alcohol, Science, and Society*, Yale University Center of Alcohol Studies, ed. Westport, Conn.: Greenwood Press.

Bailey, Margaret B. 1961. "Alcoholism and Marriage: A Review of Research and Progressional Literature." *Quarterly Journal of Studies on Alcohol* 22: 81–97.

Bales, Robert F. 1946. "Cultural Differences in Rates of Alcoholism." *Quarterly Journal of Studies on Alcohol* 6 (March): 480–499.

———. 1962. "Attitudes toward Drinking in the Irish Culture." In *Society, Culture, and Drinking Patterns*, David J. Pittman and Charles R. Snyder, eds. New York: Wiley.

Bandura, Albert 1965. "Influence of Models' Reinforcement Contingencies on the Acquisition of Imitative Responses." *Journal of Personality and Social Psychology* 1: 589–95.

Barnes, Grace M., and Marcia Russel. 1978. "Drinking Patterns in Western New York State: Comparison with National Data." *Journal of Studies on Alcohol* 39,no.7: 1148–57.

Barnett, Milton L. 1955. "Alcoholism in the Cantonese of New York City: An

Anthropological Study." In *Etiology of Chronic Alcoholism*, Oskar Diethelm, ed. Springfield, Ill.: Charles C. Thomas.

Barraclough, B., J. Bunch, B. Nelson, and P. Sainsbury. 1974. "A Hundred Cases of Suicide: Clinical Aspects." *British Journal of Psychiatry* 125: 355–73.

Barron, Milton L. 1956. *The Juvenile Delinquent in Society*. New York: Alfred A. Knopf.

Bateman, Nils I., and David M. Peterson. 1972. "Factors Related to Outcome of Treatment for Hospital White Male and Female Alcoholics." *Journal of Drug Issues* 2: 66–74.

Becker, Howard S. 1963. *Outsiders: Studies in the Sociology of Deviance*. New York: Free Press.

_____. 1967. "Whose Side Are We on?" *Social Problems* 14 (Winter): 239–47.

Beckman, Linda J. 1975. "Women Alcoholics: A Review of Social and Psychological Studies." *Journal of Studies on Alcohol* 36, no.7: 797–824.

_____. 1976. "Alcoholism Problems and Women: An Overview." In *Alcoholism Problems in Women and Children*, Milton Greenblatt and Marc A. Schuckit, eds. New York: Grune and Stratton.

_____. 1978. "Self-Esteem of Women Alcoholics." *Journal of Studies on Alcohol* 39, no. 3: 491–98.

Bedell, J.W. 1973. "The Alcoholic Housewife in American Culture." Abstracted in *Women and Alcohol: A Selective Annotated Bibliography*, Susan M. Issel, Andrae Mitchell, Patricia F. Shanks, and Holly J. Sherwood. Berkeley, Calif.: State Office of Alcoholism, 1976.

Belfer, Myron L., Richard I. Shrader, Mary Carroll, and Jerold Harmatz. 1971. "Alcoholism in Women." *Archives of General Psychiatry* 25 (December): 540–44.

Benton, Alan A., Eric R. Gelber, Harold H. Kelley, and Barry A. Liebling. 1969. "Reactions to Various Degrees of Deceit in a Mixed-Motive Relationship." *Journal of Personality and Social Psychology* 12: 170–80.

Berg, Norman L. 1971. "Effects of Alcohol Intoxication on Self-Concept: Studies of Alcoholics and Controls in Laboratory Conditions." *Quarterly Journal of Studies on Alcohol* 32: 442–53.

Blane, Howard T. 1968. *The Personality of the Alcoholic: Guises of Dependency*. New York: Harper and Row.

Block, Marvin A. 1952. "Alcoholism: The Physician's Duty." *General Practitioner* 6, no. 3: 55–58.

_____. 1965. *Alcoholism: Its Facets and Phases*. New York: John Day Company.

Blumer, Herbert. 1969. *Symbolic Interactionism: Perspective and Method*. Englewood Cliffs, N.J.: Prentice-Hall.

Brannigan, Gary G., and Alexander Tolor. 1971. "Sex Differences in Adaptive Styles." *Journal of Genetic Psychology* 119: 143–49.

Broom, Leonard, and Philip Selznick. 1963. *Sociology: A Text of Adapted Readings*. New York: Harper and Row.

Broverman, Inge K., Donald M. Broverman, Frank E. Clarkson, Paul S. Rosenkranz, and Susan R. Vogel. 1970. "Sex-Role Stereotypes and Clinical Judgments of Mental Health." *Journal of Consulting and Clinical Psychology* 34, no.1: 1–7.

Buikhuisen, Wouter, and Fokke P.H. Dijksterhuis. 1971. "Delinquency and Stigmatisation." *British Journal of Criminology* 11, no.2: 185–87.

Bunzel, Ruth. 1940. "The Role of Alcohol in Two Central American Cultures."

Psychiatry 3 (August): 220–37.

Burnum, John F. 1974. "Outlook for Treating Patients with Self-Destructive Habits." *Annals of Internal Medicine* 81, no.3: 387–93.

Burtle, Vasanti, ed. 1979. *Women Who Drink: Alcoholic Experience and Psychotherapy.* Springfield, Ill.: Charles C. Thomas.

Burtle, Vasanti, Doris Whitlock, and Violet Franks. 1974. "Modification of Low Self-Esteem in Women Alcoholics: A Behavior Treatment Approach." *Psychotherapy: Theory, Research, and Practice* 11, no.1: 36–40.

Cahalan, Don, Ira H. Cisin, and Helen M. Crossley. 1967. *American Drinking Practices: A National Survey of Behavior and Attitudes Related to Alcoholic Beverages.* Social Science Group Report no.3. Washington, D.C.: Washington University Press.

―――. 1969. *American Drinking Practices: A National Study of Drinking Behavior and Attitudes.* Monograph No. 6. New Brunswick, N.J.: Rutgers Center of Alcohol Studies.

Cahn, Sidney. 1970. *The Treatment of Alcoholics: An Evaluative Study.* New York: Oxford University Press.

Camberwell Council on Alcoholism. 1980. *Women and Alcohol.* London: Tavistock Publications.

Cameron, Paul 1970. "The Generation Gap: Which Generation Is Believed Powerful versus Generational Members' Self-Appraisals of Power." *Developmental Psychology* 3: 403–4.

Cara. 1979. "Women and Alcohol: A Close-up." In *Women Who Drink: Alcoholic Experience and Psychotherapy,* Vasanti Burtle, ed. Springfield, Ill.: Charles C. Thomas.

Cartwright, Lillian Kaufman 1970. "Women in Medical School." Ph.D. diss., University of California, Berkeley.

Carver, Virginia. 1977. "The Female Alcoholic in Treatment." *Canadian Psychological Review* 18, no.1: 96–103.

Chalfant, H. Paul; and Brent S. Roper. 1980. *Social and Behavioral Aspects of Female Alcoholism: An Annotated Bibliography,* Westport, Conn.: Greenwood Press.

Chambliss, William J., and Robert B. Seidman. 1971. *Law, Order, and Power.* Reading, Mass.: Addison-Wesley.

Christenson, Susan J., and Alice Q. Swanson. 1974. "Women and Drug Use: An Annotated Bibliography." *Journal of Psychedelic Drugs* 16, no.4: 371–414.

Circourel, Aaron. 1968. *The Social Organization of Juvenile Justice.* New York: Wiley.

Clark, Walter C. 1967. "Sex Roles and Alcoholic Beverage Usage," Working paper no.16. Mental Research Institute Drinking Practices Study.

Clarke, Sandra K. 1974. "Self-Esteem of Women Alcoholics." *Quarterly Journal of Studies on Alcohol* 35: 1380–81.

Clemmons, Penny. 1979. "A Comprehensive Psychoanalytic Approach to Alcoholism Treatment." In *Women Who Drink: Alcoholic Experience and Psychotherapy,* Vasanti Burtle, ed. Springfield, Ill.: Charles C. Thomas.

―――. 1979. "Issues in Marriage and the Family and Child Counseling in Alcoholism." In *Women Who Drink: Alcoholic Experience and Psychotherapy,* Vasanti Burtle, ed. Springfield, Ill.: Charles C. Thomas.

Clinebell, Howard J. 1968. *Understanding and Counseling the Alcoholic through Religion and Psychology.* New York: Abingdon Press.

Cohen, Albert K. 1955. *Delinquent Boys: The Culture of the Gang,* New York: Free Press.

Cooley, Charles Horton. 1902. *Human Nature and the Social Order*. New York: Charles Scribner's Sons.

Corrigan, Eileen M. 1974. *Problem Drinkers Seeking Treatment*. New Brunswick, N.J.: Rutgers Center of Alcohol Studies.

_____. 1980. *Alcoholic Women in Treatment*. New York: Oxford University Press.

Coser, Lewis A., and Bernard Rosenberg. 1982. *Sociological Theory: A Book of Readings*. 5th ed. New York: Macmillan.

Cramer, Mary Jane, and Edward Blacker. 1966. "Social Class and Drinking Experiences of Female Drunkenness Offenders." *Journal of Health and Human Behavior* 7: 276–83.

Crawford, R. J. 1976. "Treatment Success in Alcoholism." *New Zealand Medical Journal* 84, no.569: 93–96.

Cressey, Donald R. 1970. "The Respectable Criminal." In *Modern Criminals*, James F. Short, Jr., ed. Chicago: Aldine.

Curlee, Joan. 1967. "Alcoholic Women: Some Considerations for Further Research." *Bulletin of the Menninger Clinic* 31: 154–63.

_____. 1968. "Women Alcoholics." *Federal Probation* 32, no.1: 16–20.

_____. 1969. "Alcoholism and the 'Empty Nest,'" *Bulletin of the Menninger Clinic* 33, no.3: 165–71.

_____. 1970. "A Comparison of Male and Female Patients at an Alcoholism Treatment Center." *Journal of Psychology* 74 (January): 239–47.

_____. 1971. "Sex Differences in Patient Attitudes towards Alcoholism." *Quarterly Journal of Studies on Alcohol* 32: 643–50.

Curran Frank J. 1937. "Personality Studies in Alcoholic Women." *Journal of Nervous and Mental Disease* 86, no.6: 643–67.

Cyrns, A. G. 1974. "Personality Characteristics of Heroin Addicts in a Methadone Treatment Program: An Exploratory Study." *International Journal of Addictions* 9: 255–66.

Dahlgreen, L. 1978. "Female Alcoholics. III. Development and Pattern of Problem Drinking." *Acta Psychiatrica Scandinavica* 57: 325–35.

Damm, Vernon J. 1969. "Overall Measures of Self-Actualization Derived from the Personal Orientation Inventory." *Educational and Psychological Measurement* 29: 977–81.

_____. 1972. "Overall Measures of Self-Actualization Derived from the Personal Orientation Inventory: A Replication and Refinement Study." *Educational and Psychological Measurement* 32: 485–89.

Davidson, Anne F. 1976. "Evaluation of the Treatment and Aftercare of a Hundred Alcoholics." *British Journal of Addiction* 71: 217–24.

Davies, D. L., Michael Sheperd, and Edgar Myers. 1956. "The Two-Year Prognosis of Fifty Alcohol Addicts after Treatment in Hospital." *Quarterly Journal of Studies on Alcohol* 17: 485–502.

Davis, James A. *National Data Program for the Social Sciences: Code Book for the Spring of 1972*, Chicago, Ill.: National Opinion Research Center.

Davis, Harry Grayson. 1966. "Variables Associated with Recovery in Male and Female Alcoholics Following Hospitalization." Ph.D. diss., Texas Technological College.

Davis, Nanette J. 1975. *Sociological Constructions of Deviance*, Dubuque, Iowa: Wm. C. Brown.

de Lint, Jan E.E. 1964. "Alcoholism, Birth Rank, and Parental Deprivation." *American Journal of Psychiatry* 120:1062–65.

Demone, Harold W., Jr. 1963. "Experiments in Referral to Alcoholism Clinics." *Quarterly Journal of Studies on Alcohol* 24: 495–502.

Dinitz, Simon, Russell R. Dynes, and Alfred C. Clarke. 1975. *Deviance: Studies in Definition, Management, and Treatment*. New York: Oxford University Press.

Draper, Patricia. 1975. "!Kung Women: Contrasts in Sexual Egalitarianism in Foraging and Sedentary Contexts." In *Toward an Anthropology of Women*, Rayna R. Reiter, ed. New York: Monthly Review Press.

Durkheim, Emile. 1951. *Suicide*. Glencoe, Ill.: Free Press.

Ebbe, Curtis H., and Charles E. McKeown. 1953. "An Evaluation of the Use of Tetraethylthiuram Disulfide in the Treatment of 560 Cases of Alcohol Addiction." *American Journal of Psychiatry* 109: 670–73.

Edlehertz, Herbert. 1975. "The Nature, Impact, and Prosecution of White Collar Crime." In *Deviance: Studies in Definition, Management, and Treatment*, Simon Dinitz, Russell R. Dynes, and Alfred C. Clarke, eds. New York: Oxford University Press.

Edwards, Patricia, Cheryl Harvey, and Paul C. Whitehead. 1973. "Wives of Alcoholics: A Critical Review and Analysis." *Quarterly Journal of Studies on Alcohol* 34: 112 –32.

Efron, Vera, Mark Keller, and Carol Guriolo. 1974. *Statistics on Consumption of Alcohol and on Alcoholism*. New Brunswick, N.J.: Rutgers Center of Alcohol Studies.

Elder, Thomas C. 1973. "Alcoholism and Its Onset in a Population of Admitted Alcoholics (An AA Study)." *British Journal of Addiction* 68: 291–94.

Empey, Lamar T., and Maynard L. Erickson. 1966. "Hidden Delinquency and Social Status." *Social Forces* 74, no.4: 546–54.

English, Horace, and Eva C.English. 1958. *A Comprehensive Dictionary of Psychological and Psychoanalytic Terms*. New York: Logmans, Green.

Fad, Gayle, ed. 1970. *Woman's Role in Aboriginal Society*. Australian Aboriginal Studies no.36. Canberra: Australian National Institute of Aboriginal Studies.

Farrell, Ronald A., and James F. Nelson. 1976. "A Causal Model of Secondary Deviance: The Case of Homosexuality." *Sociological Quarterly* 17 (Winter): 109–20.

Feather, N. T. 1969. "Attribution of Responsibility and Valence of Outcomes in Relation to Initial Confidence and Task Performance." *Journal of Personality and Social Psychology* 13: 129–44.

Fenchinel, Otto. 1945. *The Psychoanalytic Theory of Neurosis*. New York: Norton.

Field, Peter B. 1962. "A New Cross-Cultural Study of Drunkenness." In *Society, Culture, and Drinking Patterns*, David J. Pittman and Charles R. Snyder, eds. New York: Wiley.

Fitts, William H., J. Arney, and W. Patton. 1973. *A Self-Concept Study of Alcoholic Patients*. Research Monograph no. 6. Nashville: Dede Wallace Center.

Fitzgerald, Bernard J., Richard A. Pasework, and Robert Clark. 1971. "Four-Year Follow-up of Alcoholics Treated at a Rural State Hospital." *Quarterly Journal of Studies on Alcohol* 32: 636–42.

Fleming, E. S., and R. G. Attonen. 1971. "Teacher Expectancy as Related to the

Academic and Personal Growth of Primary-Age Children." *Monographs of Society for Research in Child Development* 36.

Fleming, Robert. 1972. "Medical Treatment of the Inebriate." In *Alcohol, Science, and Society*, Yale University, Center of Alcohol Studies, eds. Westport, Conn.: Greenwood Press.

Ford, Betty. 1978. *The Times of My Life*. New York: Harper and Row and the Reader's Digest.

Fort, Twila, and Ausin L. Porterfield. 1961. "Some Backgrounds and Types of Alcoholism among Women." *Journal of Health and Human Behavior* 2, no.1: 283–92.

Fox, Ruth. 1956. "The Alcoholic Spouse." In *Neurotic Interaction in Marriage*, Victor W. Einstein, ed. New York: Basic Books.

Fox, Vernelle. 1979. "Clinical Experiences in Working with Women with Alcoholism." In *Women Who Drink*, Vasanti Burtle, ed. Springfield, Ill.: Charles C. Thomas.

Fox, Vernelle, and Marguerite A. Smith. 1959. "Evaluation of a Chemopsychotherapeutic Program for the Rehabilitation of Alcoholics: Observations over a Two-Year Period." *Quarterly Journal of Studies on Alcohol* 20: 767–80.

Fraser, Judy. 1973. "The Female Alcoholic." *Addictions* 20: 371–414. Reprint. 1974. Toronto: Addiction Research Foundation, 1–16.

Friedland, Seymor J., Walter Crockett, and James D. Laird. 1973. "The Effects of Role and Sex on the Perception of Others." *Journal of Social Psychology* 91: 273–83.

Futterman, Samuel 1953. "Personality Trends in Wives of Alcoholics." *Journal of Psychiatric Social Work* 23: 37–41.

Galton, Lawrence. 1978. "Alcoholism in Women: The Hidden Epidemic." *Syracuse Herald-American Parade*, 5 February, 10–15.

Gardner, Joann. 1971. "Sexist Counseling Must Stop." *Personnel and Guidance Journal* 49: 705–14

Garret, Gerald R., and Howard M. Bahr. 1974. "Comparison of Self-Rating and Quantity Frequency Measures of Drinking." *Quarterly Journal of Studies on Alcohol* 35: 1294–1306.

Garske, John P. 1975. "Role Variation as a Determinant of Attributed Masculinity and Femininity." *Journal of Psychology* 91: 31–37.

Geis, Gilbert, ed. 1968. *White-Collar Criminal*. New York: Athernon.

Gerard, Donald L., and Gerhart Sanger. 1966. *Outpatient Treatment of Alcoholism*. Brookside monograph no. 4. Toronto: Univerity of Toronto Press.

Gibbs, Jack P. 1968. "Conceptions of Deviant Behavior: The Old and the New." In *Approaches to Deviance: Theories, Concepts, and Research Findings*, Mark Lefton, Jawmes K. Skipper, Jr., and Charles H. McCaghy, eds. New York: Appleton-Century-Croft.

Ginzberg, Eli 1966. *Life Styles of Educated Women*. New York: Columbia University Press.

Glaser, Barney G., and Anselm L. Strauss. 1967. *The Discovery of Grounded Theory: Strategies for Qualitative Research*. Chicago: Aldine Press.

Glassner Barry. 1982. "Labeling Theory." In *The Sociology of Deviance*, M. Michael Rosenberg, Robert A. Stebbins, and Allan Turowetz, eds. New York: St. Martin's Press.

Glassner, Barry, and Bruce Berg. 1980. "How Jews Avoid Alcohol Problems." *American Sociological Review* 45 (August): 647–64.

Glatt, M.M. 1955. "A Treatment Center for Alcoholics in a Public Mental Hospital: Its Establishment and Working." *British Journal of Addiction* 52: 55–92.

_____. 1961. "Drinking Habits of English (Middle-Class) Alcoholics." *Acta Psychiatrica Scandinavica* 37: 88–113.

_____. 1961. "Treatment Results in an English Mental Hospital Unit." *Acta Psychiatrica Scandinavica* 37: 143–67.

Godfried, Marvin R. 1969. "Prediction of Improvement in an Alcoholism Outpatient Clinic." *Quarterly Journal of Studies on Alcohol* 30: 129–39.

Goffman, Erving. 1961. *Asylums: Essays on the Social Situation of Mental Patients and Other Inmates*. Garden City, N.J.: Prentice–Hall.

_____. 1963. *Stigma: Notes on the Management of Spoiled Identity*. Englewood Cliffs, N.J.: Prentice-Hall.

Gold, Martin. 1966. "Undetected Delinquent Behavior." *Journal of Research on Crime and Delinquency* 3:44.

Gomberg, Edith S. 1974. "Women and Alcoholism." In *Women in Therapy: New Psychotherapies for a Changing Society*, Violet Franks and Vasanti Burtle, eds. New York: Brumer / Mazel.

Goss, Allen M. 1968. "Estimated versus Actual Physical Strength in Three Ethnic Groups." *Child Development* 39: 283–90.

Gouldner, Alvin W. "The Sociologist as Partisan: Sociology and the Welfare State." 1968. *American Sociologist* (May): 103–16.

Gove, Walter R. 1980. *The Labelling of Deviance: Evaluating a Perspective*. 2d ed. Beverly Hills, Calif.: Sage Publications.

Gross, William F. 1971. "Self–Concepts of Alcoholics before and after Treatment." *Journal of Clinical Psychology* (October): 539–41.

Gross, William F., and Linda O. Alder. 1970. "Aspects of Alcoholics' Self-Concepts as Measured by the Tennessee Self–Concept Scale." *Psychological Reports* 27: 431–34.

Hall, Peter M. 1966. "Identification with Delinquent Subculture and Level of Self-Evaluation." *Sociometry* 29(June): 146–58.

Hammersmith, Sue Kiefer, and Martin S. Weinberg. 1973. "Homosexual Identity: Commitment, Adjustment, and Significant Others." *Sociometry* 36, no.1: 56–79.

Hartson, Arlene La Fleur. 1976. "The Self-Concept of the Alcoholic in-Patient before and after Treatment." Master's thesis, University of California, Los Angeles.

Heath, Dwight B. 1962. "Drinking Patterns in the Bolivian Camba." In *Society, Culture, and Drinking Patterns*, David J. Pittman and Charles R. Snyder, eds. New York: Wiley.

Helson, Ravenna. 1972. "The Changing Image of the Career Woman." *Journal of Social Issues* 28, no.2: 33–46.

Hirsh, Joseph. 1962. "Women and Alcoholism." In *Problems in Addiction*, William C. Bier, ed. New York: Fordham University Press.

Horn, John L., and Kenneth W. Wanberg. 1973. "Females Are Different: On the Diagnosis of Alcoholism in Women." In *Proceedings of the First Annual Alcoholism Conference of NIAAA*, Morris Chavetz, ed. Washington, D. C.: Department of Health, Education and Welfare. Pp. 332–54.

Hornick, Edith Lynn. 1977. *The Drinking Woman*. New York: Association Press.

Hoyt, Donald, and Carroll Kennedy. 1958. "Interest and Personality Correlates of Career-Motivated College Women." *Journal of Counseling Psychology* 5: 44–48.

Jackman, Norman R., Richard O'Toole, and Gilbet T. Geis. 1963. "The Self-Image of a Prostitute." *Sociological Quarterly* 4 (Spring): 150–61.

Jackson, Joan K. 1962. "Alcoholism and the Family." In *Society, Culture, and Drinking Patterns*, David J. Pittman and Charles R. Snyder, eds. New York: Wiley.

Jacob, Andre G.; and Camil Lavoie. 1971. "A Study of Some of the Characteristics of a Group of Women Alcoholics." In *Selected Papers Presented at the General Sessions, Twenty-Second Annual Meeting, September 12–17, 1971, Hartford, Connecticut*, Ruth Brock, ed. Washington, D.C.: Alcohol and Drug Problems Association of North America. Pp. 25–32.

James, Jane E. 1975. "Symptoms of Alcoholism in Women: A Preliminary Survey of A.A. Members." *Journal of Studies on Alcohol* 36, no.11: 1564–69.

James, William. 1890. *Principles of Psychology*. Vol. 1. New York: Henry Holt.

Jellinek, Elvin M. 1952. "The Phases of Alcohol Addiction." *Quarterly Journal of Studies on Alcohol* 13: 673–84.

———. 1960. *The Disease Concept of Alcoholism*. Highland Park, N.J.: Hillhouse Press.

Johnson, Elmer H. 1964. *Crime, Correction, and Society*. Homewood, Ill.: Dorsey Press.

Johnson, Marilyn W. 1965. "Physicians, Views on Alcoholism: With Special Reference to Alcoholism in Women." *Nebraska State Medical Journal* 50, no.7: 343–47.

Johnson, Marilyn W.; Johanna C. Devries; and Mary I. Houghton. 1966. "The Female Alcoholic." *Nursing Research* 15, no.4: 343–47.

Johnson, P.B. 1978. "Working Women and Alcohol Use: Preliminary National Data." Paper presented at symposium, Psychological Issues Related to Women's Employment, American Psychological Association Convention, Toronto, August.

Jones, Mary Cover 1971. "Personality Antecedents and Correlates of Drinking Patterns in Women." *Journal of Consulting and Clinical Psychology* 36: 61–69.

Jones, Robert W. 1963. "Changing Patterns and Attitudes toward Use of Alcoholic Beverages in the U.S., 1900–1963." *Interpreting Current Knowledge about Alcohol and Alcoholism to a College Audience*. Paper read at proceedings of conference held in Albany, N.Y., (28–30 May): New York State Department of Mental Hygiene. Pp. 9–20.

Jones, Robert W.; and Alice R. Helrich. 1972. "Treatment of Alcoholism by Physicians in Private Practice: A National Survey." *Quarterly Journal of Studies on Alcohol* 33, no.1: 117–31.

Kagan, Jerome, and Howard A. Moss. 1962. *Birth and Maturity: A Study in Psychological Development*. New York: Wiley.

Kammier, Sister Mary Leo. 1977. *Alcoholism the Common Denominator: More Evidence on the Male Female Question*. Center City, Minn.: Hazelden.

Karp, Stephan A., Dorothy C. Poster, and Allan Goodman. 1963. "Differentiation in Alcoholic Women." *Journal of Personality* 31: 386–93.

Karpman, Benjamin. 1948. *The Alcoholic Woman*, Washington, D.C.: Lincare Press.

Keil, Thomas J. 1978. "Sex Role Variations and Women's Drinking: Results from a Household Survey in Pennsylvania." *Journal of Studies on Alcohol* 39, no.5: 859–68.

Keller, Mark. 1962. "The Definition of Alcoholism and the Estimation of Its Prevalence." In *Society, Culture, and Drinking Patterns*, David J. Pittman and Charles R. Synder, eds. New York: Wiley.

Keller, Mark, and Vera Efron. 1955. "The Prevalence of Alcoholism." *Quarterly Journal of Studies on Alcohol* 16, no.4: 619–44.

_____. 1958. "The Rate of Alcoholism in the U.S.A. 1954–1956." *Quarterly Journal of Studies on Alcohol* 19, no.2: 316–19.

Kenkel, William F., and Ellen Voland. 1975. *Society in Action*. San Francisco: Canfield Press.

Kent, Patricia. 1967. *An American Woman and Alcohol*. New York: Holt, Rinehart, and Winston.

Kern, Joseph C., William Schmelter, and Michael Fanelli. 1978. "A Comparison of Three Alcoholism Treatment Populations." *Journal of Studies on Alcohol* 39, no.5: 785 –92.

Kilmann, Peter K. 1974. "Self-Actualization of Female Narcotic Drug Addicts." *Journal of Clinical Psychology* 30: 308–10.

Kilty, Keith M. 1975. "Attitudes toward Alcohol and Alcoholism among Professionals and Nonprofessionals." *Quarterly Journal of Studies on Alcohol* 36, no.3: 318–27.

Kimball, Bonnie-Jean. 1978. *The Alcoholic Woman's Mad, Mad World of Denial and Mind Games*. Center City, Minn.: Hazelden.

Kinsey, Barry A. 1966. *The Female Alcoholic: A Social-Psychological Study*. Springfield, Ill.: Charles C. Thomas.

_____. 1968. "Psychological Factors in Alcoholic Women from a State Hospital Sample." *American Journal of Psychiatry* 124: 157–60.

Kirkpatrick, Jean. 1976. "Women for Sobriety." Quakertown, Penn.: Women for Sobriety, Inc.

_____. 1978. *Turnabout: Help for a New Life*. Garden City, N.Y.: Doubleday.

_____. 1980. "Women and Alcohol." In *Alcoholism in Women*, Cristen C. Eddy and John L. Ford, eds. Dubuque, Iowa: Kendall / Hunt Publishing.

Kitay, Philip M. 1940. "A Comparison of the Sexes in Their Attitude and Beliefs about Women." *Sociometry* 3, no.4: 399–407.

Kitsuse, John I. 1980. "The 'New Conception of Deviance' and Its Critics." In *The Labelling of Deviance: Evaluating a Perspective*, 2d. ed., Walter R. Gove, ed. Beverly Hills, Calif.: Sage Publications.

Knapp, Robert R. 1965. "Relationship of a Measure of Self-Actualization to Neuroticism and Extraversion." *Journal of Consulting Psychology* 29: 168–72.

_____. 1976. *Handbook for the POI*. San Diego: EdITS Publishers.

Knupfer, Genevieve. 1964. "Female Drinking Patterns." *Selected Papers Presented at the Fifteenth Annual Meeting of the North American Association of Alcoholism Programs*. Washington, D.C.: NAAAP. 140–60.

Kogan, Kate L., and Joan K. Jackson. 1965. "Stress, Personality, and Emotional Disturbance in Wives of Alcoholics." *Quarterly Journal of Studies on Alcohol* 26, no.3: 486–95.

Krasanoff, Alan. 1973. "Self-Reported Attitudes toward Drinking among Alcoholics before and after Treatment." *Quarterly Journal of Studies on Alcohol* 34: 947–50.

Kremers, M.A. 1974. "A Comparison of Members of Alcoholics Anonymous with Practicing Alcoholics and Selected Samples of Nonalcoholics, in Terms of a Positive Concept of Mental Health." Unpublished manuscript.

Kuhn, Manford H. 1960. "Self-Attitudes by Sex and Professional Training." *Sociological Quarterly* 1:39–55.

Kurtz, Richard M. 1971. "Body Attitude and Self-Esteem." *Proceedings of the 79th Annual Convention of the APA* 6: 467–68.

Kvaraceus, William. 1958. *What Research Says to the Teacher: Juvenile Delinquency.* Washington, D.C.: National Education Association.

Langone, John, and Doris Nobrega Langone. 1980. *Women Who Drink.* Reading, Mass.: Addison-Wesley.

Lawrence, J. Joseph, and Milton A. Maxwell. 1962. "Drinking and Socioeconomic Status." In *Society, Culture, and Drinking Patterns,* David J. Pittman and Charles R. Snyder, eds. New York: Wiley.

Lecky, William Edward Hartpole. 1877. Reprint. *History of European Morals from Augustus to Charlemagne.* Vol. 2. New York: Arno Press, 1975.

Leite, Evelyn. 1979. *To Be Somebody.* Center City, Minn.: Hazelden.

Lemert, Edwin M. 1951. *Social Pathology.* New York: McGraw-Hill.

_____. 1967. *Human Deviance, Social Problems, and Social Control.* Englewood Cliffs, N.J.: Prentice-Hall.

_____. 1974. "Beyond Mead: The Societal Reaction to Deviance." *Social Problems* 21 (April): 457–68.

Levine, Jacob. 1955. "Sexual Adjustment of Alcoholics: A Clinical Study of a Selected Sample." *Quarterly Journal of Studies on Alcohol* 16, no.4: 675–78.

Levy, S.J., and C.M. Doyle. 1974. "Attitudes toward Women in a Drug Abuse Treatment Program." *Journal of Drug Issues* 4: 428–34.

Lewis, Edwin C. 1968. *Developing Woman's Potential.* Ames: Iowa State University Press.

Lindbeck, Vera L. 1972. "The Woman Alcoholic: A Review of the Literature." *International Journal of Addictions* 7, no.3: 567–80.

Linton, Ralph. 1936. *The Study of Man.* New York: Appleton-Century-Crofts.

Lisansky, Edith. S. 1957. "Alcoholism in Women: Social and Psychological Concomitants." *Quarterly Journal of Studies on Alcohol* 18, no.4: 588–662.

_____. 1958. "The Woman Alcoholic." *Annals of the American Academy of Political and Social Science* 325: 73–81.

Liska, Allen E. 1981. *Perspectives on Deviance.* Englewood, N.J.: Prentice-Hall.

Lolli, Giorgio. 1961. *Social Drinking: The Effects of Alcohol.* New York: Collier.

Lolli, Giorgio, Emidio Serrianni, Ferruccio Banissoni, Grace Golder, Aldo Mariani, Raymond G. McCarthy, and Mary Toner. 1952. "The Use of Wine and Other Alcoholic Beverages by a Group of Italians and Americans of Italian Extraction." *Quarterly Journal of Studies on Alcohol* 13 (March): 27–48.

Long, B.H., E.H. Henderson, and R.C. Ziller. 1967. "Developmental Changes in Self-Concept during Middle Childhood." *Merrill-Palmer Quarterly* 13: 201–15.

Lowe, George, and H. Eugene Hodges. 1972. "Race and Treatment of Alcoholism in a Southern State." *Social Problems* 20 (Fall): 240–52.

Lundberg, Ferdinand. 1969. *The Rich and the Superrich.* New York: Bantam.

Lynn, D.B. 1959. "A Note on Sex Differences in the Development of Masculine and Feminine Identification." *Psychological Review* 64: 356–63.

Maccoby, Elanor Emmons, and Carol Nagy Jacklin. 1974. *The Psychology of Sex Differences.* Stanford: Stanford University Press.

Maccoby, Eleanor Emmons, and Wayne C. Wilson. 1957. "Identification and Observational Learning from Films." *Journal of Abnormal and Social Psychology* 55: 76–87.

Mackey, Richard A. 1969. "Views of Caregiving and Mental-Health Groups about Alcoholics." *Quarterly Journal of Studies on Alcohol* 39, no.3: 665–71.

Mangin, William. 1957. "Drinking among Andean Indians." *Quarterly Journal of Studies on Alcohol* 18 (March): 55–65.

Mankoff, Milton. 1971. "Societal Reaction and Career Deviance: A Critical Analysis." *Sociological Quarterly* 12 (Spring): 204–18.

Manheimer, Dean I., Glen D. Mellinger, and Mitchell B. Balter. 1968. " Psychotherapeutic Drugs: Use among Adults in California." *California Medicine* 109: 445–51.

Martindale, Don. 1960. *The Nature and Types of Sociological Theory.* Boston: Houghton Mifflin.

Maslow, Abraham H. 1968. *Toward a Psychology of Being.* New York: Van Nostrand Reinhold.

_____. 1970. *Motivation and Personality.* 2d ed. New York: Harper and Row.

_____. 1971. *The Farther Reaches of Human Nature.* New York: Viking.

Matza, David. 1969. *Becoming Deviant.* Englewood Cliffs, N.J.: Prentice–Hall.

Maxwell, Ruth. 1976. *The Booze Battle.* New York: Praeger.

Mayer, Joseph, David J. Myerson, Merrill A. Needham, and Marion M. Fox. 1966. "The Treatment of the Female Alcoholic: The Former Prisoner." *American Journal of Orthopsychiatry* 36: 248–49.

McCord, William, and Joan McCord. 1960. *Origins of Alcoholism.* Stanford: Stanford University Press.

McDonald, Robert L. 1968. "Effects of Sex, Race, and Class on Self, Ideal-Self, and Parental Ratings in Southern Adolescents." *Perceptual and Motor Skills* 27: 15–25.

McGuire, William J. 1968. "Personality and Susceptibility to Social Influence." In *The Handbook of Personality Theory and Research,* Edgar F. Borgatta and William W. Lambert, eds. Chicago: Rand McNally.

McKee, John. P., and Alex C, Sherriffs. 1957. "The Differential Evaluations of Males and Females." *Journal of Personality* 25: 356–71.

_____. 1959. "Men's and Women's Beliefs, Ideals, and Self-Concepts." *American Journal of Sociology* 64, no. 4: 356–63.

Mead, George Herbert. 1967. *Mind, Self, and Society.* Charles W. Morris, ed. Chicago: University of Chicago Press.

Mead, Margaret. 1935. *Sex and Temperament in Three Primitive Societies.* New York: William Morrow and Company.

Merton, Robert K. 1957. *Social Theory and Social Structure.* 9th ed. Glencoe, Ill.: Free Press.

Mihanovich, Clemet S. 1947. "Who Is the Juvenile Delinquent?" *Social Science* 22:45–50.

Mischel, H. N. 1972. "Professional Sex Bias and Sex Role Stereotypes in the U.S. and Israel. Corrected draft.

Miyamoto, S. Frank, and Sanford M. Dornbush. 1956. "A Test of Interactionist Hypotheses of Self-Conception." *American Journal of Sociology* 61, no.5: 399–403.

Mizruchi, Ephraim H., and Robert Perrucci. 1968. "Prescription, Proscription, and Permissiveness: Aspects of Norms and Deviant Drinking Behavior." In *Approaches to*

Deviance, Mark Lefton, James K. Skipper, Jr., and Charles H. McCaghy, eds. New York: Appleton-Century-Crofts.

Mogar, E., Wayne Wilson, and Stanley T. Helm. 1970. "Personality Subtypes of Male and Female Alcoholic Patients." *International Journal of Addictions* 5, no.1: 99–113.

Monahan, Lynn, Deanna Kuhn, and Phillip Shaver. 1974. "Intrapsychic versus Cultural Explanations of the 'Fear of Success' Motive." *Journal of Personality and Social Psychology* 29: 60–64.

Moore, Marv. 1966. "Aggression Themes in a Binocular Rivalry Situation." *Journal of Personality and Social Psychology* 3: 685–88.

Mulford, Harold A. 1964. "Drinking and Deviant Drinking, U.S.A. 1963." *Quarterly Journal of Studies on Alcohol* 25: 634–50.

National Institute on Alcohol Abuse and Alcoholism. 1977. *Women in Treatment for Alcoholism: A Profile*. Rockville, Md.: NIAAA.

Nazro, Richard A. 1979. "Gestalt Therapy, Self-Esteem, and the Alcoholic Woman." In *Women Who Drink: Alcoholic Experience and Psychotherapy*, Vasanti Burtle, ed. Springfield, Ill.: Charles C. Thomas.

Nel, Elizabeth, Robert Helmreich, and Elliot Aronson. 1969. "Opinion Change in the Advocate as a Function of the Personality of the Audience: A Clarification of the Meaning of Dissonance." *Journal of Personality and Social Psychology* 12: 117–24.

Nero, Jack. 1977. *If Only My Wife Could Drink Like a Lady*. Minneapolis: Comp Care Publications.

Nettler, Gwynn. 1974. *Explaining Crime*. New York: McGraw-Hill.

New York Narcotic Addiction Control Commission. *Differential Drug Use within the New York State Labor Force*. 1971. Albany, N.Y.: NYNACC.

Newman, Donald J. 1957. "Public Attitudes toward a Form of White-Collar Crime." *Social Problems* 4: 228–32.

Nunnally, Jim C., Jr. 1961. *Popular Conceptions of Mental Health*. New York: Holt, Rinehart, and Winston.

_____. 1967. "What the Mass Media Present." In *Mental Illness and Social Process*, Thomas J. Scheff., ed. New York: Harper and Row.

Nye, Ivan F., James F. Short, and Virgil Olson. 1957. "Socioeconomic Status and Delinquent Behavior." *American Journal of Sociology* 63, no.3: 381–89.

O'Brien, Robert, and Morris Chavetz. 1982. *The Encyclopedia of Alcoholism*. New York: Facts on File Publications.

Orford, Jim, Seta Waller, and Julian Peto. 1974. "Drinking Behavior and Attitudes and Their Correlates among University Students in England: I—Principle Components Domain. II—Personality and Social Influences. III—Sex Differences." *Quarterly Journal of Studies on Alcohol* 35: 1316–74.

Page, Ronald D. 1971. "Prognosis of the Alcoholic as Indicated by the Tennessee Self-Concept Scale." Master's thesis, Purdue University.

Parker, Fredrick. 1972. "Sex Role Adjustment in Women Alcoholics." *Quarterly Journal of Studies on Alcohol* 33, no.3: 647–57.

Parry, Hugh J., Mitchell B. Balter, Glen D. Mellinger, Ira H. Cissin, and Dean I. Manheimer. 1973. "National Patterns of Psychotherapeutic Drug Use." *Archives of General Psychiatry* 28: 769–83.

Pastor, Paul Anthony, Jr. 1976. "The Control of Public Drunkenness: A Comparison of the Legal and Medical Models." Ph.D. diss., Yale University.

Pattison, E. Mansell, Ronald Coe, and Robert J. Rhodes. 1969. "Evaluation of Alcoholism Treatment." *Archives of General Psychiatry* 20: 478–88.

Pemberton, D. A. 1967. "A Comparison of the Outcome of Treatment in Female and Male Alcoholics." *British Journal of Psychiatry* 113, no.479: 367–73.

Peterson-Hart, Sandra. 1976. "The Relationship of Self-Esteem and Achievement Behavior among Low-Income Youth," Ph.D. diss., Syracuse University.

Pishkin, Vladimir, and Frederick C. Thorne. 1977. "A Factorial Structure of the Dimensions of Femininity in Alcoholic, Schizophrenic, and Normal Populations." *Journal of Clinical Psychology* 33, no.1: 10–17.

Pittman, David J., and Muriel J. Sterne. 1967. "Analysis of Various Community Approaches to the Problem of Alcoholism in the U.S." In *Alcoholism*, David J. Pittman, ed. New York: Harper and Row.

Pivilian, Irving, and Scott Briar. 1964. "Police Encounters with Juveniles." *American Journal of Sociology* 69 (September): 206–14.

President's Commission on Law Enforcement and the Administration of Justice. 1967. *The Challenge of Crime in a Free Soceity.* Washington, D.C.: Government Printing Office.

Rathod N.H., and I.G. Thomson. 1971. "Women Alcoholics: A Clinical Study." *Quarterly Journal of Studies on Alcohol* 32: 45–52.

Reckless, Walter C., Simon Dinitz, and Ellen Murray. 1956. "Self-Concept as an Insulator against Delinquency." *American Sociological Review* 21: 744–46.

Reingold, Joseph C. 1964. *The Fear of Being a Woman: A Theory of Maternal Destruction.* New York: Grune & Stratton.

Reiss, Albert J., Jr. 1961. "The Social Integration of Queers and Peers." *Social Problems* 13 (Spring): 102–20.

Ridlon, Florence. 1982. "Status Insularity and Stigmatization among Female Alcoholics." Ph.D. diss., Syracuse University.

Riley, John W., and Charles F. Marden. "The Social Pattern of Alcoholic Drinking." 1947. *Quarterly Journal of Studies on Alcohol* 8, no.2: 265–73.

Rimmer, John, Ferris N. Pitts, Theodore Reich, and George Winokur. 1971. "Alcoholism II: Sex, Socioeconomic Status, and Race in Two Hospitalized Samples." *Quarterly Journal of Studies on Alcohol* 32, no.4: 942–52.

———. 1971. "Alcoholism III. Diagnosis and Familial Psychiatric Illness in 259 Alcoholic Probands." *Archives of General Psychiatry* 23, no.2: 104–11.

Rimmer, John, Theodore Reich, and George Winokur. 1972. "Alcoholism V. Diagnosis and Clinical Variations among Alcoholics." *Quarterly Journal of Studies on Alcohol* 33, no.3: 658–66.

Robins, Lee N. 1980. "Alcoholism and Labelling Theory." In *The Labelling of Deviance: Evaluating a Perspective*, 2d. ed., Walter R. Gove, ed. Beverly Hills, Calif.: Sage Publications.

Robinson, Sophia M. 1936. *Can Delinquency Be Measured?* New York: Columbia University Press.

Rose, Arnold M. 1962. "A Social-Psychological Theory of Neurosis." In *Human Behavior and Social Process, an Interactionist Approach*, Arnold Rose, ed., Boston: Houghton Mifflin.

———. 1962. "A Systematic Symmary of Symbolic Interaction Theory." In *Human Behavior and Social Process, an Interactionist Approach*, Arnold Rose, ed., Boston: Houghton Mifflin.

Rose, Arnold M., ed. 1962. *Human Behavior and Social Process, an Interactionist Approach.* Boston: Houghton Mifflin.

Rosenhan, D.L. 1973. "On Being Sane in Insane Places." *Science* 179, no.4070: 250–58.

Rosenkrantz, S. Paul, Susan Vogel, H. Bee, Inge K. Broverman. 1968. "Sex Role Stereotypes and Self-Concepts in College Students." *Journal of Consulting and Clinical Psychology* 32: 287–95.

Rubington, Earl. 1968. "Variations in Bottle-Gang Controls." In *Deviance: The Interactionist Perspective,* Earl Rubington and Martin S. Wienberg, eds. New York: MacMillan.

———. 1972. "The Hidden Alcoholic." *Quarterly Journal of Studies on Alcohol* 33: 667–83.

Ryan, William. 1971. *Blaming the Victim.* New York: Vintage.

Sacks, Karen. 1982. *Sisters and Wives: The Past and Future of Sexual Equality.* Chicago: University of Illinois Press.

Sandmaier, Marian. 1980. *The Invisible Alcoholics: Women and Alcohol Abuse in America.* New York: McGraw-Hill.

Sanford, Nevitt 1956. "Personality Development during the College Years." *Journal of Social Issues* 12, no.4: 3–12

Sarbin, Theodore R.; and James C. Mancuso. 1970. "Failure of Moral Enterprise: Attitudes of the Public toward Mental Illness." *Journal of Consulting and Clinical Psychology* 35:159–73.

Scheff, Thomas J. 1974. "The Labeling of Mental Illness." *American Sociological Review* 39: 444–52.

Schmidt, Wolfgang, and Jan de Lint. 1969. "Mortality Experiences of Male and Female Alcoholic Patients." *Quarterly Journal of Studies on Alcohol* 30 no.1: 112–18.

Schuckit, Marc A. 1972. "The Alcoholic Woman: A Literature Review." *Psychiatry in Medicine* 3, no.1: 37–43.

———. 1972. "Sexual Disturbance in the Woman Alcoholic." *Medical Aspects of Human Sexuality* 6, no.9: 44–65.

———. 1973. "Depression and Alcoholism in Women." In *Proceedings of the First Annual Alcoholism Conference of the National Institute on Alcohol Abuse and Alcoholism, June 1971,* Washington, D.C.: Department of Health, Education, and Welfare.

Schuckit, Marc A., and Elizabeth R. Morrisey. 1976. "Alcoholism in Women: Some Clinical and Social Perspectives with an Emphasis on Possible Subtypes." In *Alcoholism Problems in Women and Children,* Milton Greenblatt and Marc A. Schuckit eds. New York: Grune and Stratton.

Schuckit, Marc A., Ferris N. Pitts, Jr., Theodore Reich, Luch J. King, and George Winokar. 1969. "Alcoholism: I. Two Types of Alcoholism in Women." *Archives of General Psychiatry* 20: 301–6.

Schuckit, Marc A., and George Winokur. 1972. "A Short-Term Follow-up of Women Alcoholics." *Diseases of the Nervous System* 33: 672–78.

Schultz, Ardelle M. 1975. "Radical Feminism: A Treatment Modality for the Addicted Woman." In *Developments in the the Field of Drug Abuse,* Edward C. Senay, Vernon Shorty, and Harold Alksae, eds. Cambridge, Mass.: Schenkman.

Schur, Edwin M. 1965. *Crimes without Victims.* Englewood Cliffs, N.J.: Prentice-Hall.

———. 1971. *Labeling Deviant Behavior: Its Sociological Implications.* New York: Harper and Row.

_____. 1980. "Comments." In *The Labelling of Deviance: Evaluating a Perspective*, 2d. ed., Walter R. Gove, ed. Beverly Hills, Calif.: Sage Publications.

_____. 1984. *Labeling Women Deviant: Gender Stigma and Social Control*. New York: Random House.

Schwartz, Edward. 1945. "A Community Experiment in the Measurement of Juvenile Delinquency." *National Probation Association Yearbook*, Marjorie Bell, ed. New York: National Probation Association.

Schwartz, Luis M., and Stanton Fjeld. 1969. "The Alcoholic Patient in the Psychiatric Hospital Emergency Room." *Quarterly Journal of Studies on Alcohol* 30, no.1: 104–11.

Schwartz, Michael, Gordon F. Fearn, and Sheldon Stryker. 1966. "A Note on Self-Conception and the Emotionally Disturbed Role." *Sociometry* 29 (September): 300–305.

Schwartz, Richard D., and Jerome H. Skolnick. 1962. "Two Studies of Legal Stigma." *Social Problems* 10:133–142.

Sclare, A. Balfour. 1970. "The Female Alcoholic." *Journal of Addictions* 65, no.2: 99–127.

Secretary of Health, Education, and Welfare, 1971. "Extent and Patterns of Use and Abuse of Alcohol. In *The First Special Report to the U.S. Congress on Alcohol and Health*, Mark Keller, ed. Washington, D.C.: National Institute on Alcohol Abuse and Alcoholism. Pp. 21–36.

Selzer, Melvin L. 1975. "Treatment-Related Factors in Alcoholic Populations." Paper presented at American Psychiatric Association's 128th Annual Meeting, Anaheim, California. Rockville, Md.: *National Institute on Alcohol Abuse and Alcoholism*.

Senseman, Lawrence A. 1966. "The Housewife's Secret Illness: How to Recognize the Female Alcoholic." *Rhode Island Journal of Medicine* 49, no.1: 40–42.

Shalloo, Jeremiah. 1937. "Youth and Crime." *Annals of the American Academy of Political and Social Science* 194 (November): 79–86.

Sherfey Mary Jane. 1955. "Psychopathology and Character Structure in Chronic Alcoholism." In *Etiology of Chronic Alcoholism*, Oskar Diethelm, ed. Springfield, Ill.: Charles C. Thomas.

Sherriffs, Alex C., and John P. McKee. 1953. "Sex Differences in Attitudes about Sex Differences." *Journal of Psychology* 35: 161–68.

_____. 1957. "Quantitative Aspects of Beliefs about Men and Women." *Journal of Personality* 25: 451–64.

Shostrom, Everett L. 1974, *Manual for the Personal Orientation Inventory*, San Diego: Educational and Industrial Testing Service.

_____. 1974. *Personal Orientation Inventory: An Inventory for the Measurement of Self-Actualization*. San Diego: Educational and Industrial Testing Service.

Siass, Iradj, Guido Crocetti, and Herzl R. Spino. 1973. "Drinking Patterns and Alcoholism in a Blue-Collar Population." *Quarterly Journal of Studies on Alcohol* 34, no.3: 916–26.

Southerby, Norm, and Alexandra Southerby. 1975. *Twelve Young Women*. Long Beach, Calif.: Norm Southerby Associates.

Snyder, Charles R. 1962 "Culture and Jewish Sobriety: The Ingroup-Outgroup

Factor." In *Society, Culture, and Drinking Patterns*, David J. Pittman and Charles R. Snyder, eds. New York: Wiley.

Spain, David M. 1945. "Portal Cirrhosis of the Liver: A Review of Two Hundred Fifty Necropsies with Reference to Sex Differences." *American Journal of Clinical Pathology* 15: 215–18.

Spitzer, Stephen P. 1969. "Test Equivalence of Unstructured Self-Evaluation Instruments." *Sociological Quarterly* 10, no.2: 204–15.

Sterne, Muriel W., and David J. Pittman. 1972. *Drinking Patterns in the Ghetto*. Vol. 2. St. Louis: Social Science Institute, Washington University.

Straus, Robert, and Seldon D. Bacon. 1954. *Drinking in College*. New Haven, Conn.: Yale University Press.

Sutherland, Edwin H. 1949. *White Collar Crime*. New York: Holt, Rinehart, and Winston.

Swartz, Richard D., and Jerome H. Skolnick. 1962. "Two Studies of Legal Stigma." *Social Problems* 10: 133–42.

Sykes, Gresham M., and David Matza, 1957. "Techniques of Neutralization: A Theory of Delinquency." *American Sociological Review* 22 (December): 664–70.

Tamasi, Barbara. 1982. *I'll Stop Tomorrow*, Orleans, Mass.: Paraclete Press.

Tamerin, John S., P. Neumann, and M. H. Marshall. 1971. "The Upper-Class Alcoholic: A Syndrome in Itself?" *Psychometrics* 12: 200–204.

Tamerin, John S., Alexander Tolor, and Betsy Harrington. 1976. "Sex Differences in Alcoholics: A Comparison of Male and Female Alcoholics' Self and Spouse Perceptions." *American Journal of Drug and Alcohol Abuse* 3, no.3: 457–72.

Tangri, Sandra Schwartz 1972. "Determinants of Occupational Role-Innovation among College Women." *Journal of Social Issues* 28, no.2: 177–99.

Tavarone, Antonia Regina. 1983. "The Role of Family Members in the Treatment of Women Alcoholics." Ph.D. diss., Syracuse University.

Taylor, Howard F. 1970. *Balance in Small Groups*. New York: Van Nostrand-Reinhold.

Taylor, Ian, Paul Walton, and Jack Young. 1973. *The New Criminology: For A Social Theory of Deviance*. New York: Harper and Row.

Taylor, Laurie, and Paul Walton. 1971. "Industrial Sabotage: Motives and Meanings." In *Images of Deviance*, Stanley Cohen, ed. Harmondsworth, England: Penguin.

Trice, Harrison. 1966. *Alcoholism in America*. New York: McGraw-Hill.

Trice, Harrison M., and Paul Michael Roman. 1970. "Delabeling, Relabeling, and Alcoholics Anonymous." *Social Problems* 17 (Spring): 123–43.

Ullman, Albert D. 1958. "Sociocultural Backgrounds of Alcoholism." *Annals of the American Academy of Politial and Social Sciences* 315: 48–54.

———. 1960. *To Know the Difference*. New York: St. Martin's Press.

Unsigned. 1973. "Alcoholism in Women." *Journal of the American Medical Association*. 225 (20 August): 988.

U.S. Bureau of Census. 1950, 1960, 1970, and 1982. *S'atistical Abstract of the United States*. Washington, D.C.: Government Printing Office.

U.S. Department of Health and Human Services. 1981. "Tailoring Alcoholism Therapy to Client Needs." Washington, D.C.: Government Printing Office.

U.S. National Highway Traffic Safety Administration. 1974. *Factors Influencing Alcohol Safety Action Project Police Officers' DWI Arrests*. Washington, D.C.: Department of Transportation.

U.S. Senate Subcommittee on Alcoholism and Narcotics of the Committee on Labor and Public Welfare, 94th Congress. 1976. *Alcohol Abuse among Women: Special Problems and Unmet Needs*. Washington, D.C.: U.S. Government Printing Office.

Vanderpool, James A. 1966. "Self-Concept Differences in the Alcoholic under Varying Conditions of Drinking and Sobriety." Ph.D. diss., Loyola University.

_____. 1969. "Alcoholism and Self-Concept." *Quarterly Journal of Studies on Alcohol* 30: 59–77.

Voegtlin, Walter L. , and William R. Broz. 1949. "The Conditioned Reflex Treatment of Chronic Alcoholism. X. An Analysis of 3,125 Admissions over a Period of Ten-and-a-Half Years." *Annals of Internal Medicine* 30: 580–97.

Vogel, Sidney. 1968. "Psychiatric Treatment of Alcoholism." *Annals of the American Academy of Political and Social Sciences* 315: 99–107.

Wall, James H. 1937. "A Study of Alcoholism in Women." *American Journal of Psychiatry* 93, no.4: 941–55.

Waller, S., and B. Lorch. 1978. "Social and Psychological Characteristics of Alcoholics: A Male-Female Comparison." *International Journal of Addictions* 13: 201–12.

Walliman, Isidor, Howard Rosenbaum, Nicholas Tatsis, and George Zito. 1980. "Misreading Weber: The Concept of 'Macht'." *Sociology: The Journal of the British Sociological Association* 14, no.2: 261–75.

Wallston, Kenneth A., Barbara S. Wallston, and Brenda M. Devellis. 1976. "Effect of Negative Stereotype on Nurses' Attitudes toward an Alcoholic Patient." *Journal of Studies on Alcohol* 37, no.5: 659–65.

Wanberg, Kenneth W., and John L. Horn. 1970. "Alcoholism Symptom Patterns of Men and Women." *Quarterly Journal of Studies on Alcohol* 31: 40–61.

_____. 1973. "Alcoholism Syndromes Related to Sociological Classifications." *International Journal of Addictions* 8: 99–120.

Wanberg, Kenneth W., and John Knapp. 1970. "Differences in Drinking Symptoms and Behavior of Men and Women Alcoholics." *British Journal of Addiction* 64: 347–55.

Wasserstein, Bruce, and Mark J. Green, eds. 1972. *Justice for Some*. Boston: Beacon.

Wechsler, Henry , Harold W. Demone, Jr., and Nell Gottlieb. 1978. "Drinking Patterns of Greater Boston Adults: Subgroup Differences on the QFV Index." *Journal of Studies on Alcohol* 39, no.7: 1158–65.

Weir, William R. 1965. "The Use of a Measure of Self-Actualization in the Treatment of Alcoholics and Their Spouses in an Out-Patient Agency." Master's thesis, University of North Dakota.

Weir, William R., and Eldon M. Gade. 1969. "An Approach to Counseling Alcoholics." *Rehabilitation Counseling Bulletin* 12 (June): 227–30.

Wells, L. Edward, and Gerald Marwell. 1976. *Self-Esteem: Its Conceptualization and Measurement*. Beverly Hills, Calif.: Sage Publications.

Wesley, Carol. 1975. "The Woman's Movement and Psychotherapy." *Social Work* 20: 120–24.

White, Lynn Townsend. 1950. *Educating Our Daughters*, New York: Harper.

Wienberg, Martin S. 1968. "Sexual Modesty, Social Meanings, and the Nudist Camp." In *Approaches to Deviance: Theories, Concepts, and Research Findings*, Mark Lefton, James K. Skipper, Jr., and Charles H. McCaghy, eds. New York: Appleton-Century-Crofts.

Wilkinson, P., J. N. Santamaria, and J. G. Rankin. 1969. "Epidemiology of Alcoholic Cirrhosis." *Australas. Ann. Med.* 18: 222–26.

_____. 1969. "Epidemiology of Alcoholism: Social Data and Drinking Patterns of a Sample of Australian Alcoholics." *Medical Journal of Austrailia* 1: 1020–25.

Williams, Juanita H. 1983. *Psychology of Women: Behavior in a Biosocial Context.* New York: W.W. Norton and Company.

Wilsnak, Sharon C. 1973. "Femininity in the Bottle." *Psychology Today* 6, no. 11: 39–102.

_____. 1973. "The Needs of the Female Drinker: Dependency, Power, or What?" In *Proceedings of the Second Annual Conference of the NIAAA*, Morris Chavetz, ed. Washington, D.C.: Department of Health, Education, and Welfare.

_____. 1973. "Sex Role Identification in Female Alcoholism." *Journal of Abnormal Psychology* 82, no.2: 253–61.

———. 1976. "The Impact of Sex Roles on Women's Alcohol Use and Abuse," In *Alcoholism Problems in Women and Children*, Milton Greenblatt and Marc A. Schuckit, eds. New York: Grune and Stratton.

Windseth, J.C., and J. Mayer. 1971. "Drinking Behavior and Attitudes toward Delinquent Girls." *International Journal of Addictions* 6: 453–61.

Winokur, George, and Paula Clayton. 1967. "Family History Studies. II. Sex Differences and Alcoholism in Primary Affective Illness." *British Journal of Psychiatry* 113, no.500: 973–79.

_____. 1968. "Family History Studies. IV. Comparison of Male and Female Alcoholics." *Quarterly Journal of Studies on Alcohol* 29, no. 3: 885–91.

Winokur, George, Theodore Reich, John Rimmer, and Ferris Pitts. 1970. "Alcoholism III. Diagnosis and Familial Psychiatric Illness in 259 Alcoholic Probands." *Archives of General Psychiatry* 23, no.2: 104–11.

Wolff, Sulammith and Lydia Holland. 1964. "A Questionnaire Follow-up of Alcohol Patients." *Quarterly Journal of Studies on Alcohol* 25: 108–19.

Wolfgang, Marvin E. 1964. *Crime and Race: Conceptions and Misconceptions.* New York: Institute on Human Relations.

Wood, Howard P., and Edward L. Duffy. 1966. "Psychological Factors in Alcoholic Women." *American Journal of Psychiatry* 123, no.3: 341–45.

Woodruff, Robert A., Jr., Samuel B. Guze, and Paula J. Clayton, "Divorce among Psychiatric out-Patients." *British Journal of Psychiatry* 121, no.562: 289–92.

World Health Organization Expert Committee on Mental Health, Alcoholism Subcommittee. 1952. *Technical Report Series No. 48*, 2d report. Geneva: World Health Organization.

Youcha, Geraldine. 1978. *A Dangerous Pleasure.* New York: Hawthorn Books.

Zaccaria, Joseph S., and William R. Weir. 1967. "A Comparison of Alcoholics and Selected Sample of Nonalcoholics in Terms of Positive Concept of Mental Health." *Journal of Social Psychology* 71: 151–57.

Zeldich, Morris, Jr. 1968. "Status, Social," In *International Encyclopedia of the Social Sciences.* New York: Macmillan and Free Press.

Zelen, Seymour L., Jack Fox, J. Edward Gould, and Ray W. Olson. 1966. "Sex-Contingent Differences between Male and Female Alcoholics." *Journal of Clinical Psychology* 22: 160–65.

Subject Index

Name Index

Anthony, Susan B., 28

Bateman, Nils I., 84
Becker, Howard S., 55, 99
Beckman, Linda J., 82
Bedell, J. W., 81
Blane, Howard T., 81
Blumer, Herbert, 74–76
Broverman, Inge K., 23–24, 30, 60, 69
Burtle, Vasanti, 80–82, 84

Cahalan, Don, 107
Carver, Virginia, 146 n.42
Chambliss, William J., 92, 96, 99, 100
Clarke, Alfred C., 95–96
Clarke, Sandra K., 82
Clayton, Jan, 27
Clemmons, Penny, 144 n.20
Cooley, Charles Horton, 72, 74, 75, 149-
    50 n.12
Corrigan, Eileen M., 61, 153 n.87
Coser, Lewis A., 20, 134 n.1
Curlee, Joan, 79

Davis, Nanette J., 55, 88–89, 97, 101
Dinitz, Simon, 95–96
Doyle, C. M., 137 n.46
Duffy, Edward L., 78
Durkheim, Emile, 85, 126
Dynes, Russell, 95–96

Edlehertz, Herbert, 96

Farrell, Ronald A., 133–34 n.40
Fearn, Gordon F., 134 n.43
Fitts, William H., 71
Ford, Betty, 46
Fraser, Judy, 35

Geis, Gilbert T., 150–51 n.41
Gibbs, Jack P., 56
Glaser, Barney G., 76
Glassner, Barry, 56

Glat, M. M., 70
Goffman, Erving, 99
Gomberg, Edith S., 65
Gouldner, Alvin W., 53, 55, 99–100
Gove, Walter R., 51, 52

Hall, Peter M., 134 n.43, 150–51 n.41
Hammersmith, Sue Kiefer, 133–34 n.40
Hirsh, Joseph, 26
Horn, John L., 144 n.20

Jacklin, Carol Nagy, 151 n.43
Jackman, Norman R., 150–51 n.41
James, William, 72–73
Jellinek, Elvin M., 78
Johnson, Marilyn W., 46

Kammier, Sister Mary Leo, 131 n.1
Kenkel, William F., 96
Kinsey, Barry A., 78–79
Kirkpatrick, Jean, 43, 62
Kitsuse, John I., 51, 52, 56
Knupfer, Genevieve, 25, 29, 78
Kuhn, Manford H., 72, 75–77, 157 n.19

Langone, Doris Nobrega, 82
Langone, John, 82
Lecky, William, 49
Lemert, Edwin M., 16–19, 52, 54, 58,
    67–68, 72, 74
Levy, S. J., 137 n. 46
Linton, Ralph, 134 n.1
Lisansky, Edith S., 68–69

Maccoby, Elanor Emmons, 151 n.43
McCord, Joan, 140–41 n.22
McCord, William, 140–41 n.22
McKee, John P., 135 n.9
Martindale, Don, 72
Marwell, Gerald, 71
Maslow, Abraham H., 107–8
Maxwell, Ruth, 65
Mead, Geroge Herbert, 72–75, 77